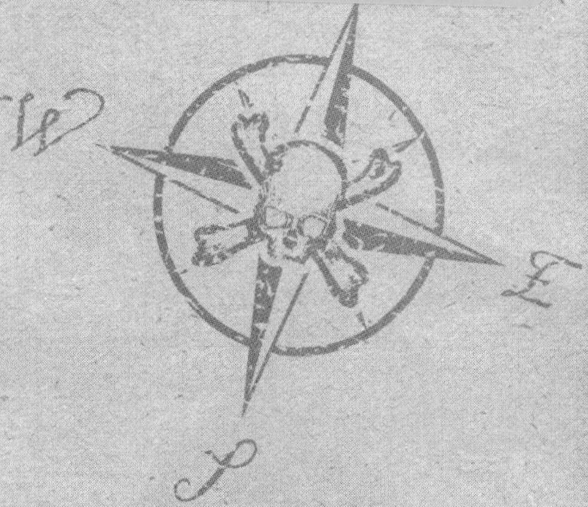
W
E
S

SEA OF RED™

No Quarter

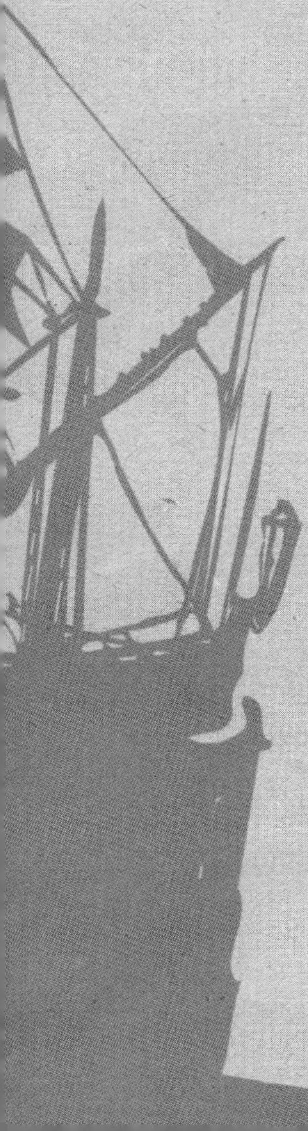

For Image Comics

Erik Larsen - Publisher
Todd McFarlane - President
Marc Silvestri - CEO
Jim Valentino - Vice-President

Eric Stephenson - Executive Director
Jim Demonakos - PR & Marketing Coordinator
Mia MacHatton - Accounts Manager
Laurenn McCubbin - Art Director
Allen Hui - Production Artist
Joe Keatinge - Traffic Manager
Jonathan Chan - Production Assistant
Drew Gill - Production Assistant
Traci Hui - Administrative Assistant

www.imagecomics.com

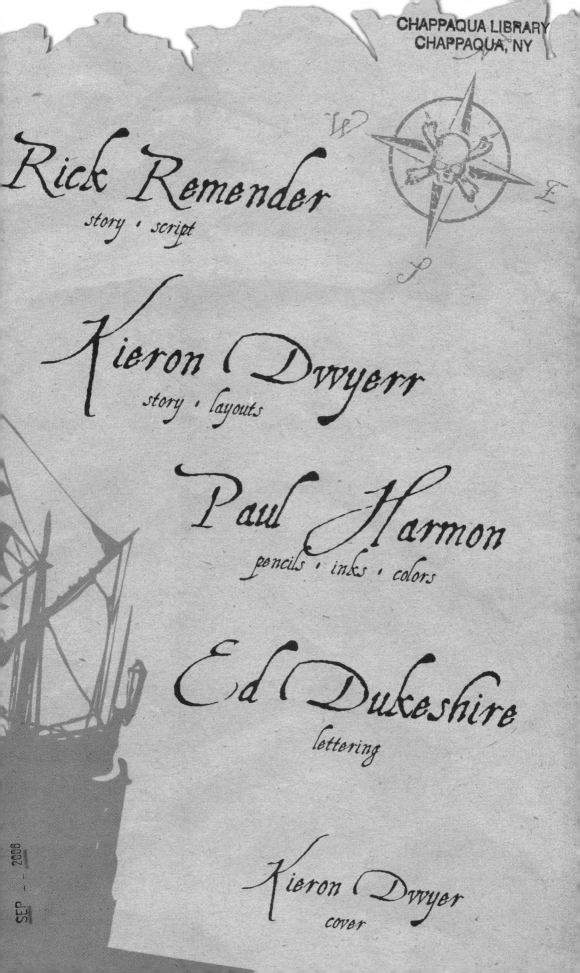

Rick Remender
story · script

Kieron Dwyerr
story · layouts

Paul Harmon
pencils · inks · colors

Ed Dukeshire
lettering

Kieron Dwyer
cover

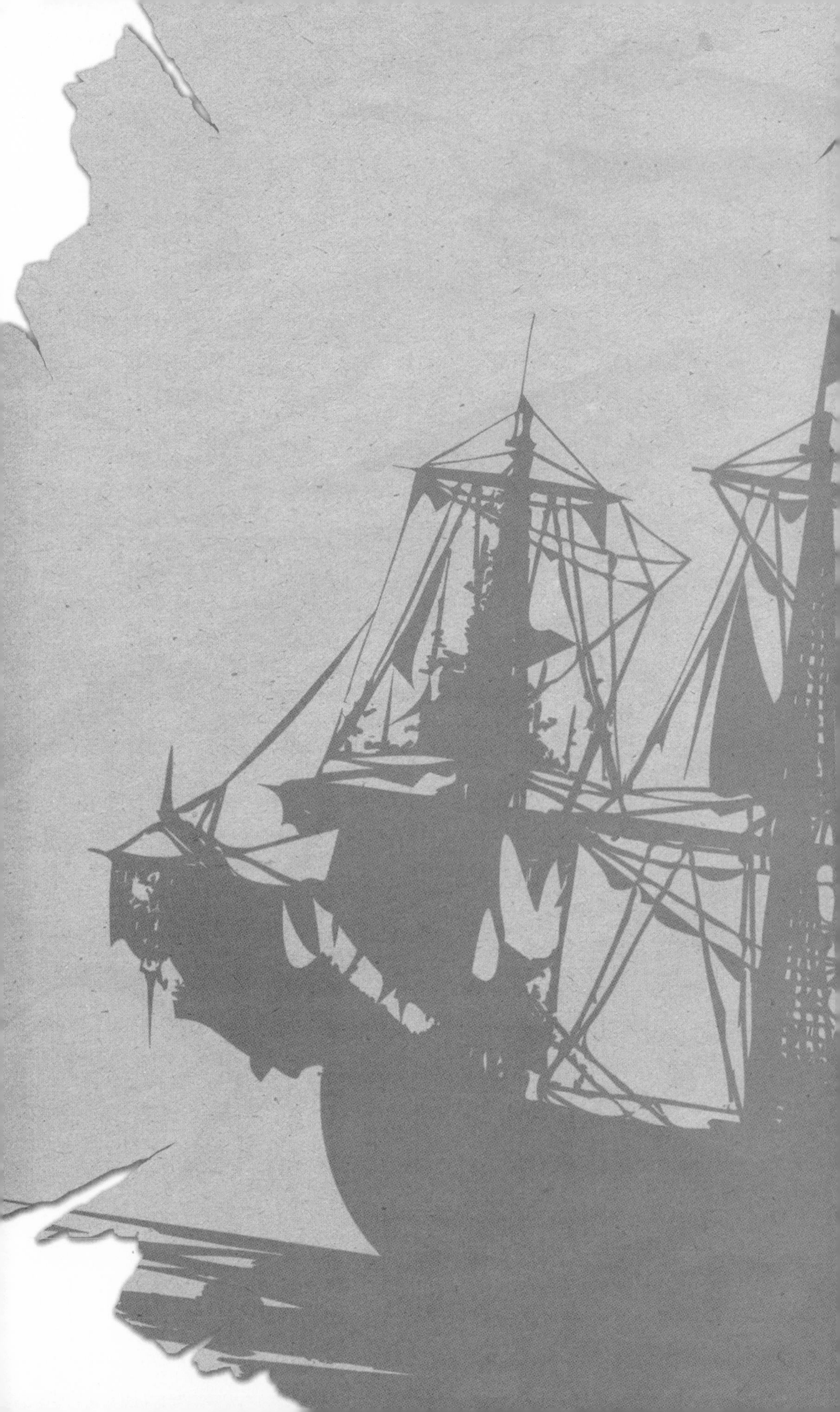

Five

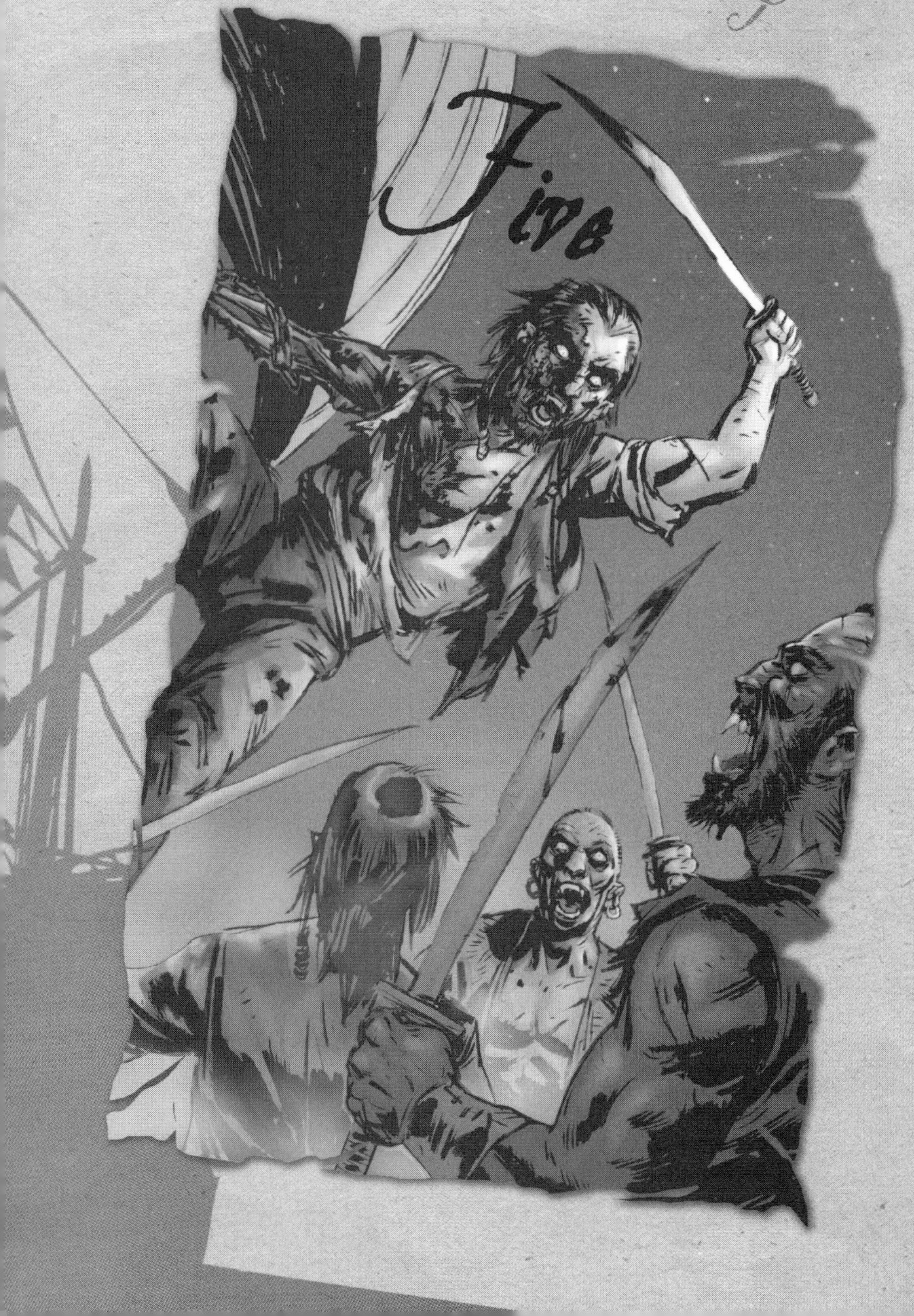

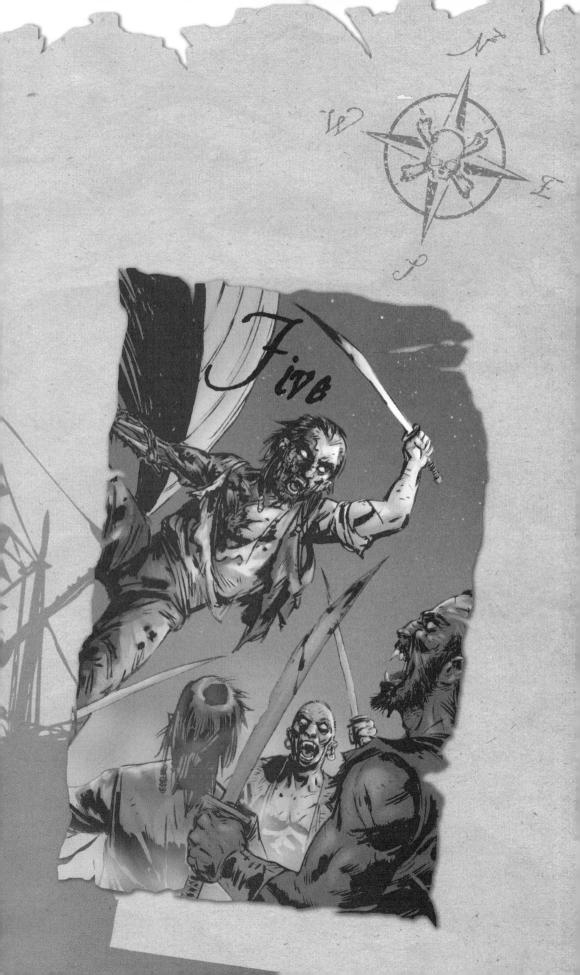

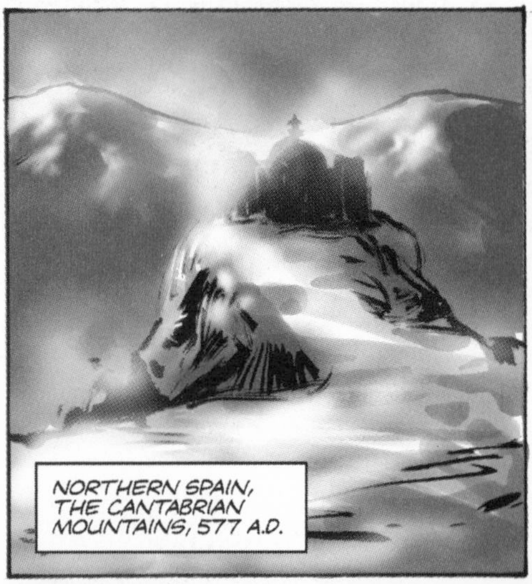
NORTHERN SPAIN, THE CANTABRIAN MOUNTAINS, 577 A.D.
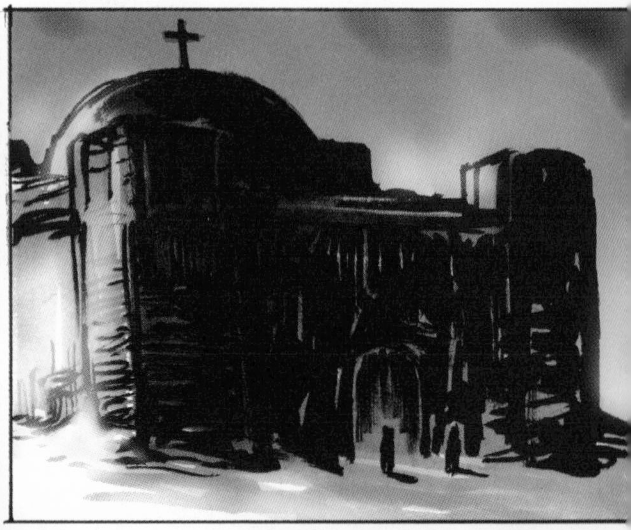
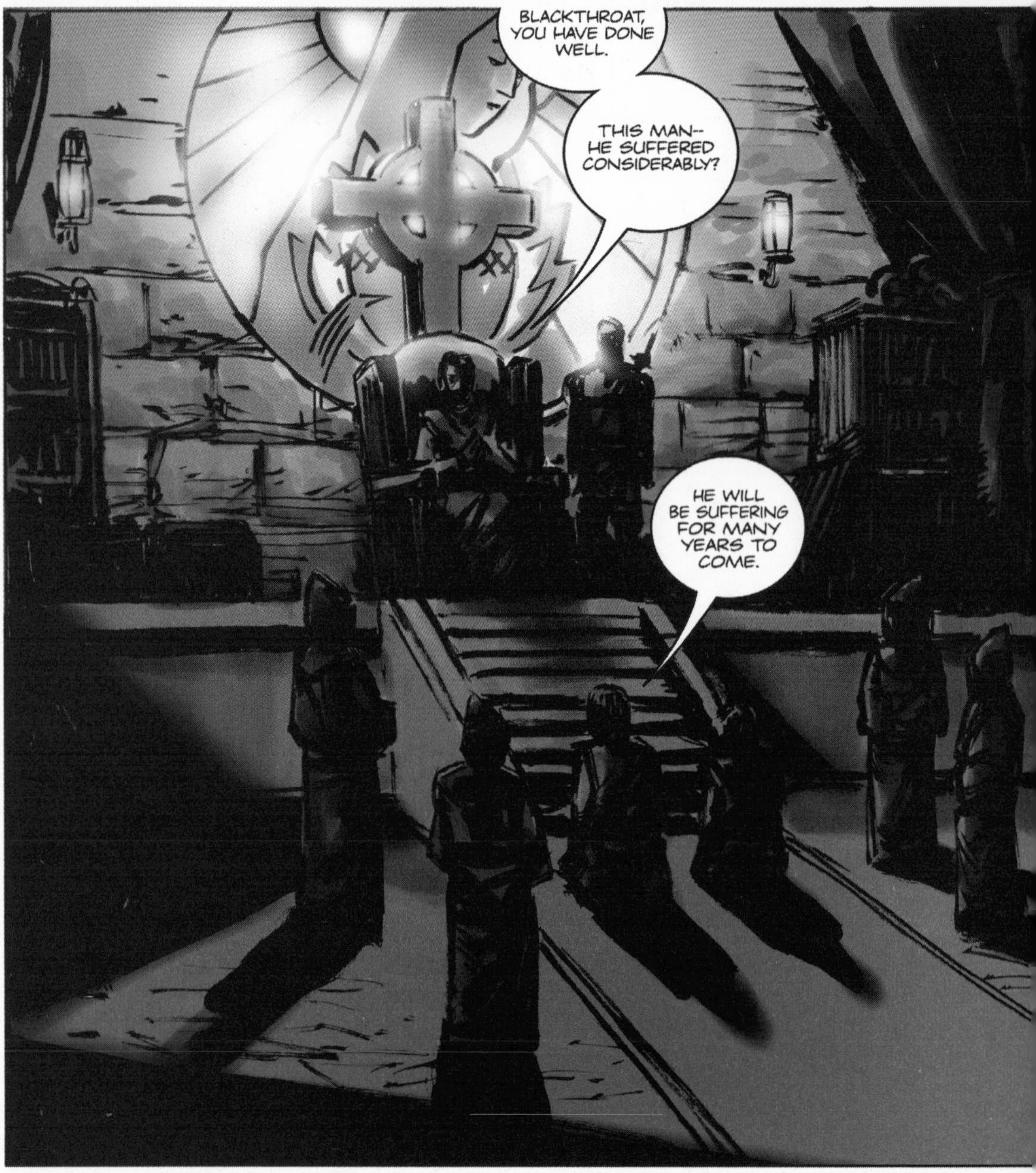
BLACKTHROAT, YOU HAVE DONE WELL.
THIS MAN-- HE SUFFERED CONSIDERABLY?
HE WILL BE SUFFERING FOR MANY YEARS TO COME.

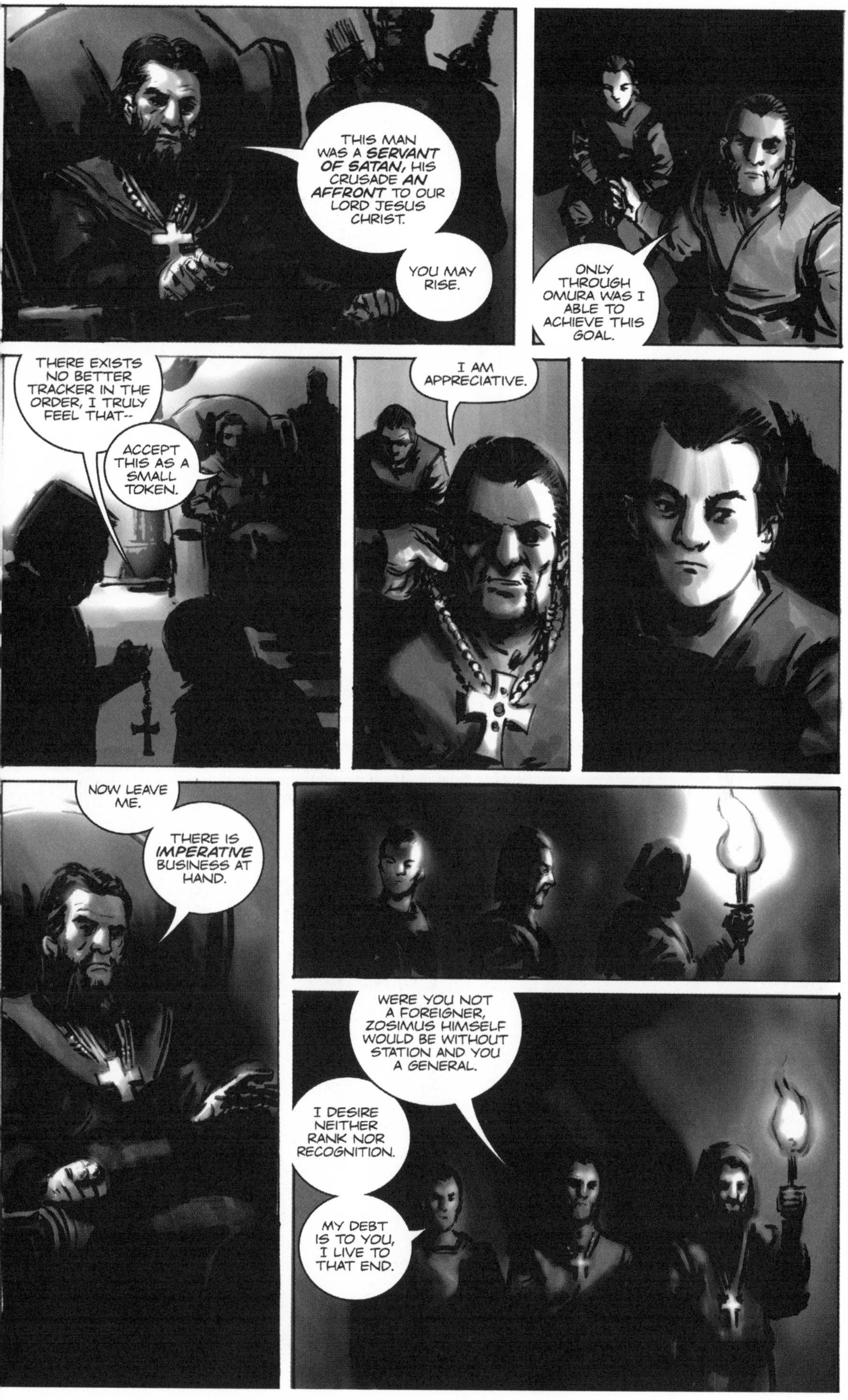
THIS MAN WAS A SERVANT OF SATAN, HIS CRUSADE AN AFFRONT TO OUR LORD JESUS CHRIST.
YOU MAY RISE.
ONLY THROUGH OMURA WAS I ABLE TO ACHIEVE THIS GOAL.
THERE EXISTS NO BETTER TRACKER IN THE ORDER, I TRULY FEEL THAT--
ACCEPT THIS AS A SMALL TOKEN.
I AM APPRECIATIVE.
NOW LEAVE ME.
THERE IS IMPERATIVE BUSINESS AT HAND.
WERE YOU NOT A FOREIGNER, ZOSIMUS HIMSELF WOULD BE WITHOUT STATION AND YOU A GENERAL.
I DESIRE NEITHER RANK NOR RECOGNITION.
MY DEBT IS TO YOU, I LIVE TO THAT END.

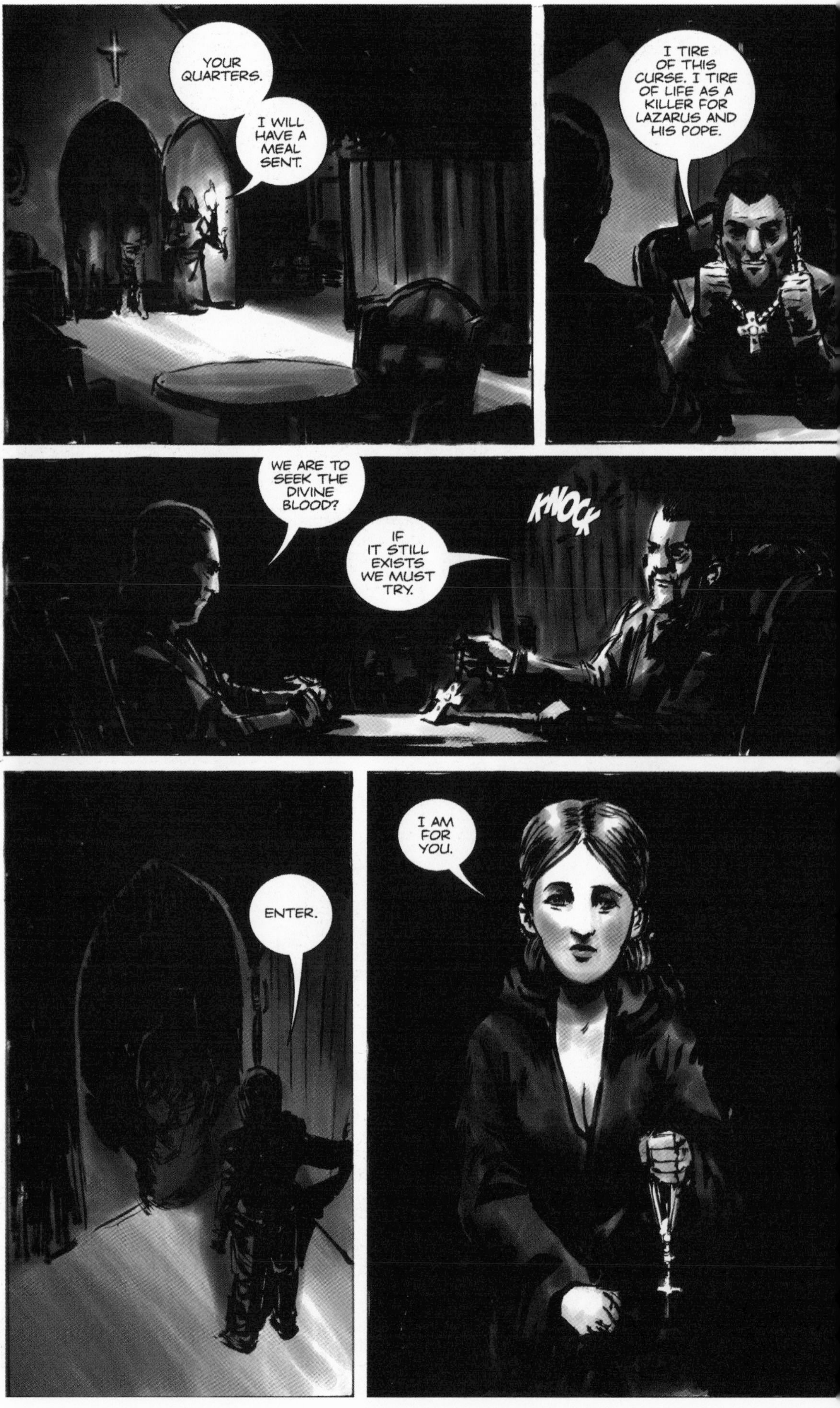
YOUR QUARTERS.
I WILL HAVE A MEAL SENT.
I TIRE OF THIS CURSE. I TIRE OF LIFE AS A KILLER FOR LAZARUS AND HIS POPE.
WE ARE TO SEEK THE DIVINE BLOOD?
KNOCK
IF IT STILL EXISTS WE MUST TRY.
ENTER.
I AM FOR YOU.

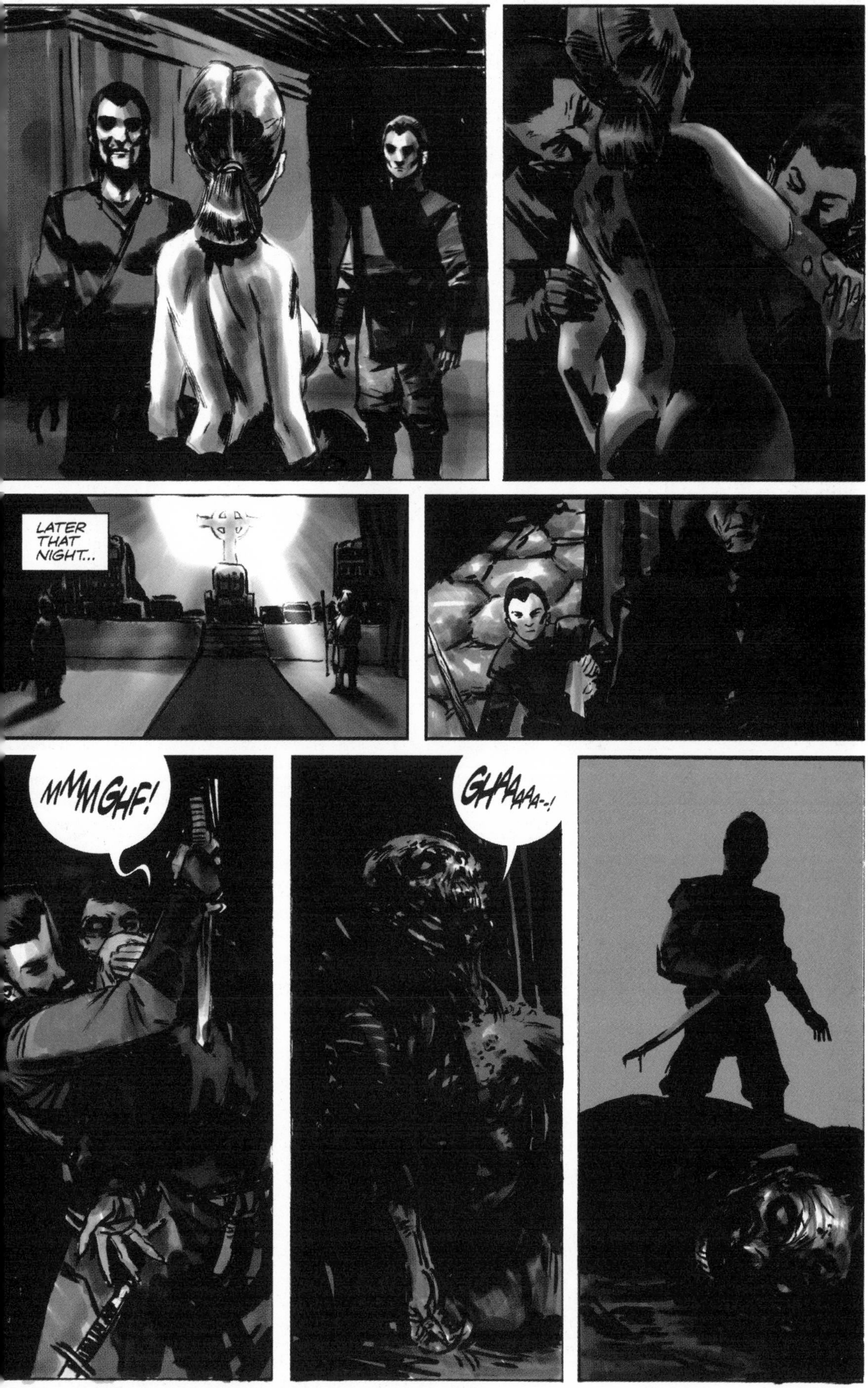
LATER THAT NIGHT...
MMMGHF!
GHAAAAA-!

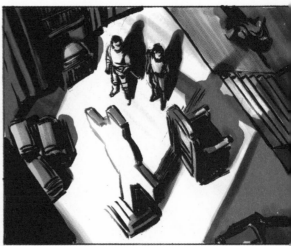

THIS IS THE ONE.

MAKE HASTE.

CREEEEAK

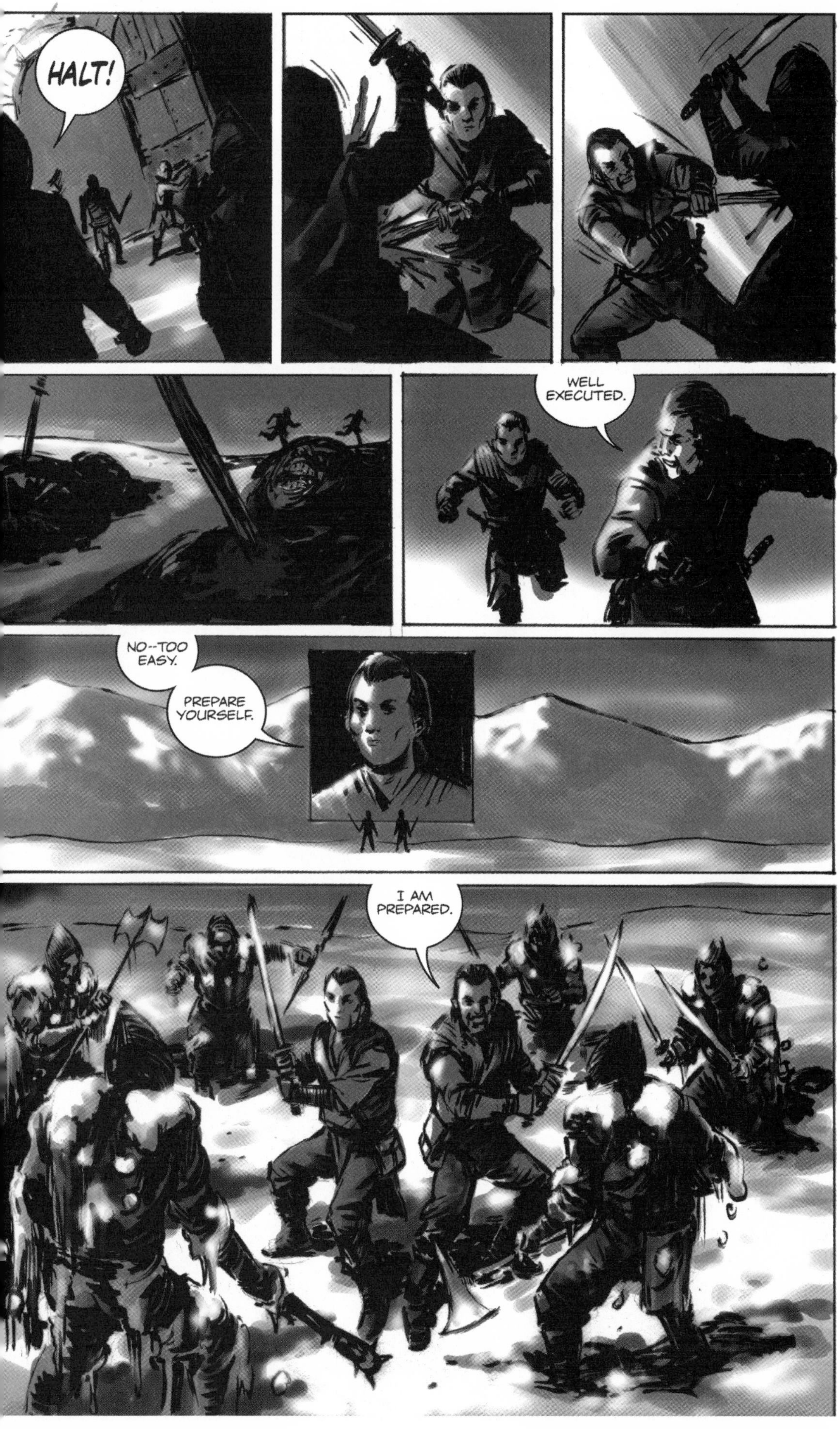
HALT!
WELL EXECUTED.
NO--TOO EASY.
PREPARE YOURSELF.
I AM PREPARED.

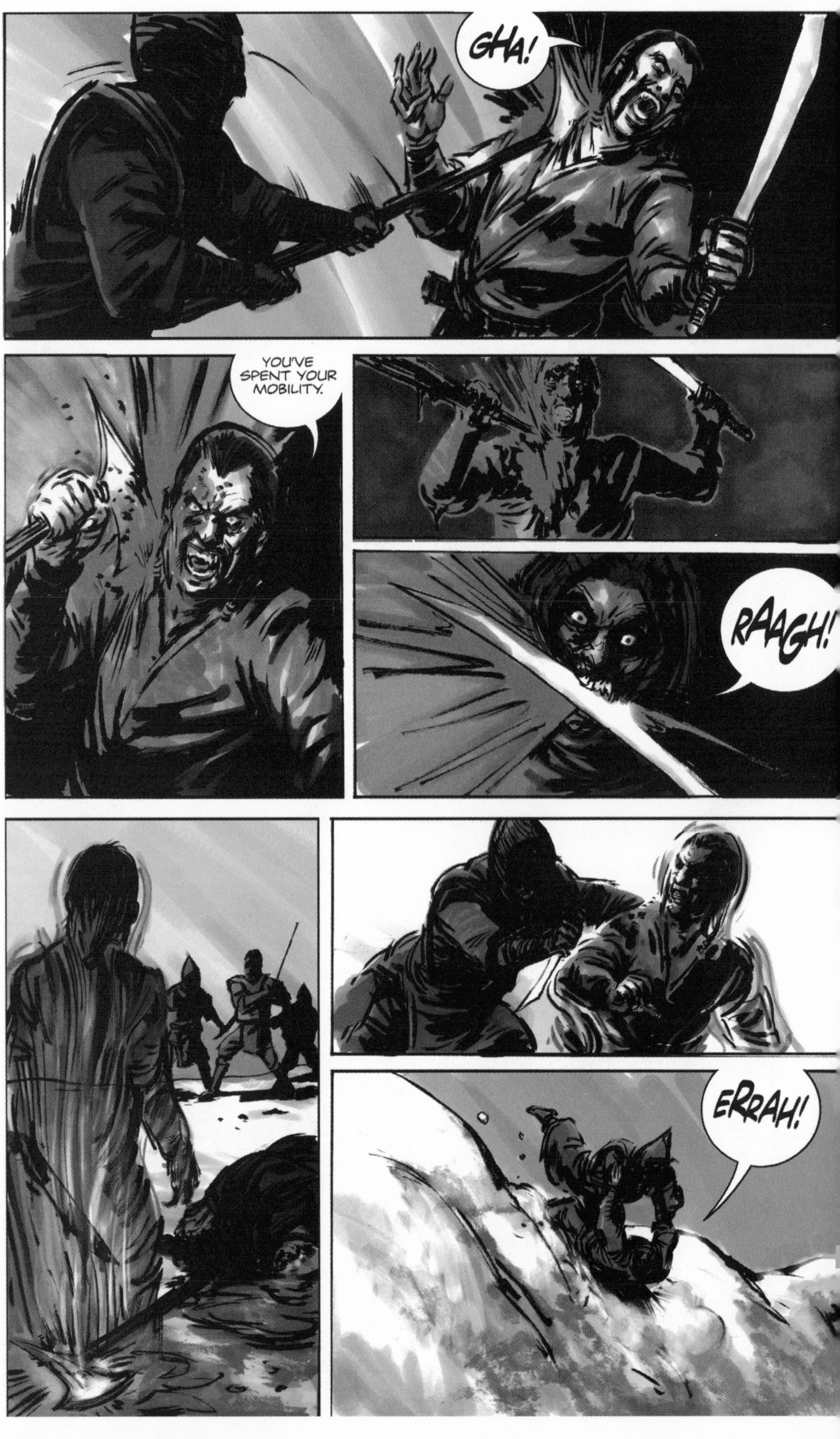
GHA!
YOU'VE SPENT YOUR MOBILITY.
RAAGH!
ERRAH!

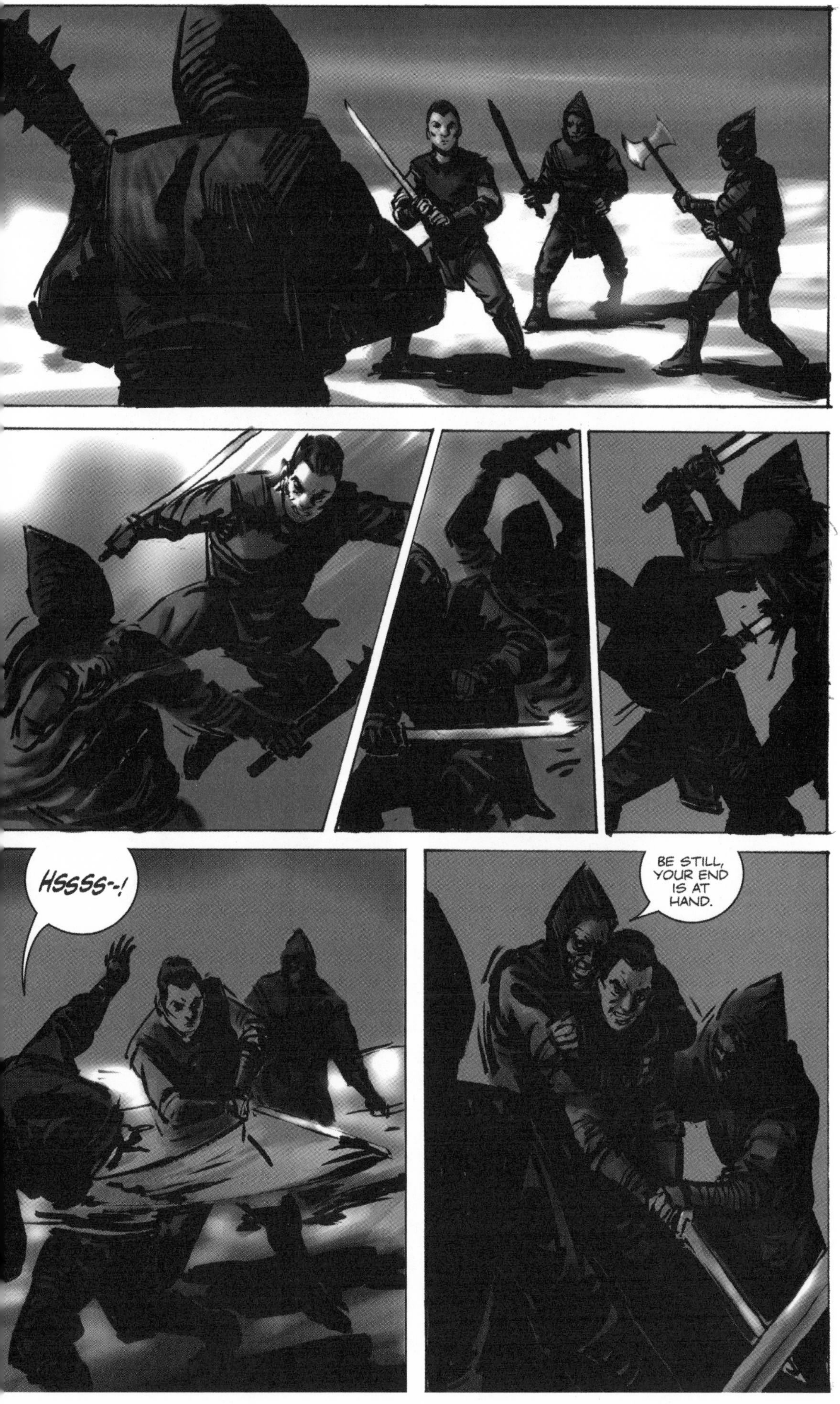
HSSSS-!
BE STILL, YOUR END IS AT HAND.

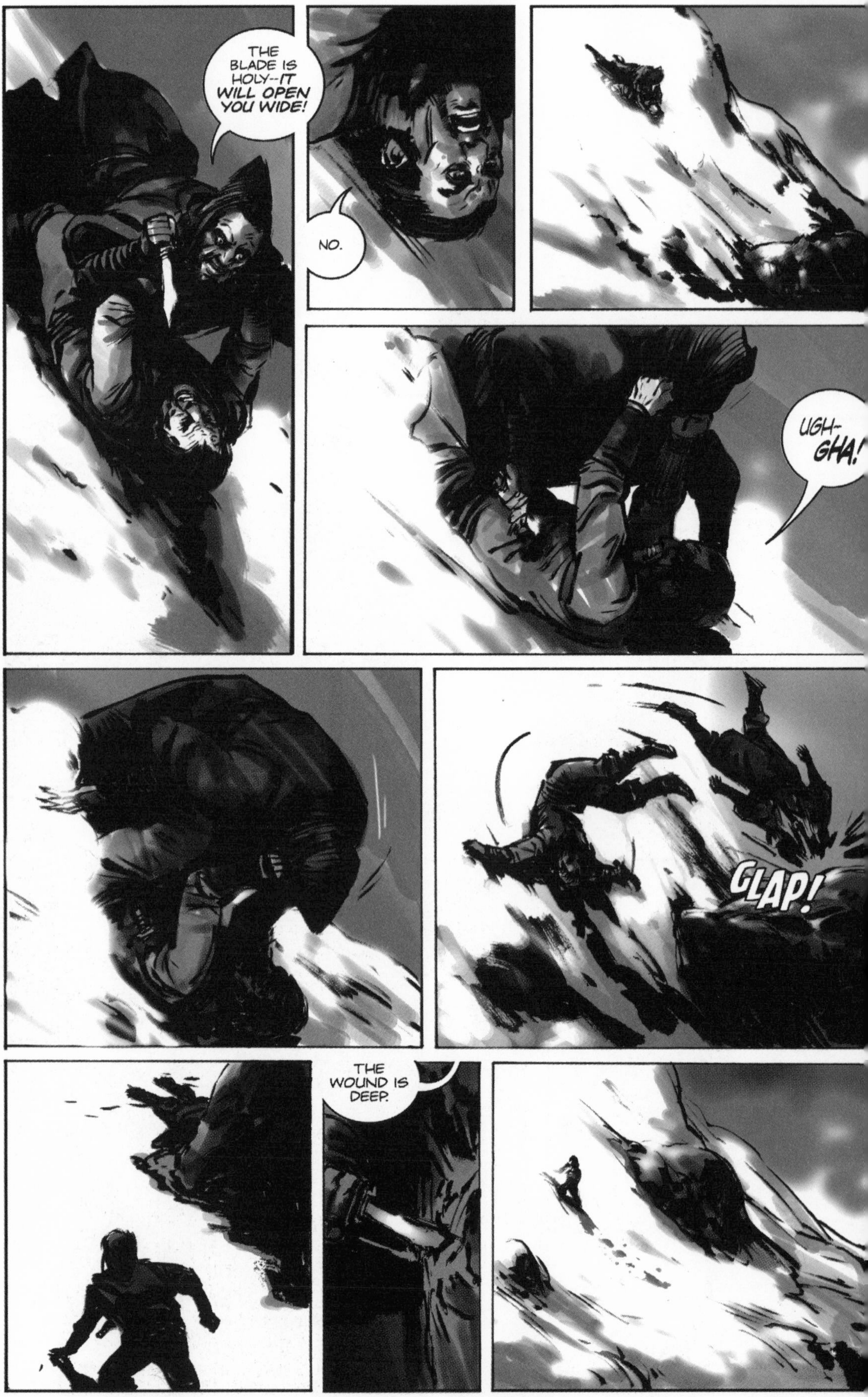

THE BLADE IS HOLY--IT WILL OPEN YOU WIDE!
NO.
UGH-GHA!
GLAP!
THE WOUND IS DEEP.

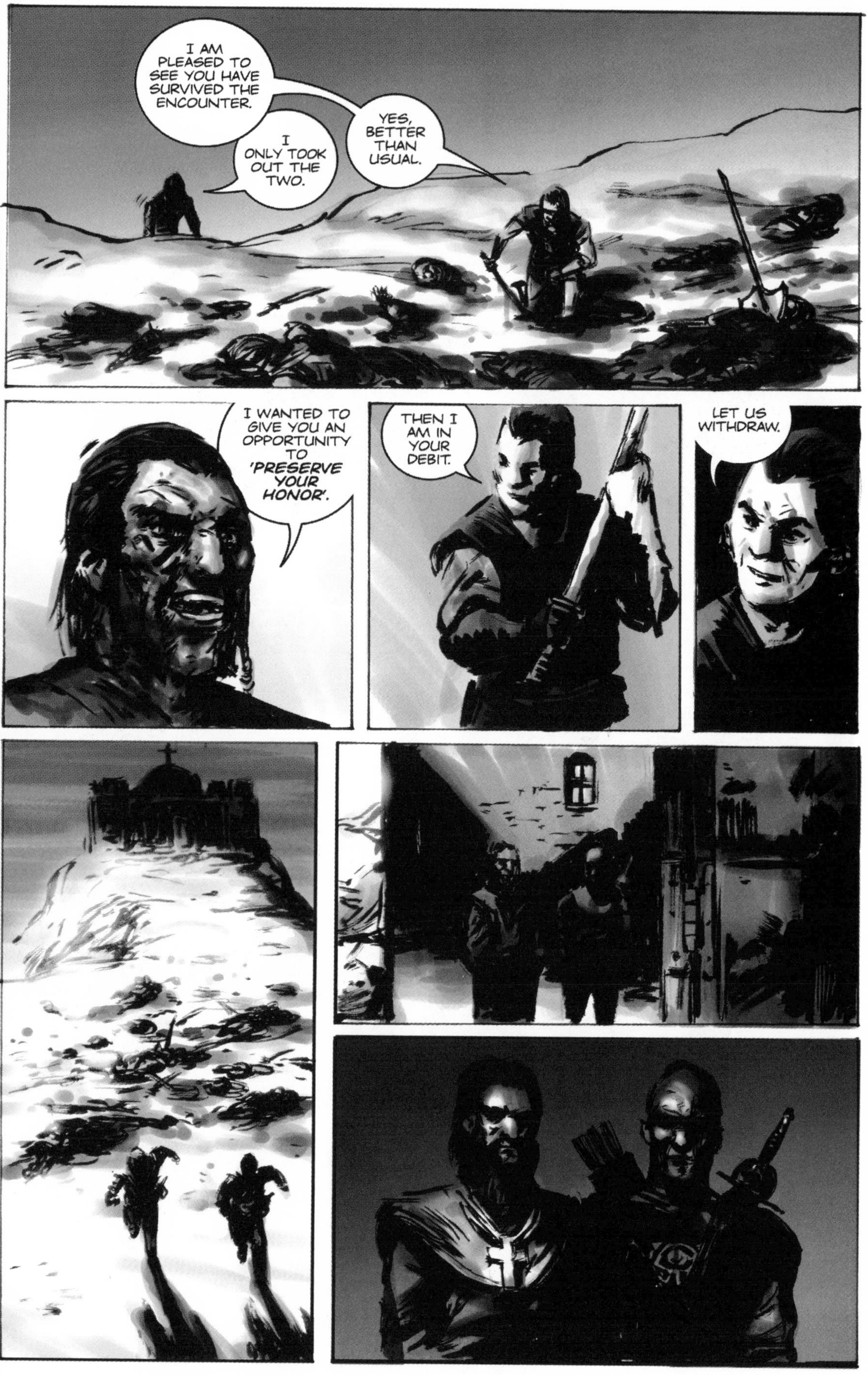
I AM PLEASED TO SEE YOU HAVE SURVIVED THE ENCOUNTER.
YES, BETTER THAN USUAL.
I ONLY TOOK OUT THE TWO.
I WANTED TO GIVE YOU AN OPPORTUNITY TO *'PRESERVE YOUR HONOR'*.
THEN I AM IN YOUR DEBIT.
LET US WITHDRAW.

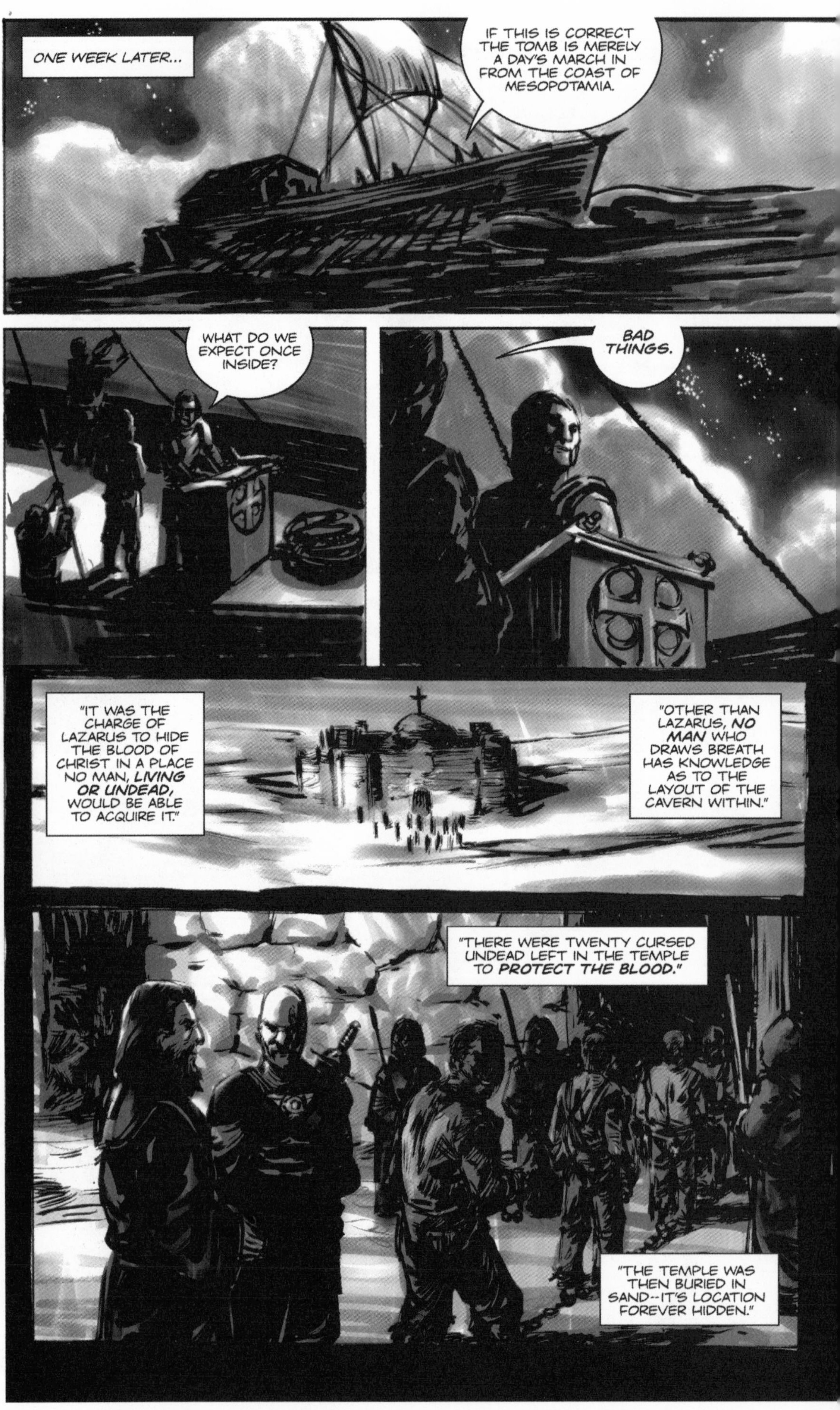
ONE WEEK LATER...
IF THIS IS CORRECT THE TOMB IS MERELY A DAY'S MARCH IN FROM THE COAST OF MESOPOTAMIA.
WHAT DO WE EXPECT ONCE INSIDE?
BAD THINGS.
"IT WAS THE CHARGE OF LAZARUS TO HIDE THE BLOOD OF CHRIST IN A PLACE NO MAN, LIVING OR UNDEAD, WOULD BE ABLE TO ACQUIRE IT."
"OTHER THAN LAZARUS, NO MAN WHO DRAWS BREATH HAS KNOWLEDGE AS TO THE LAYOUT OF THE CAVERN WITHIN."
"THERE WERE TWENTY CURSED UNDEAD LEFT IN THE TEMPLE TO PROTECT THE BLOOD."
"THE TEMPLE WAS THEN BURIED IN SAND--IT'S LOCATION FOREVER HIDDEN."

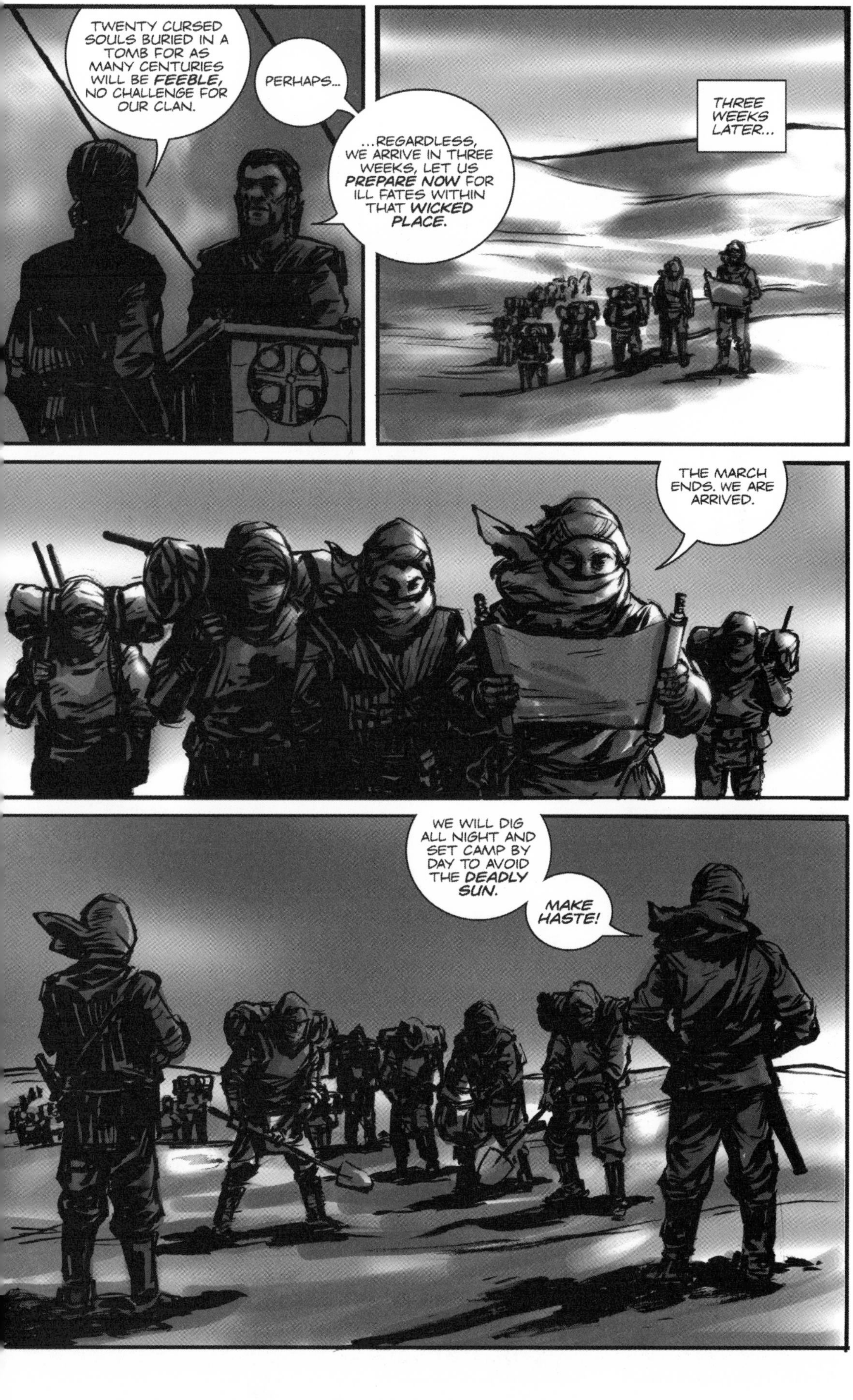
TWENTY CURSED SOULS BURIED IN A TOMB FOR AS MANY CENTURIES WILL BE FEEBLE, NO CHALLENGE FOR OUR CLAN.
PERHAPS...
...REGARDLESS, WE ARRIVE IN THREE WEEKS, LET US PREPARE NOW FOR ILL FATES WITHIN THAT WICKED PLACE.
THREE WEEKS LATER...
THE MARCH ENDS. WE ARE ARRIVED.
WE WILL DIG ALL NIGHT AND SET CAMP BY DAY TO AVOID THE DEADLY SUN.
MAKE HASTE!

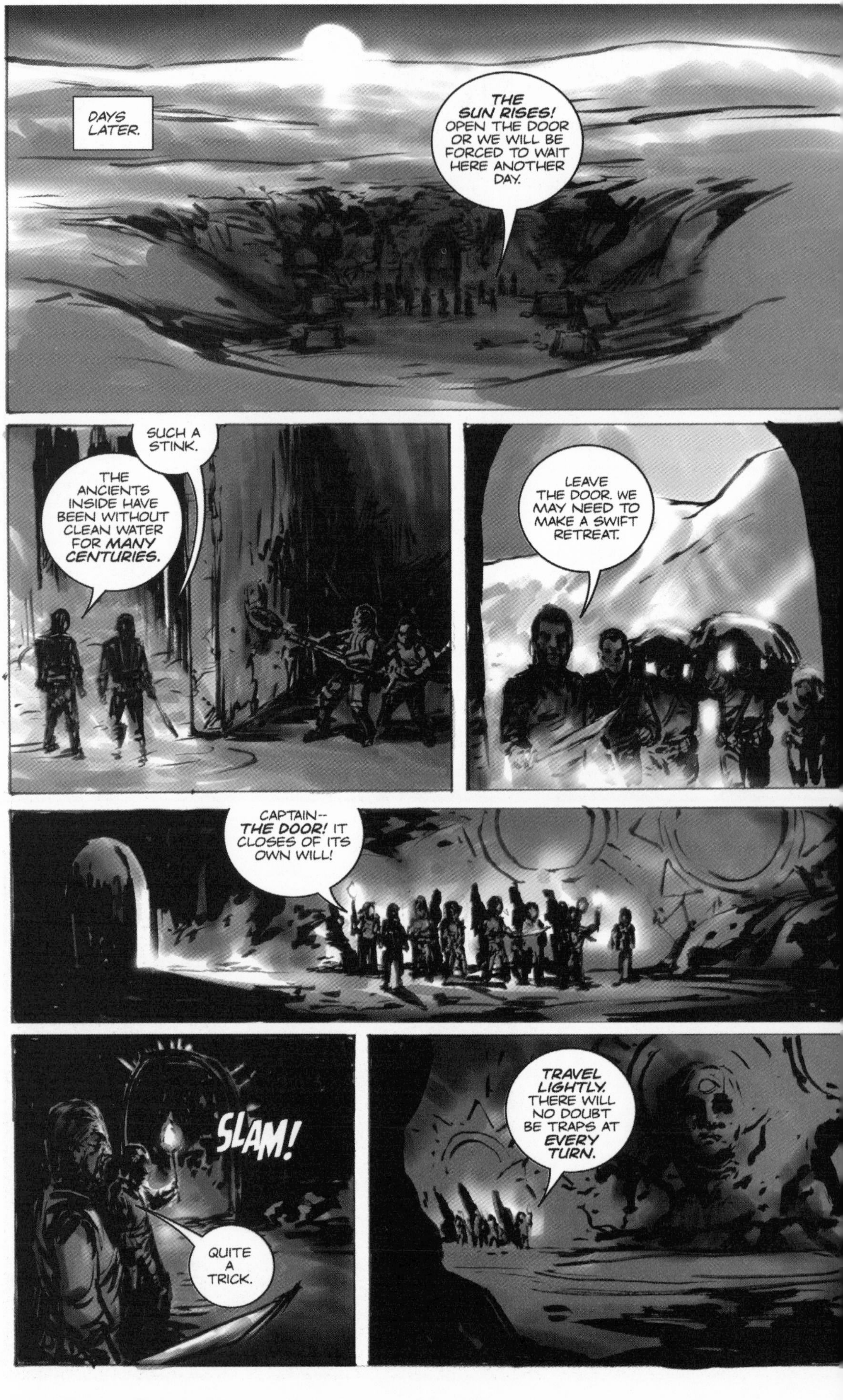
DAYS LATER.
THE SUN RISES! OPEN THE DOOR OR WE WILL BE FORCED TO WAIT HERE ANOTHER DAY.
SUCH A STINK.
THE ANCIENTS INSIDE HAVE BEEN WITHOUT CLEAN WATER FOR MANY CENTURIES.
LEAVE THE DOOR. WE MAY NEED TO MAKE A SWIFT RETREAT.
CAPTAIN-- THE DOOR! IT CLOSES OF ITS OWN WILL!
SLAM!
QUITE A TRICK.
TRAVEL LIGHTLY. THERE WILL NO DOUBT BE TRAPS AT EVERY TURN.

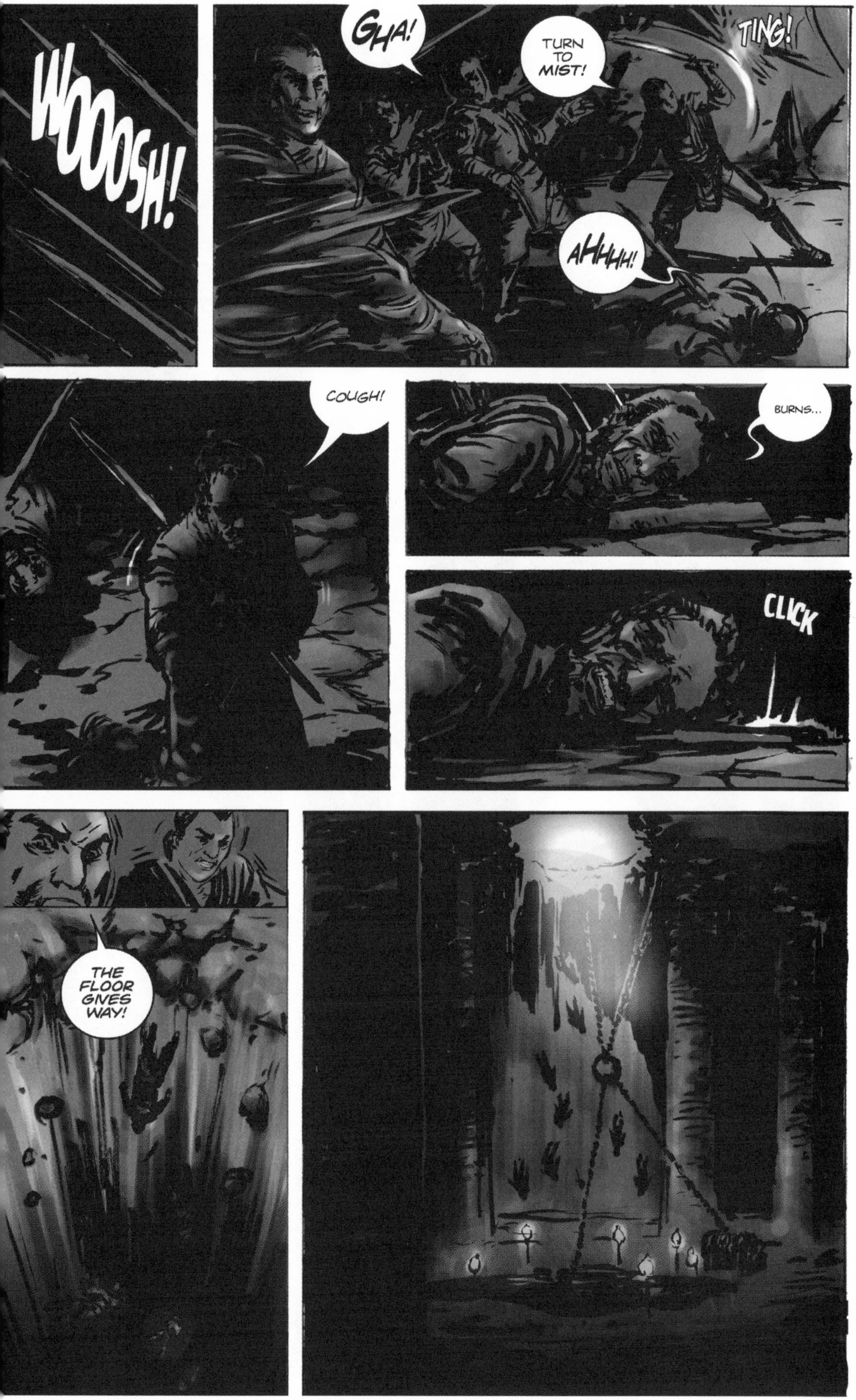
WOOOSH!
GHA!
TURN TO MIST!
TING!
AHHHH!
COUGH!
BURNS...
CLICK
THE FLOOR GIVES WAY!

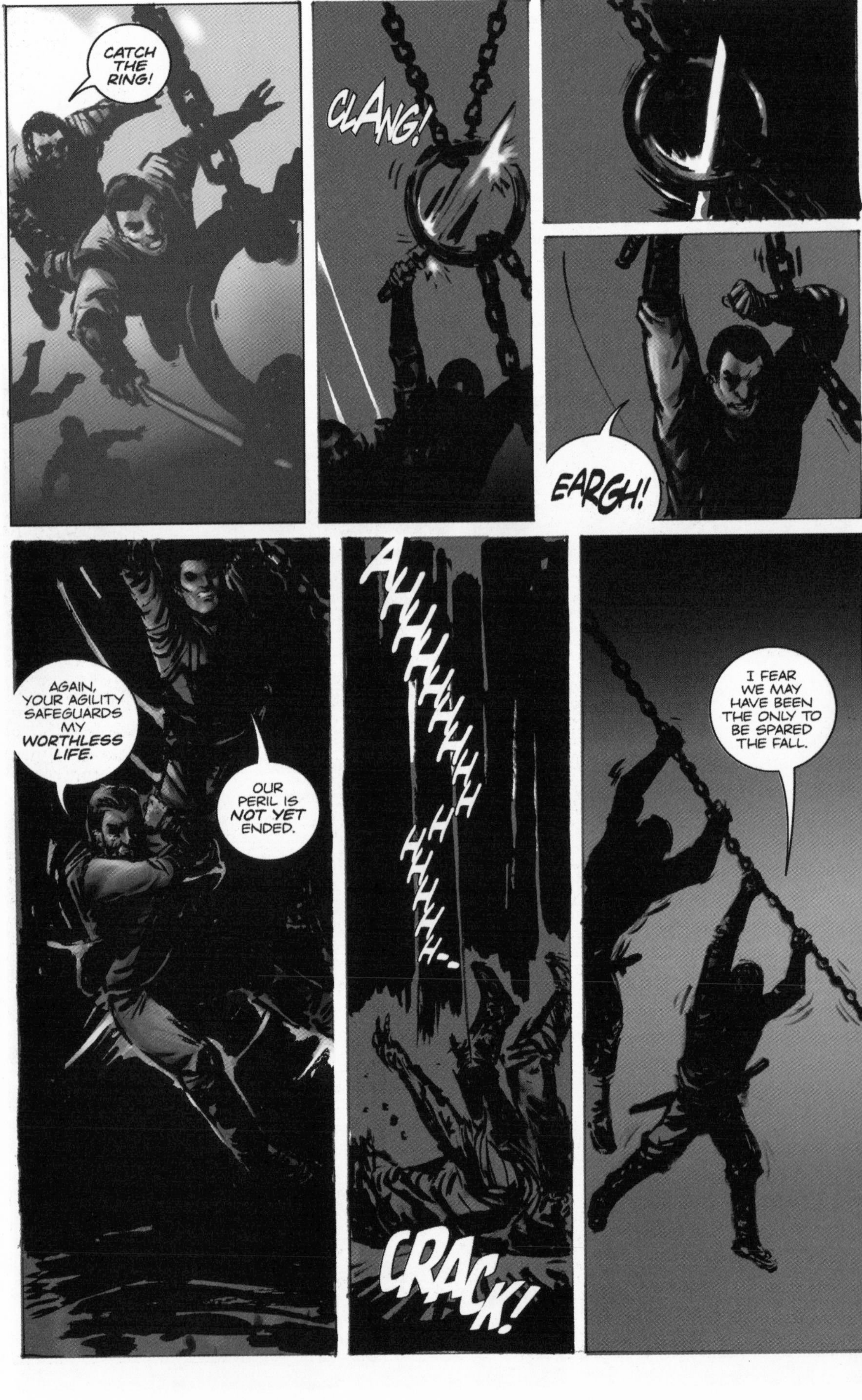
CATCH THE RING!
CLANG!
EARGH!
AGAIN, YOUR AGILITY SAFEGUARDS MY WORTHLESS LIFE.
OUR PERIL IS NOT YET ENDED.
AHHHHHHHHHHHHHHHHHHH--
CRACK!
I FEAR WE MAY HAVE BEEN THE ONLY TO BE SPARED THE FALL.

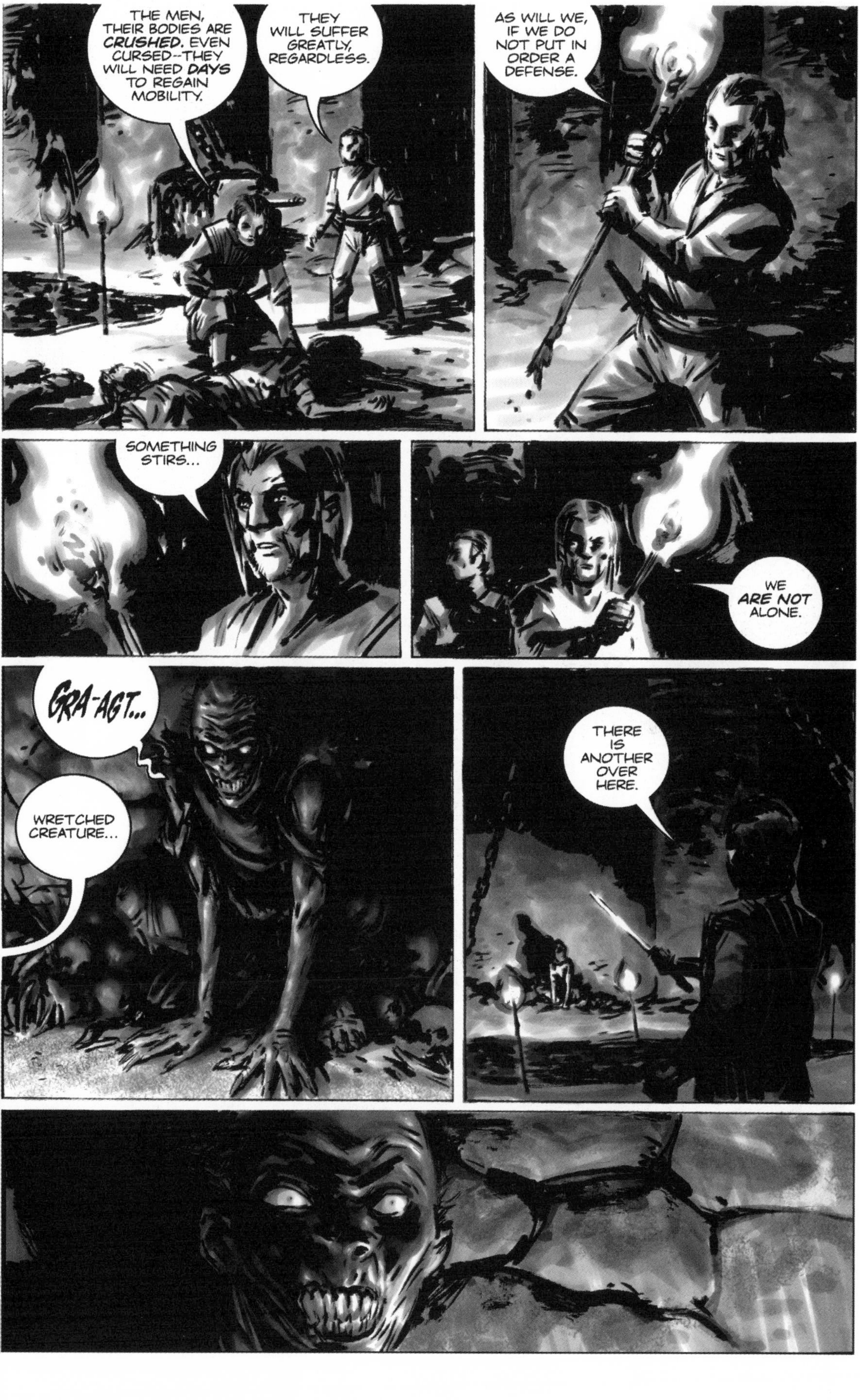
THE MEN, THEIR BODIES ARE CRUSHED. EVEN CURSED--THEY WILL NEED DAYS TO REGAIN MOBILITY.
THEY WILL SUFFER GREATLY, REGARDLESS.
AS WILL WE, IF WE DO NOT PUT IN ORDER A DEFENSE.
SOMETHING STIRS...
WE ARE NOT ALONE.
GRA-AGT...
WRETCHED CREATURE...
THERE IS ANOTHER OVER HERE.

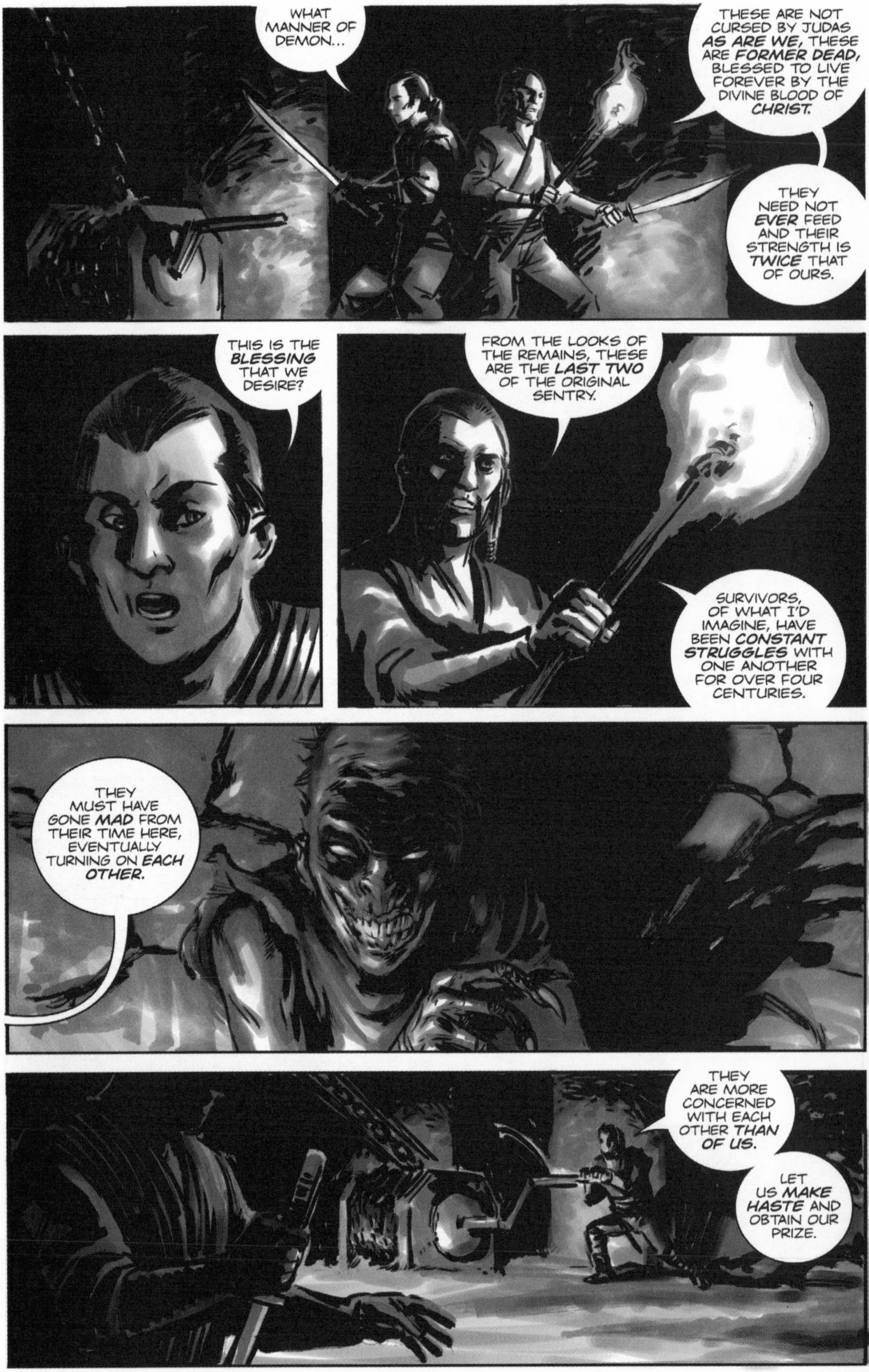
WHAT MANNER OF DEMON...
THESE ARE NOT CURSED BY JUDAS AS ARE WE, THESE ARE FORMER DEAD, BLESSED TO LIVE FOREVER BY THE DIVINE BLOOD OF CHRIST.
THEY NEED NOT EVER FEED AND THEIR STRENGTH IS TWICE THAT OF OURS.
THIS IS THE BLESSING THAT WE DESIRE?
FROM THE LOOKS OF THE REMAINS, THESE ARE THE LAST TWO OF THE ORIGINAL SENTRY.
SURVIVORS, OF WHAT I'D IMAGINE, HAVE BEEN CONSTANT STRUGGLES WITH ONE ANOTHER FOR OVER FOUR CENTURIES.
THEY MUST HAVE GONE MAD FROM THEIR TIME HERE, EVENTUALLY TURNING ON EACH OTHER.
THEY ARE MORE CONCERNED WITH EACH OTHER THAN OF US.
LET US MAKE HASTE AND OBTAIN OUR PRIZE.

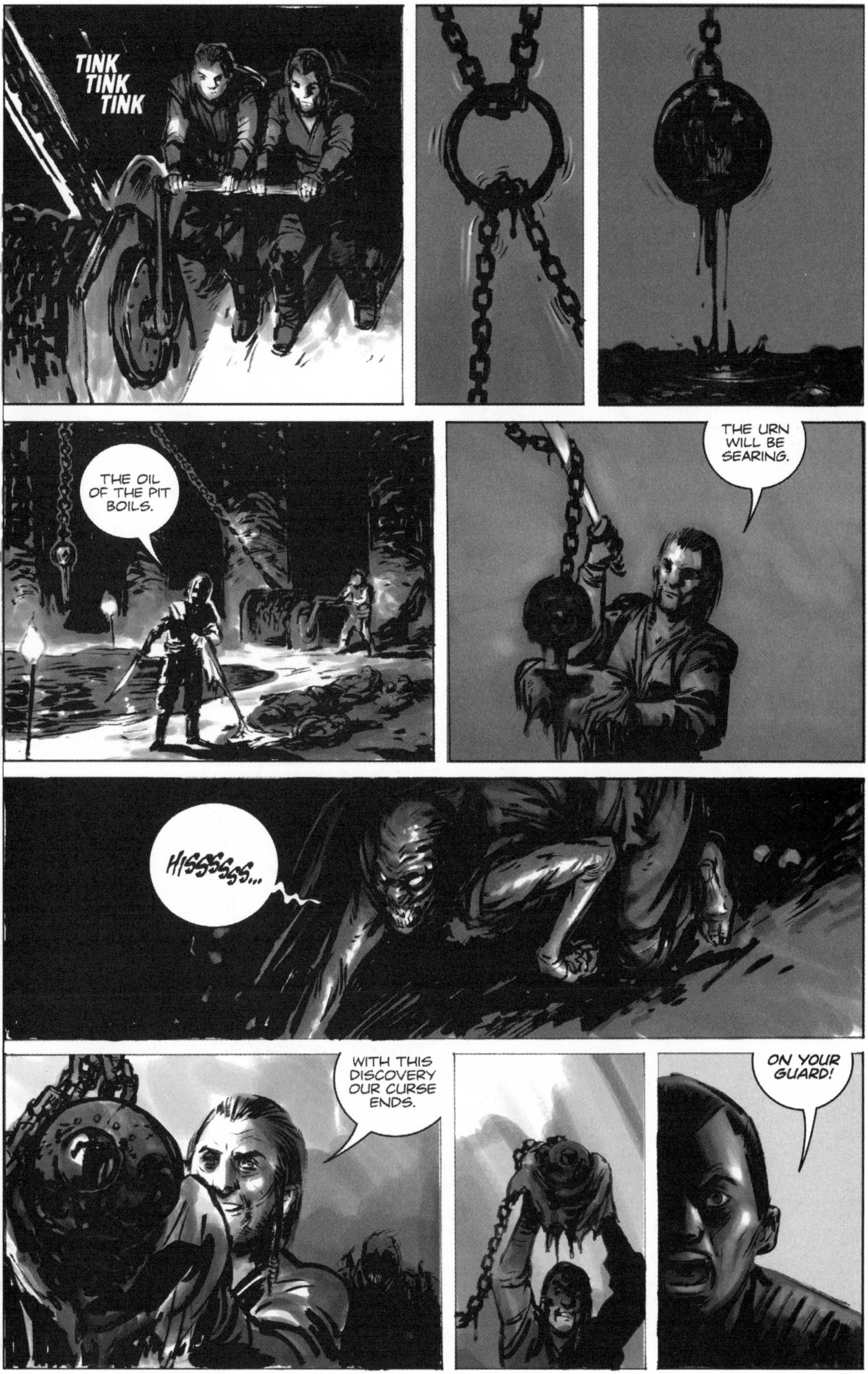
TINK TINK TINK
THE OIL OF THE PIT BOILS.
THE URN WILL BE SEARING.
HISSSSSS...
WITH THIS DISCOVERY OUR CURSE ENDS.
ON YOUR GUARD!

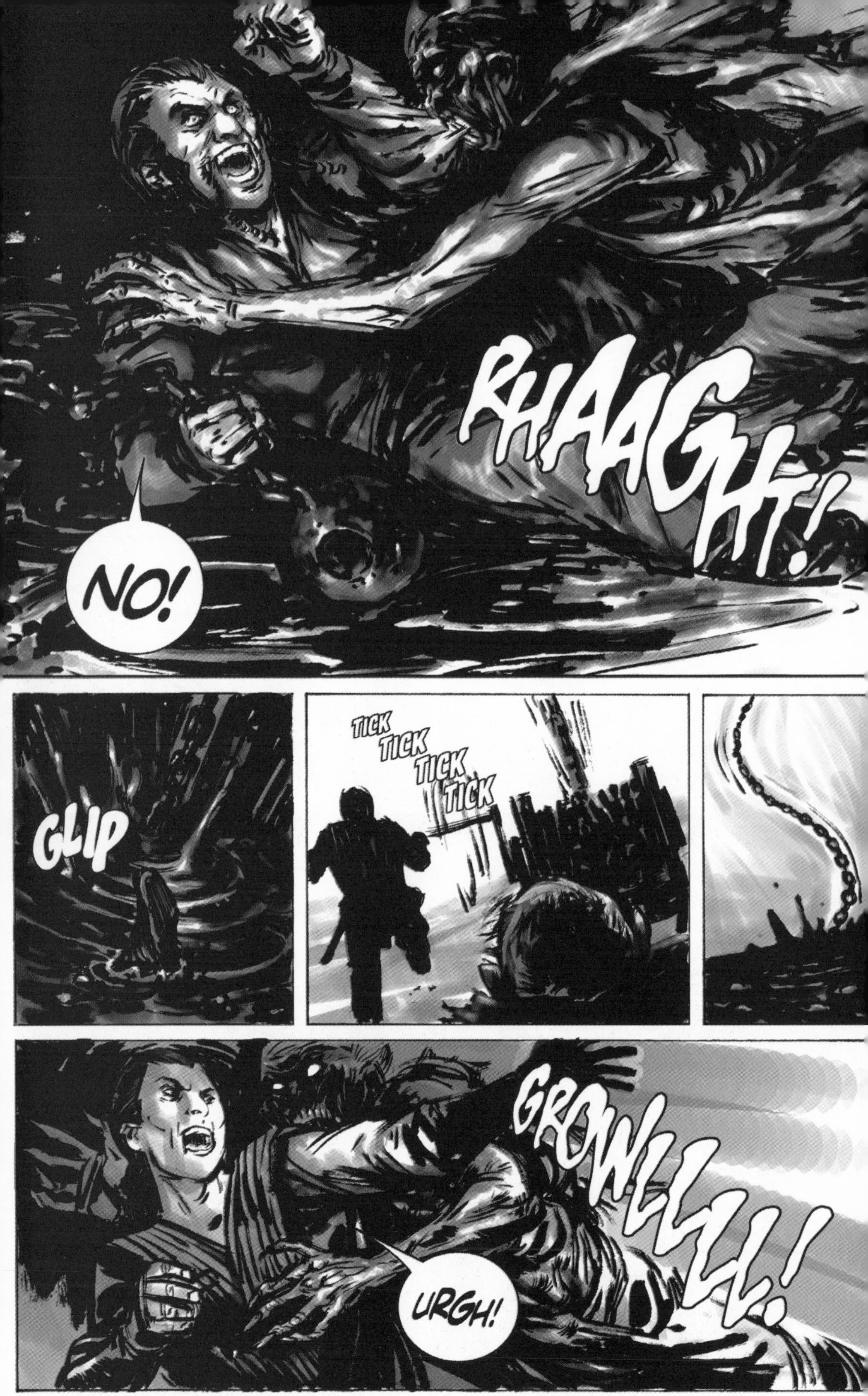
RHAAGHH!
NO!
GLIP
TICK
TICK
TICK
TICK
GROWLLLLL!
URGH!

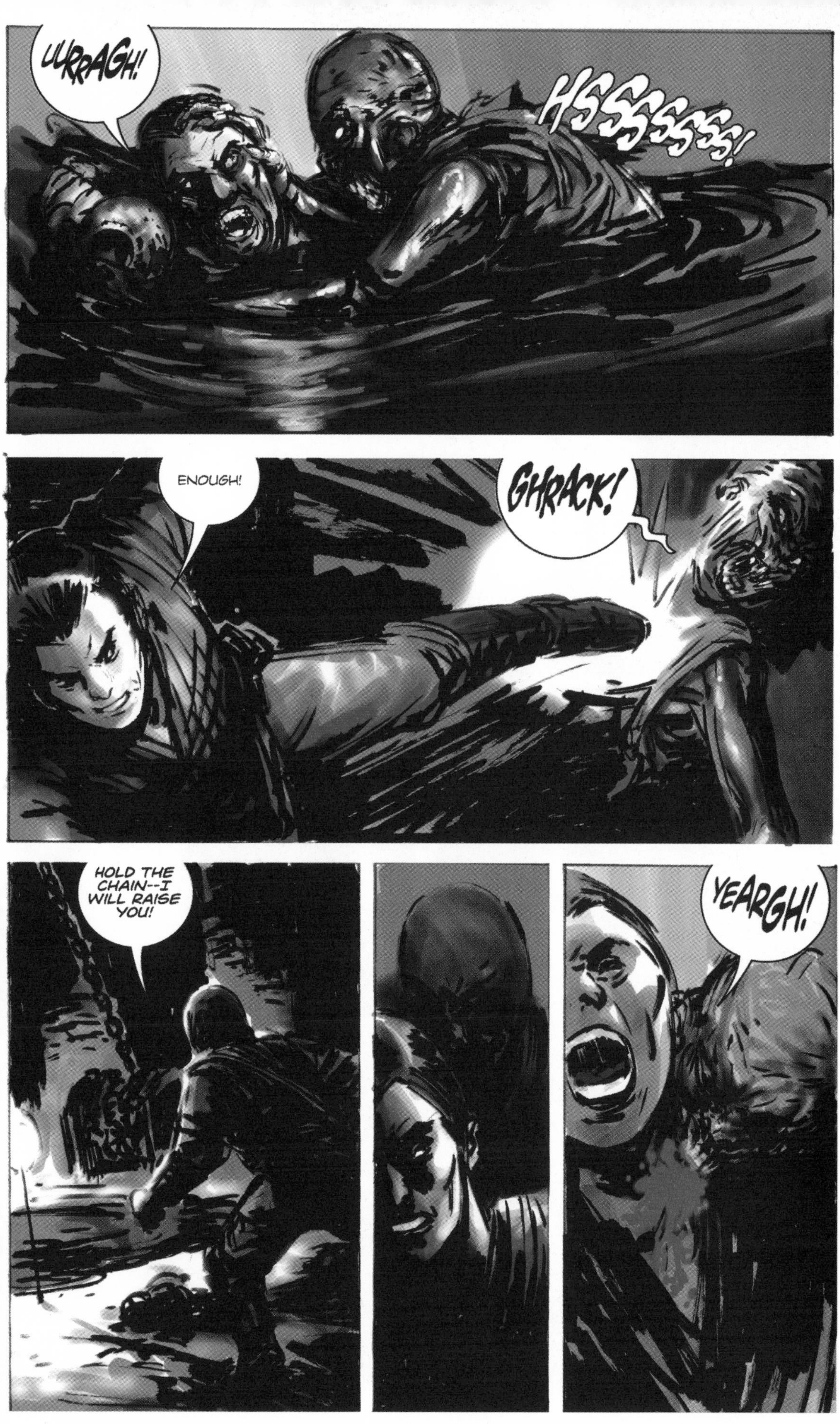
UURRAGH!
HSSSSSSS!
ENOUGH!
GHRACK!
HOLD THE CHAIN--I WILL RAISE YOU!
YEARGH!

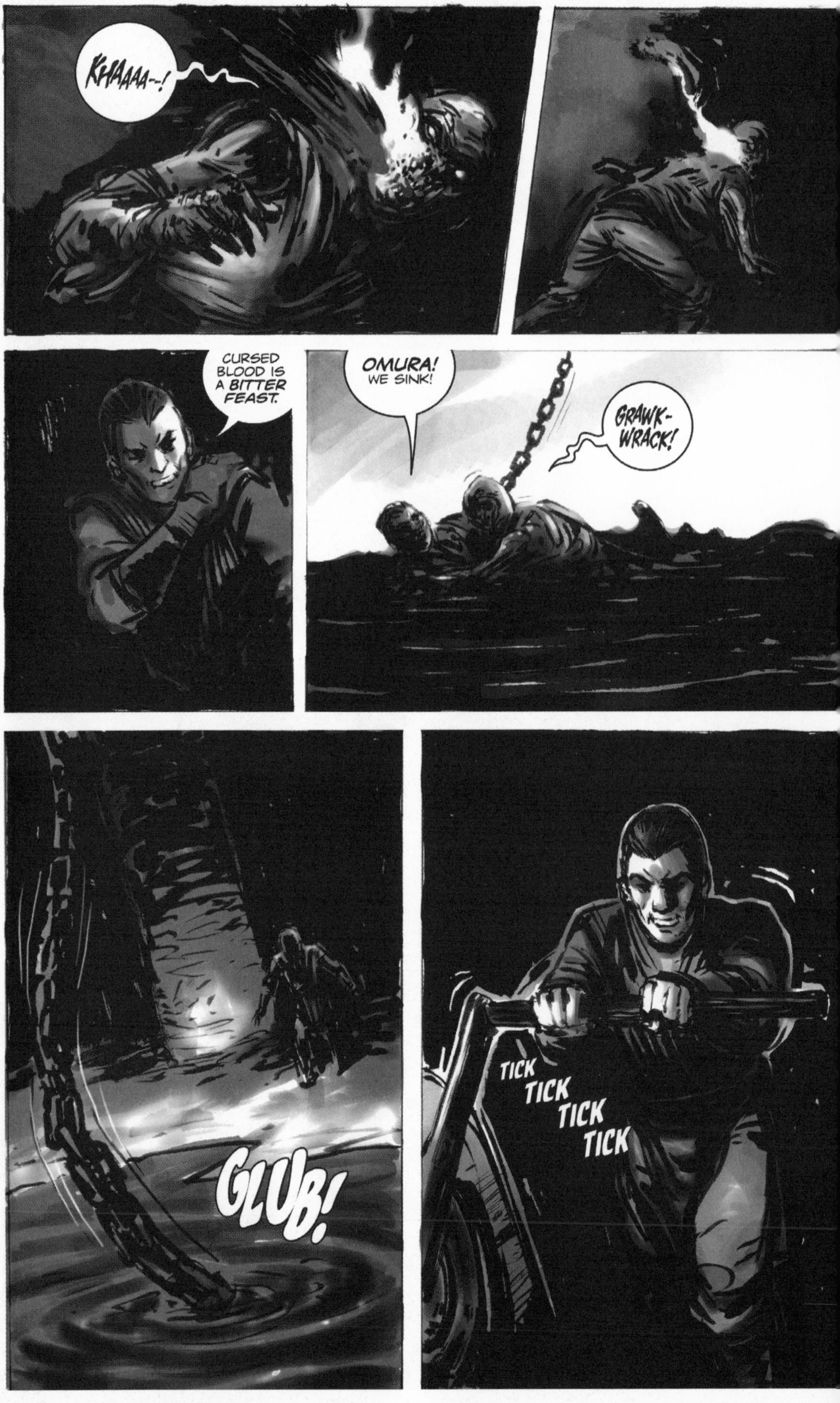
KHAAAA--!
CURSED BLOOD IS A BITTER FEAST.
OMURA! WE SINK!
GRAWK-WRACK!
GLUB!
TICK TICK TICK TICK

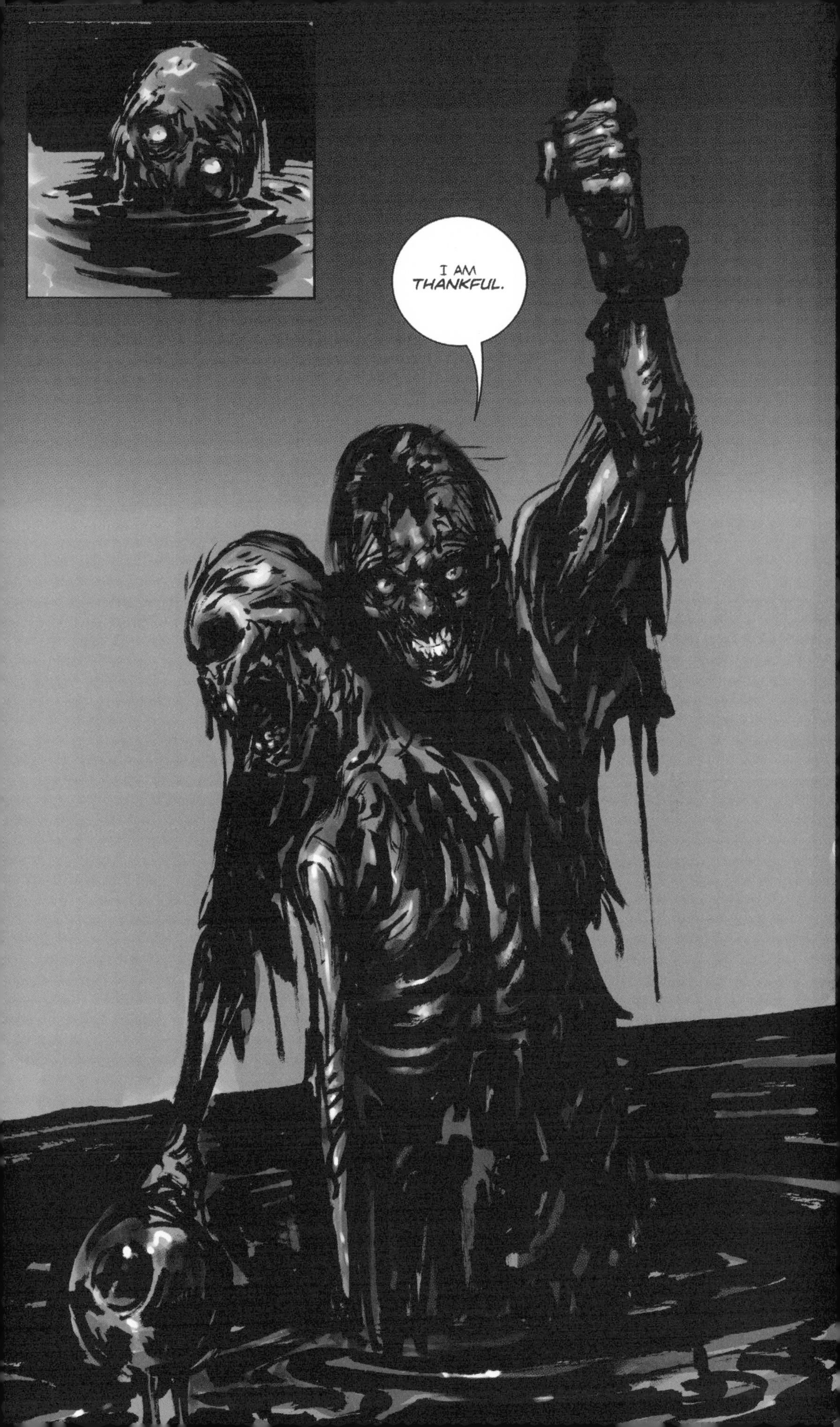
I AM THANKFUL.

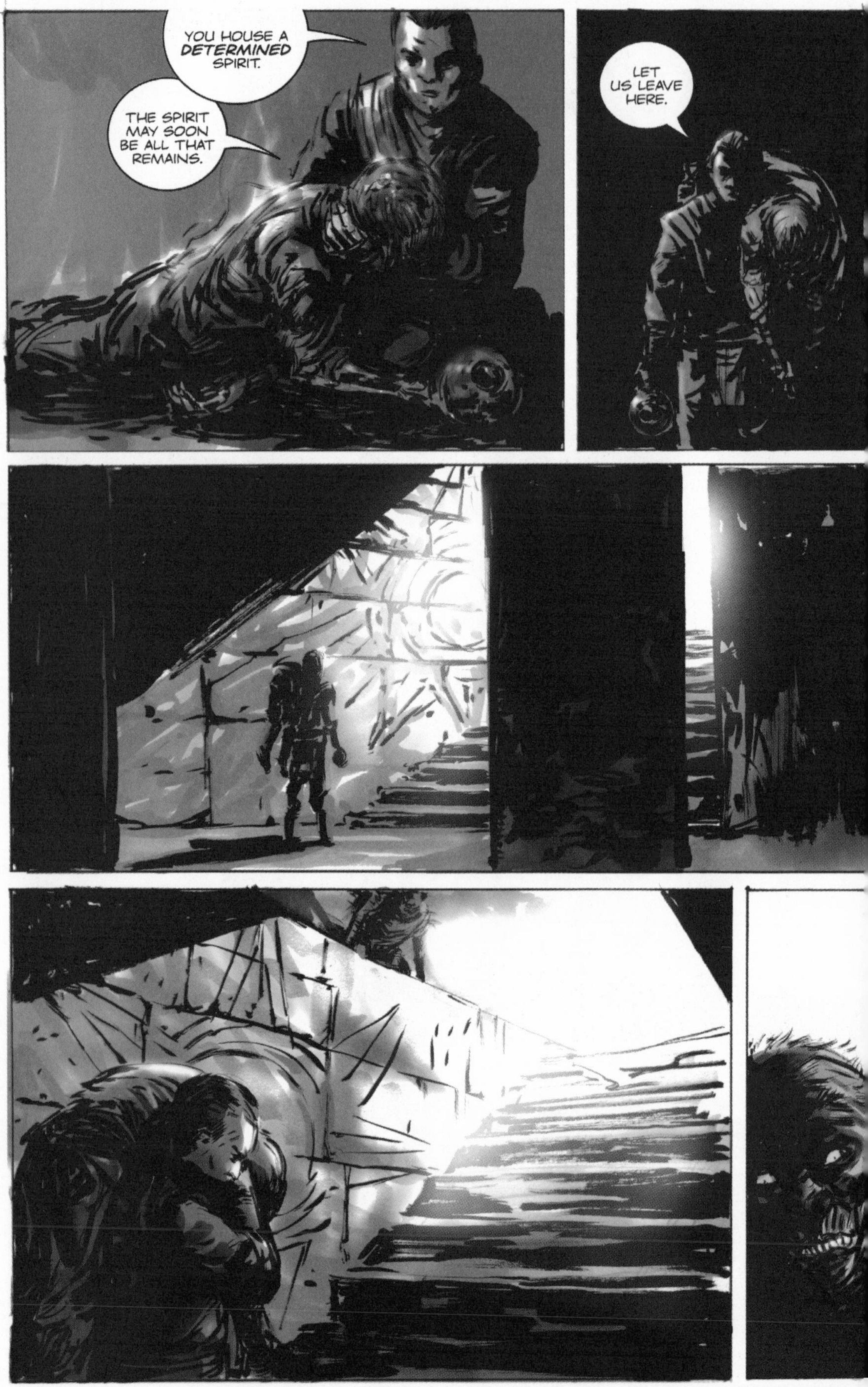

YOU HOUSE A *DETERMINED* SPIRIT.
THE SPIRIT MAY SOON BE ALL THAT REMAINS.
LET US LEAVE HERE.

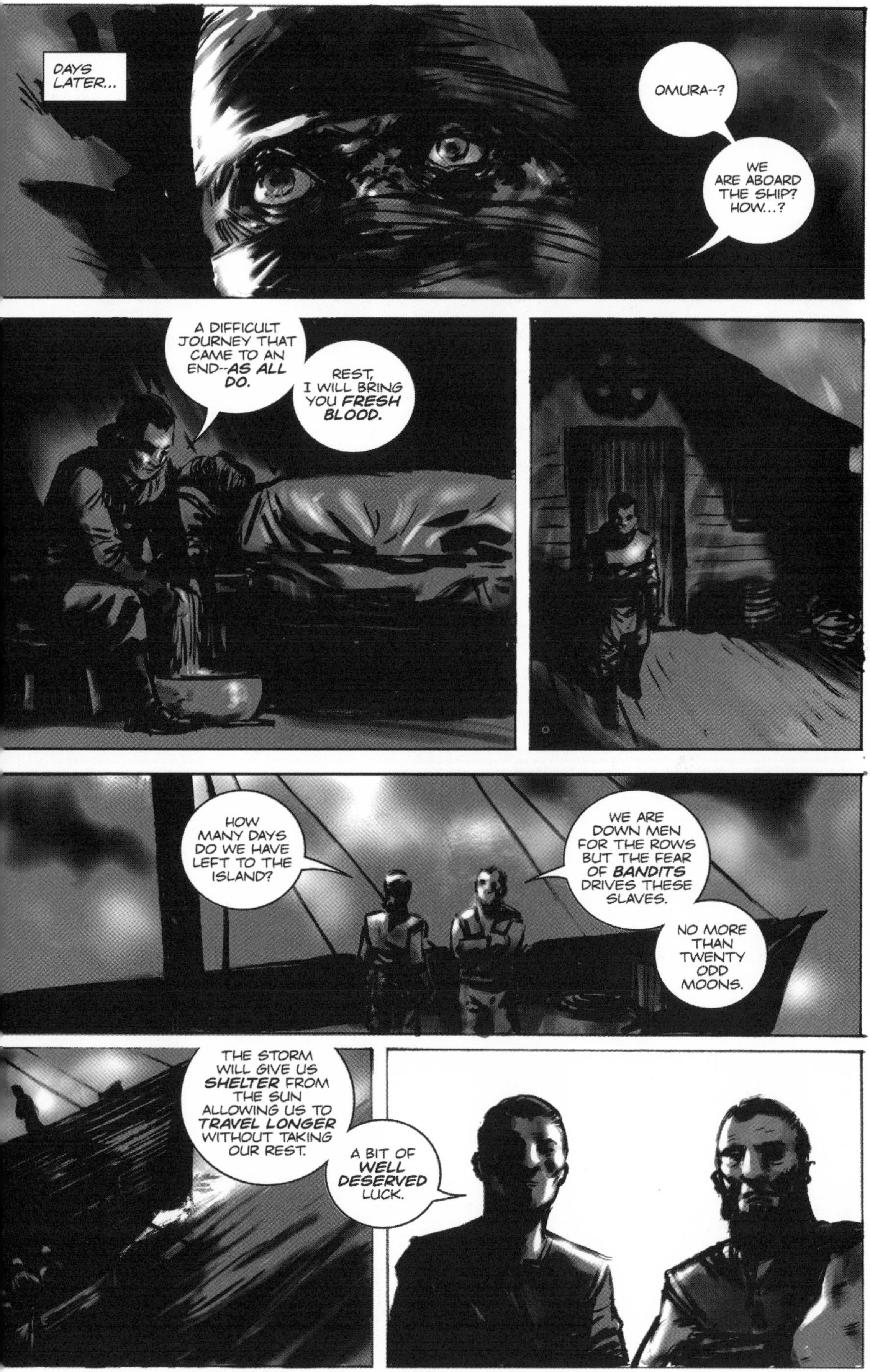
DAYS LATER...
OMURA--?
WE ARE ABOARD THE SHIP? HOW...?
A DIFFICULT JOURNEY THAT CAME TO AN END--AS ALL DO.
REST, I WILL BRING YOU FRESH BLOOD.
HOW MANY DAYS DO WE HAVE LEFT TO THE ISLAND?
WE ARE DOWN MEN FOR THE ROWS BUT THE FEAR OF BANDITS DRIVES THESE SLAVES.
NO MORE THAN TWENTY ODD MOONS.
THE STORM WILL GIVE US SHELTER FROM THE SUN ALLOWING US TO TRAVEL LONGER WITHOUT TAKING OUR REST.
A BIT OF WELL DESERVED LUCK.

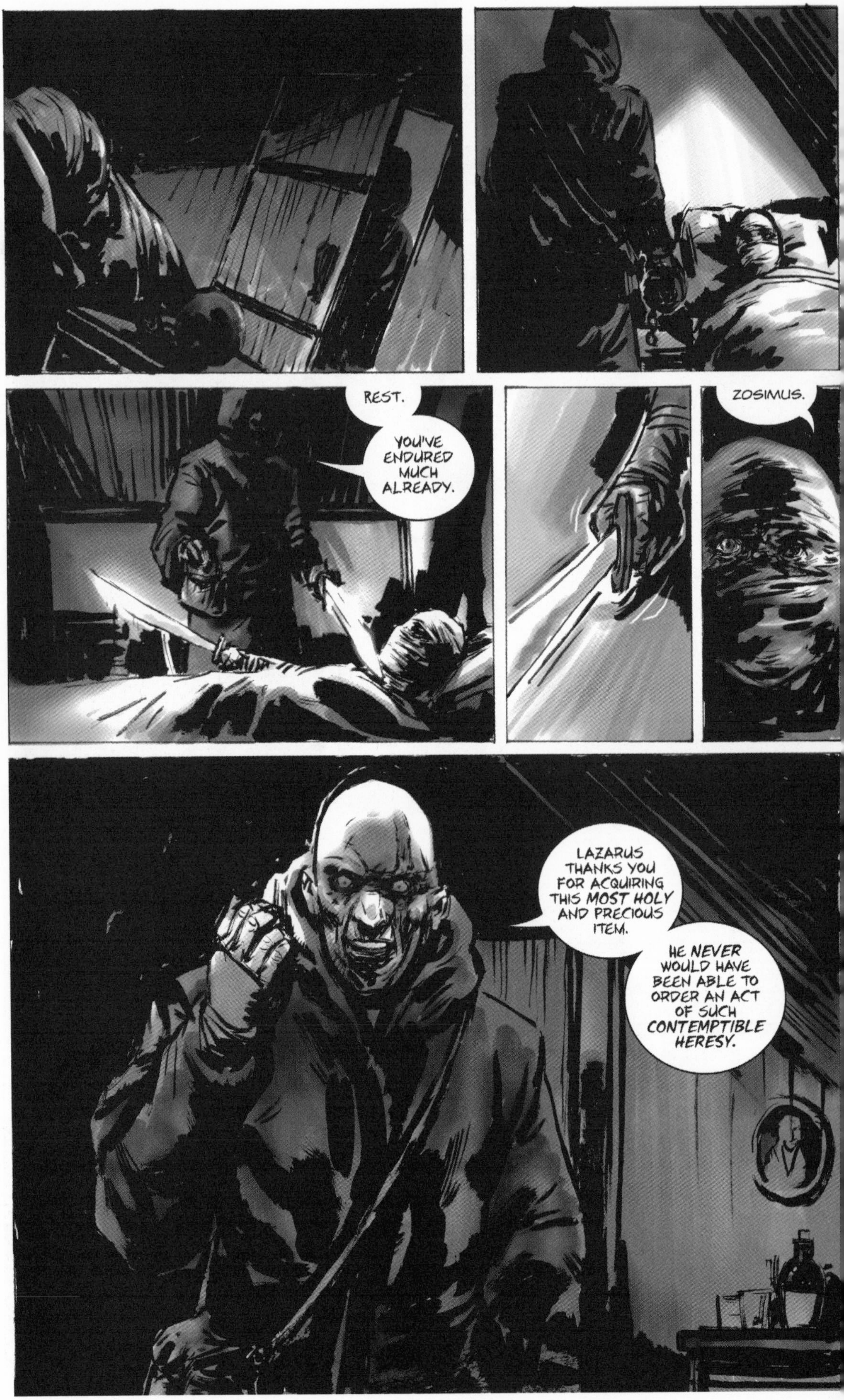
REST.
YOU'VE ENDURED MUCH ALREADY.
ZOSIMUS.
LAZARUS THANKS YOU FOR ACQUIRING THIS MOST HOLY AND PRECIOUS ITEM.
HE NEVER WOULD HAVE BEEN ABLE TO ORDER AN ACT OF SUCH CONTEMPTIBLE HERESY.

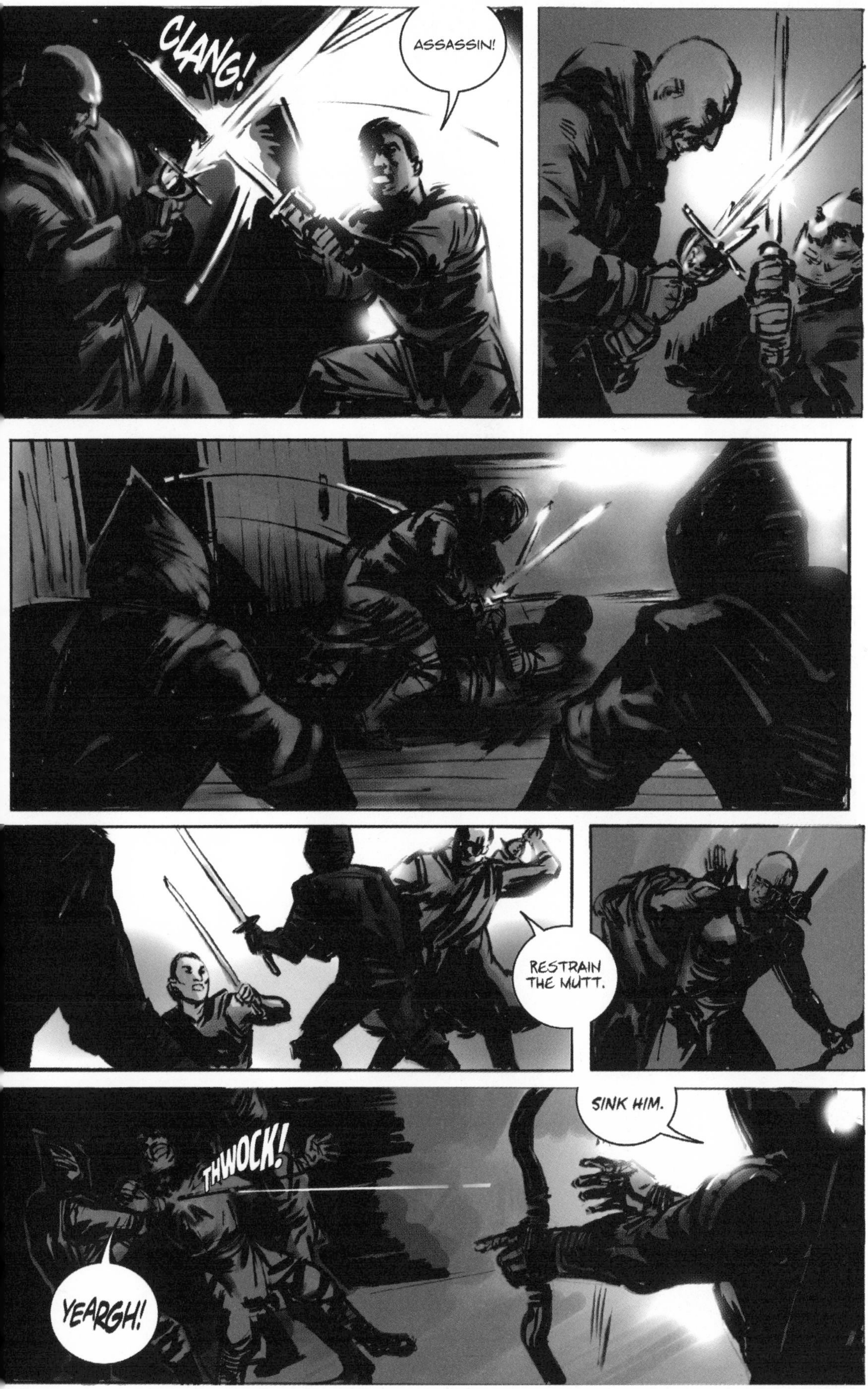
CLANG!
ASSASSIN!
RESTRAIN THE MUTT.
SINK HIM.
THWOCK!
YEARGH!

QUICKLY.

THE ANOINTED ARROW'S EFFECTS WILL ONLY PREVENT HIM FROM MISTING FOR MOMENTS.

YOU WILL SINK LIKE A ROCK.

PERHAPS...

TOK.

I'LL NOT BE ALONE!

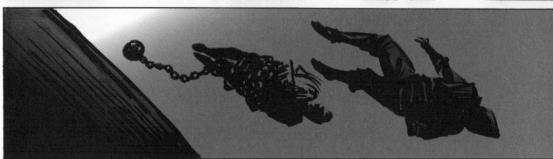

YOU ARE STRONG.

I WOULD ENSURE YOU DO NOT SURVIVE TO SEEK ME OUT.

HE WILL NOT NEED TO...

SWUCT!

YOU WILL BE DEAD.

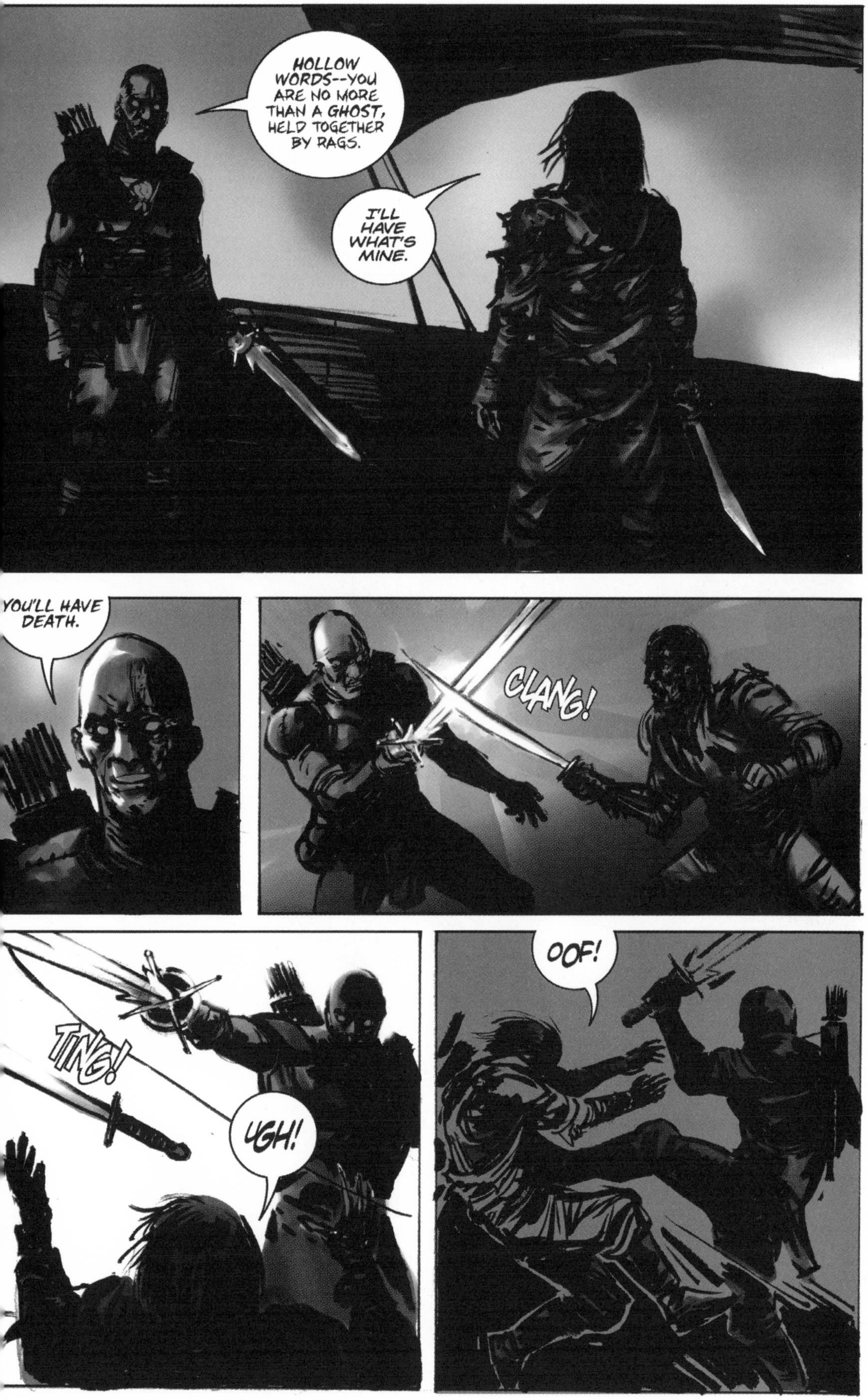
HOLLOW WORDS--YOU ARE NO MORE THAN A GHOST, HELD TOGETHER BY RAGS.
I'LL HAVE WHAT'S MINE.
YOU'LL HAVE DEATH.
CLANG!
TING!
UGH!
OOF!

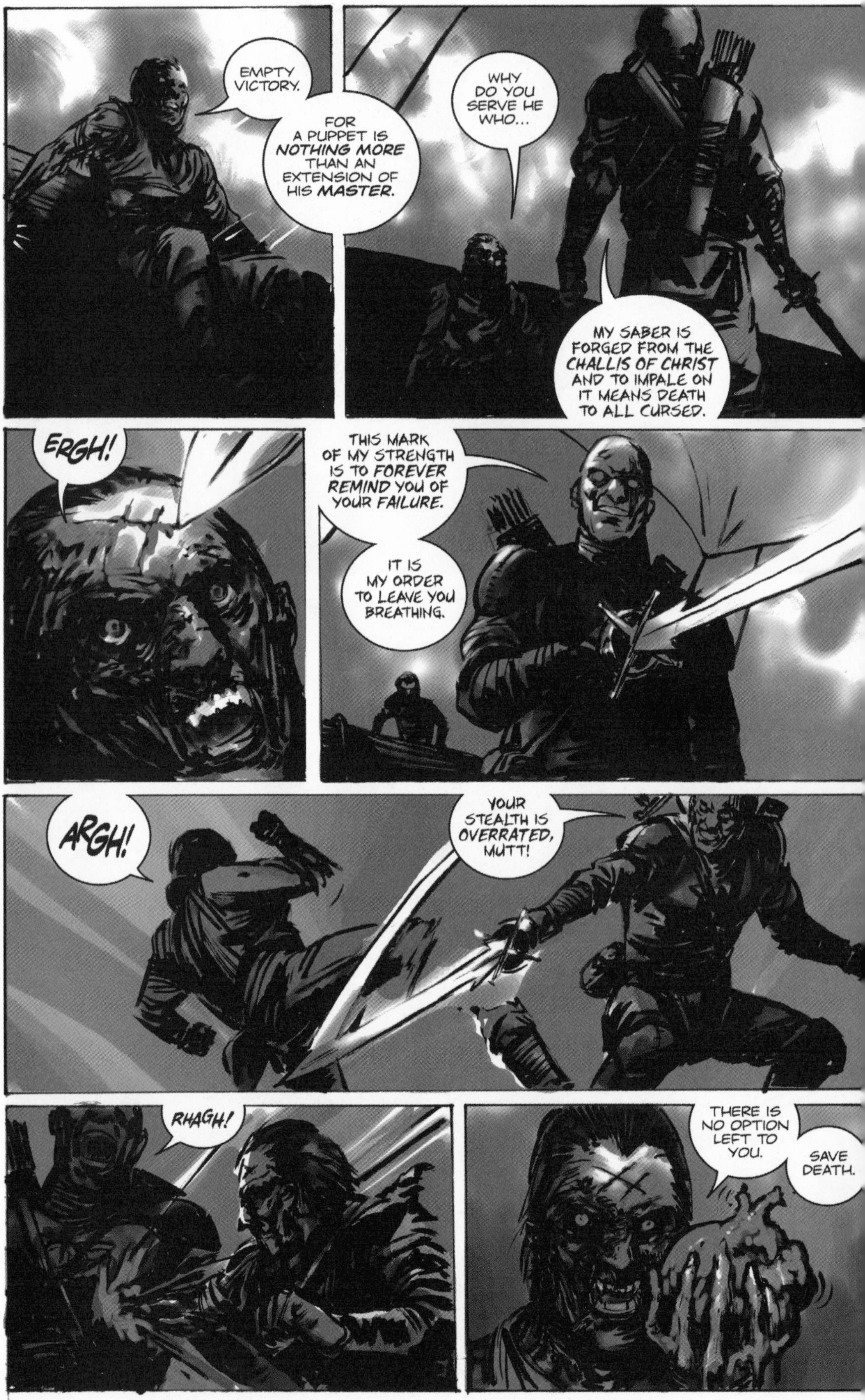
EMPTY VICTORY.
FOR A PUPPET IS NOTHING MORE THAN AN EXTENSION OF HIS MASTER.
WHY DO YOU SERVE HE WHO...
MY SABER IS FORGED FROM THE CHALLIS OF CHRIST AND TO IMPALE ON IT MEANS DEATH TO ALL CURSED.
ERGH!
THIS MARK OF MY STRENGTH IS TO FOREVER REMIND YOU OF YOUR FAILURE.
IT IS MY ORDER TO LEAVE YOU BREATHING.
ARGH!
YOUR STEALTH IS OVERRATED, MUTT!
RHAGH!
THERE IS NO OPTION LEFT TO YOU.
SAVE DEATH.

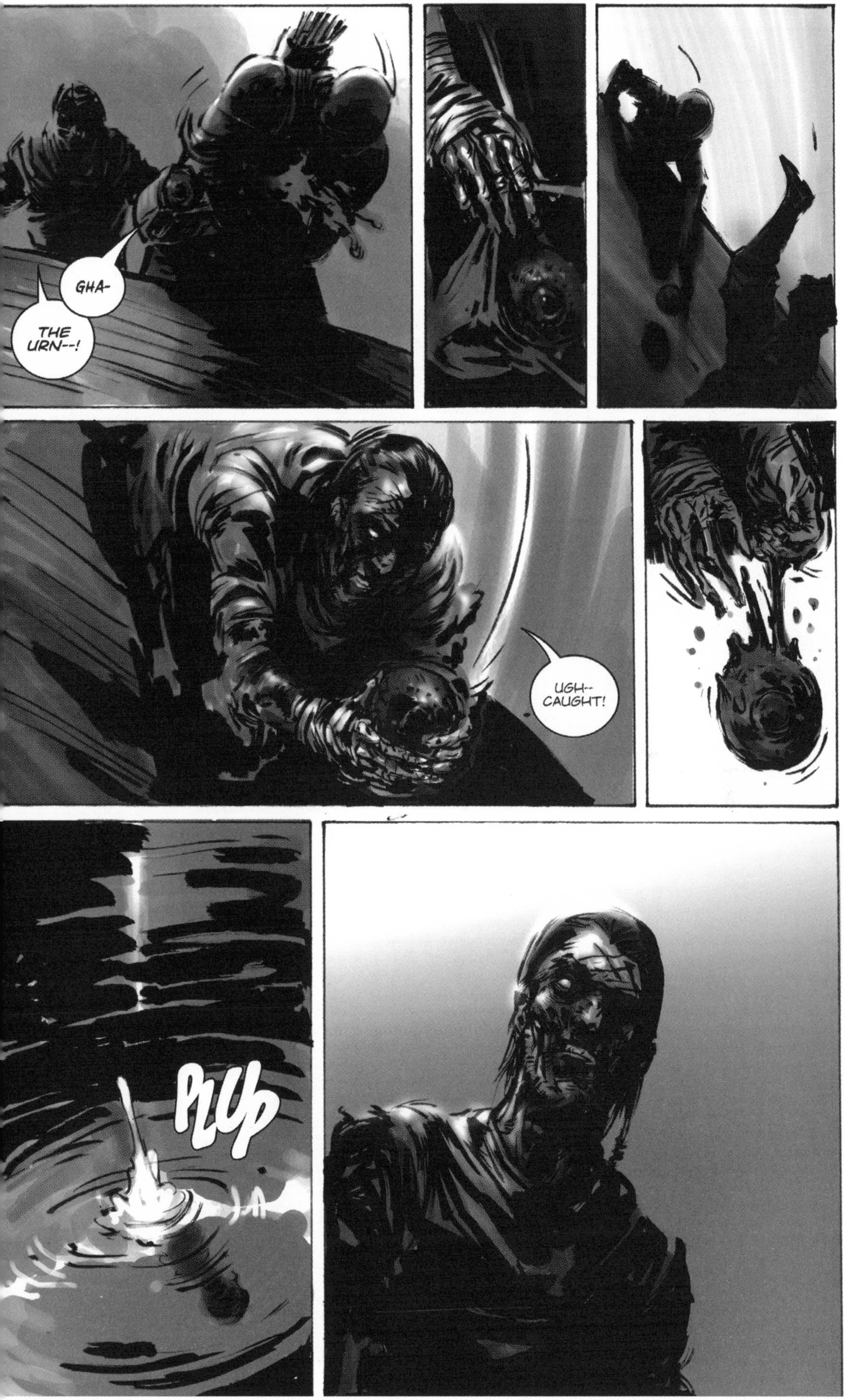
GHA-
THE URN--!
UGH--
CAUGHT!
PLUP

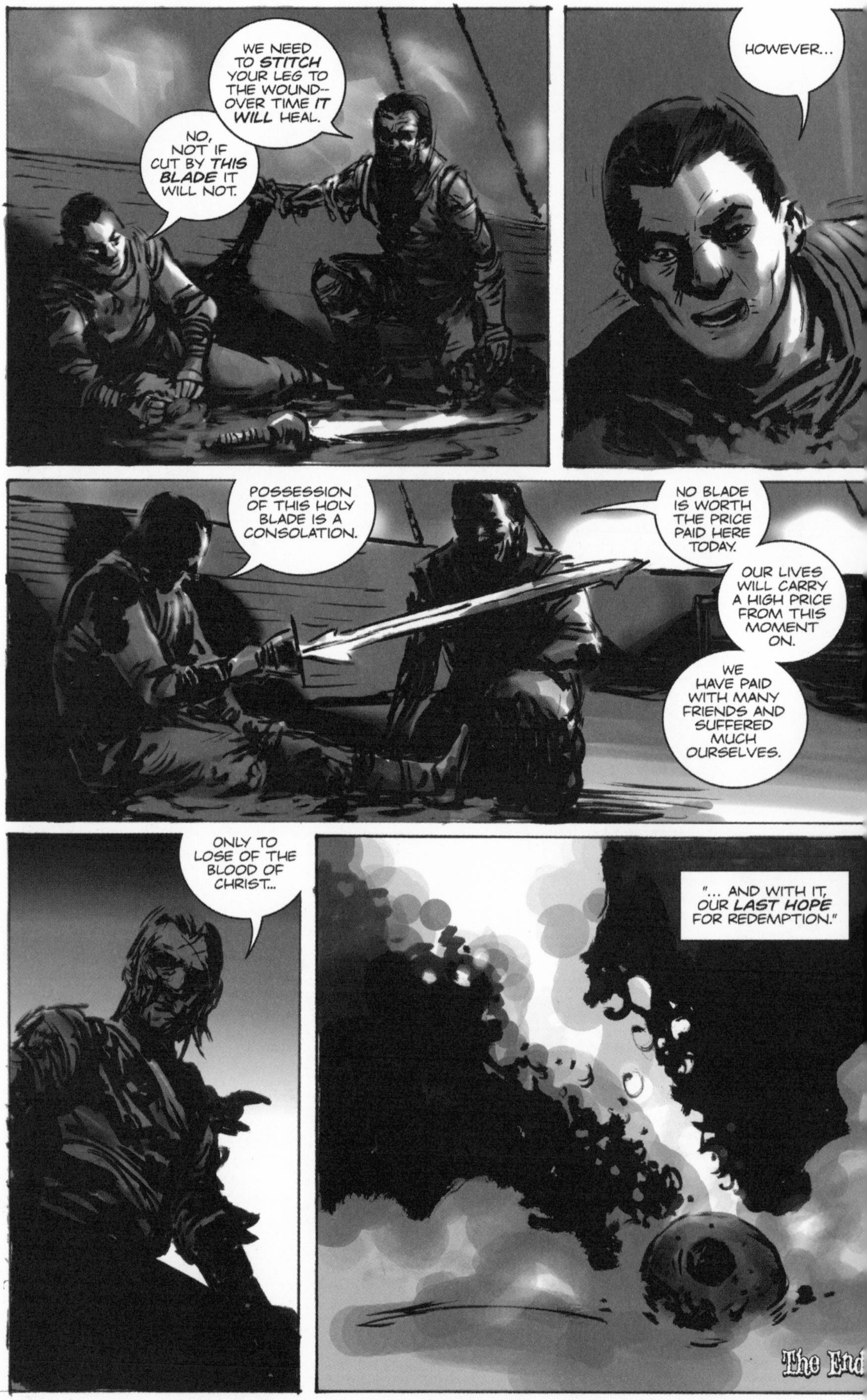
WE NEED TO STITCH YOUR LEG TO THE WOUND-- OVER TIME IT WILL HEAL.
NO, NOT IF CUT BY THIS BLADE IT WILL NOT.
HOWEVER...
POSSESSION OF THIS HOLY BLADE IS A CONSOLATION.
NO BLADE IS WORTH THE PRICE PAID HERE TODAY.
OUR LIVES WILL CARRY A HIGH PRICE FROM THIS MOMENT ON.
WE HAVE PAID WITH MANY FRIENDS AND SUFFERED MUCH OURSELVES.
ONLY TO LOSE OF THE BLOOD OF CHRIST...
"... AND WITH IT, OUR LAST HOPE FOR REDEMPTION."
The End

Six

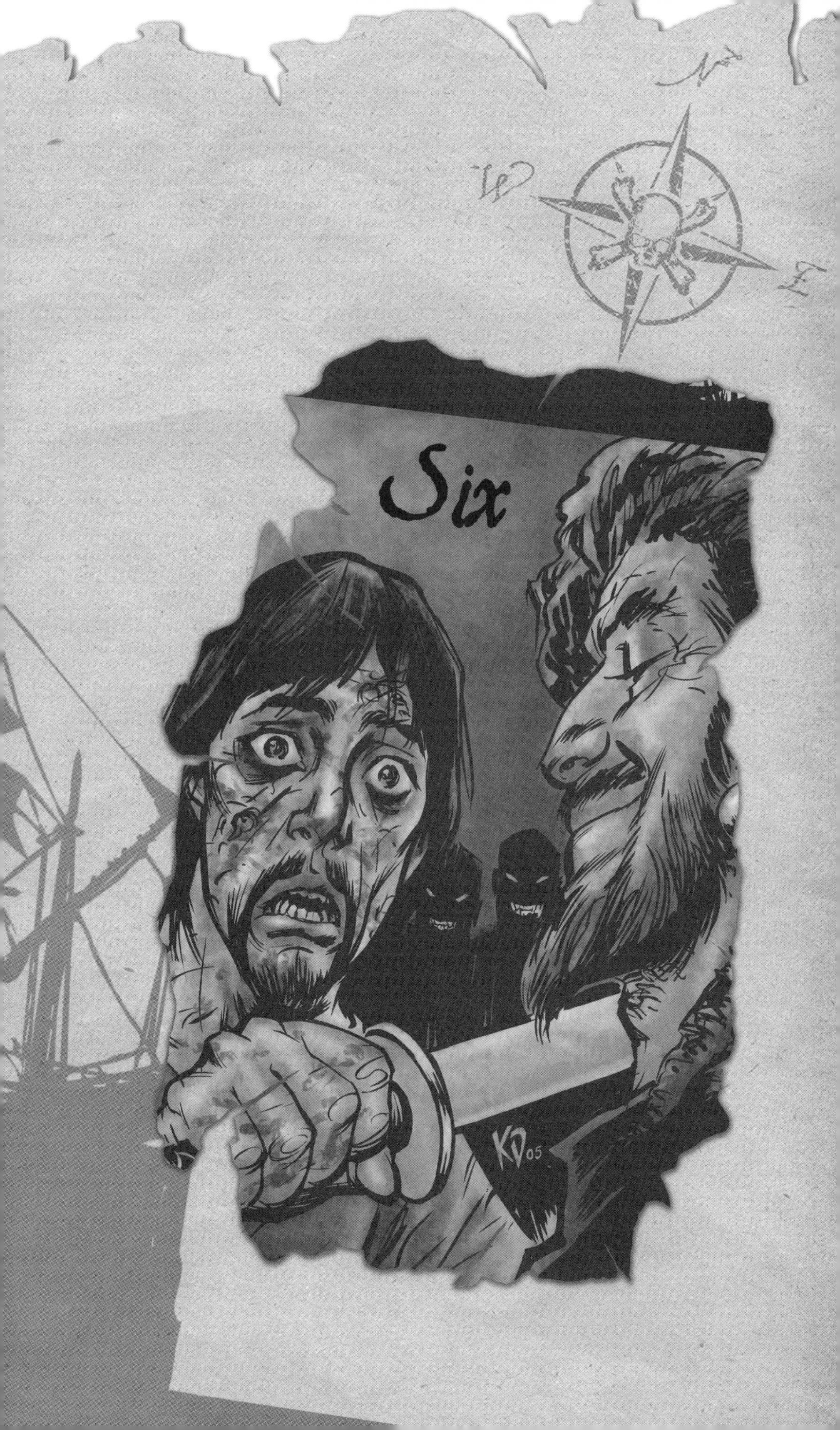

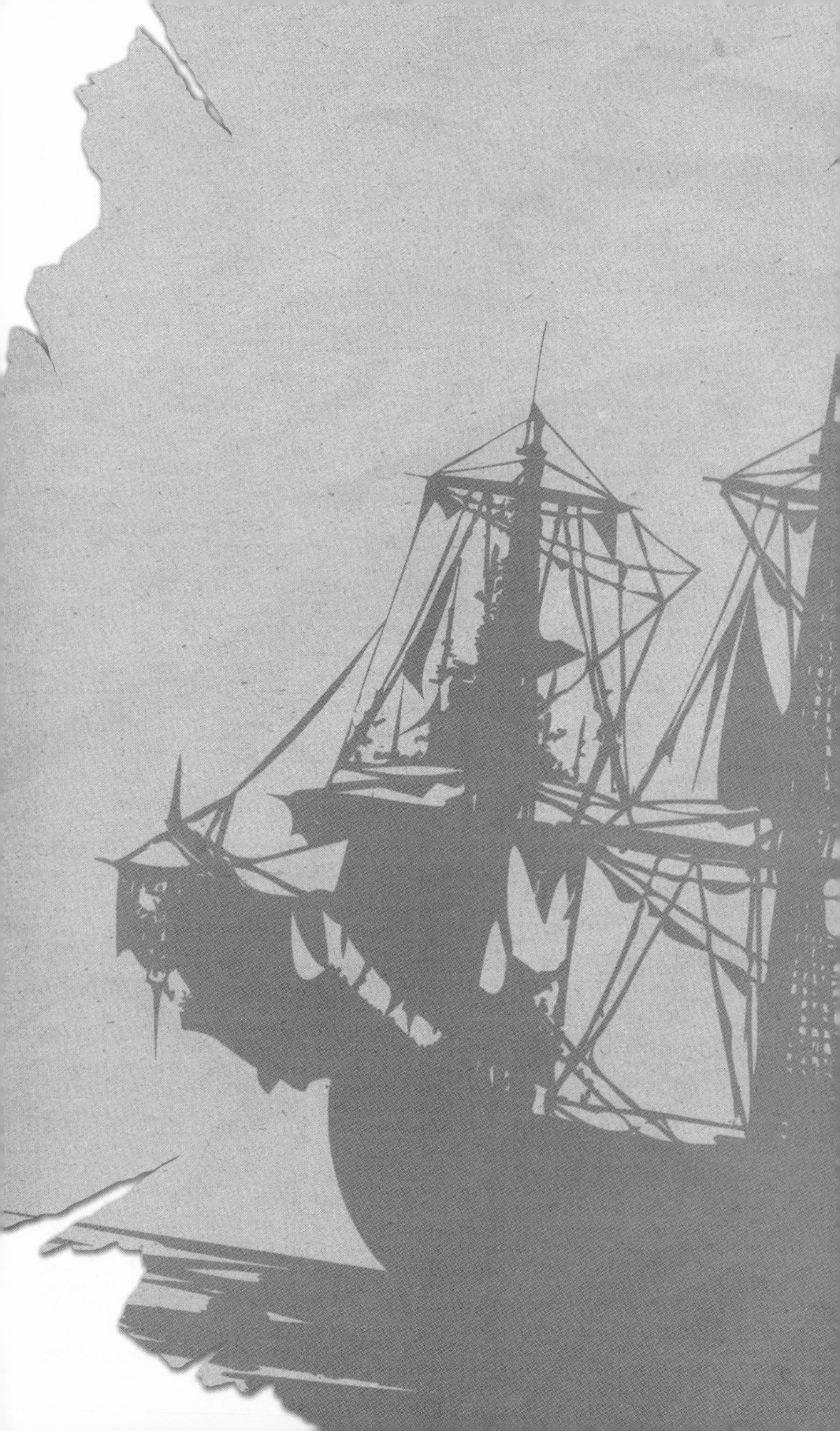

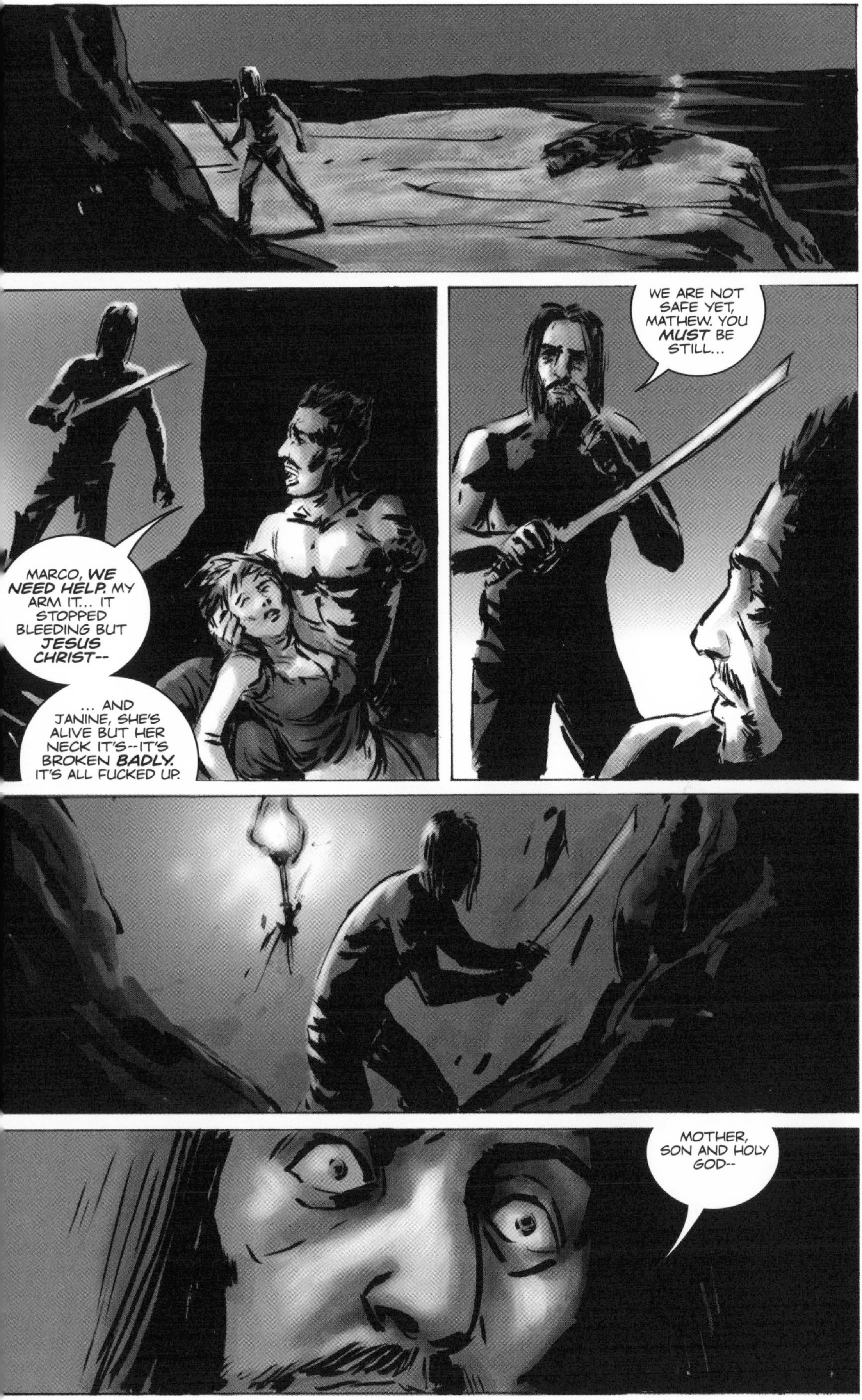
MARCO, **WE NEED HELP.** MY ARM IT... IT STOPPED BLEEDING BUT **JESUS CHRIST--**
... AND JANINE, SHE'S ALIVE BUT HER NECK IT'S--IT'S BROKEN **BADLY.** IT'S ALL FUCKED UP.
WE ARE NOT SAFE YET, MATHEW. YOU **MUST** BE STILL...
MOTHER, SON AND HOLY GOD--

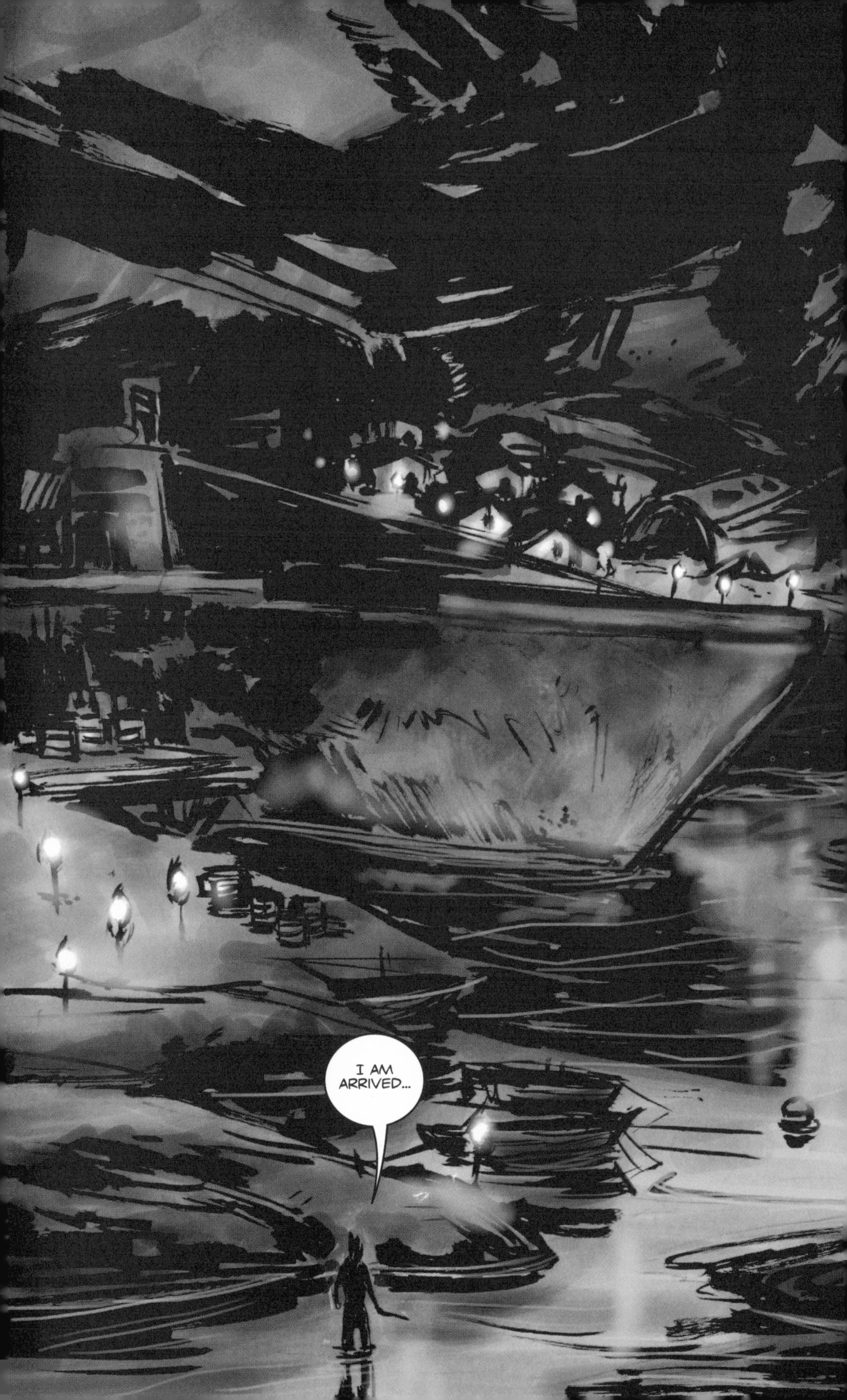
I AM ARRIVED...

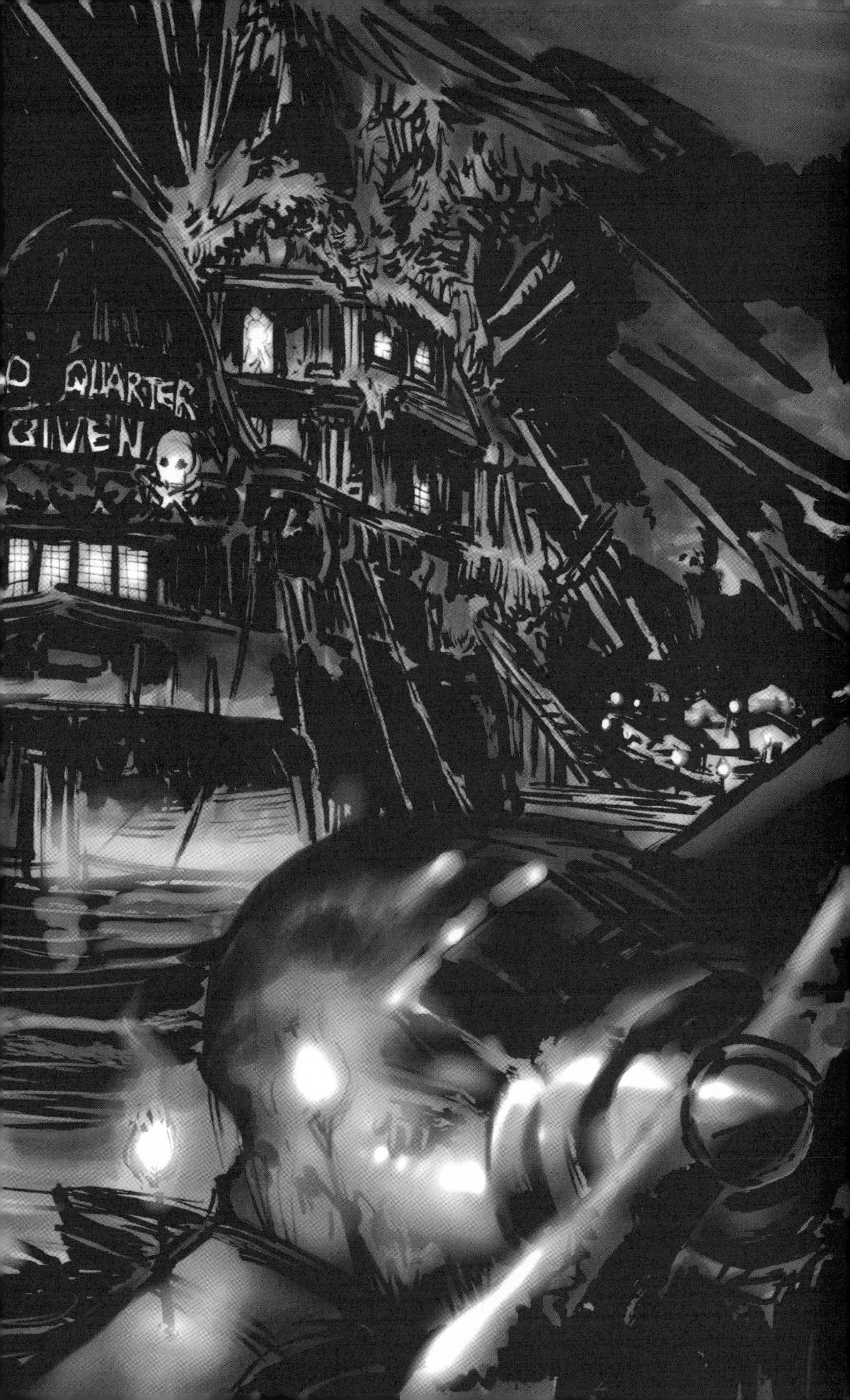
O QUARTER
GIVEN

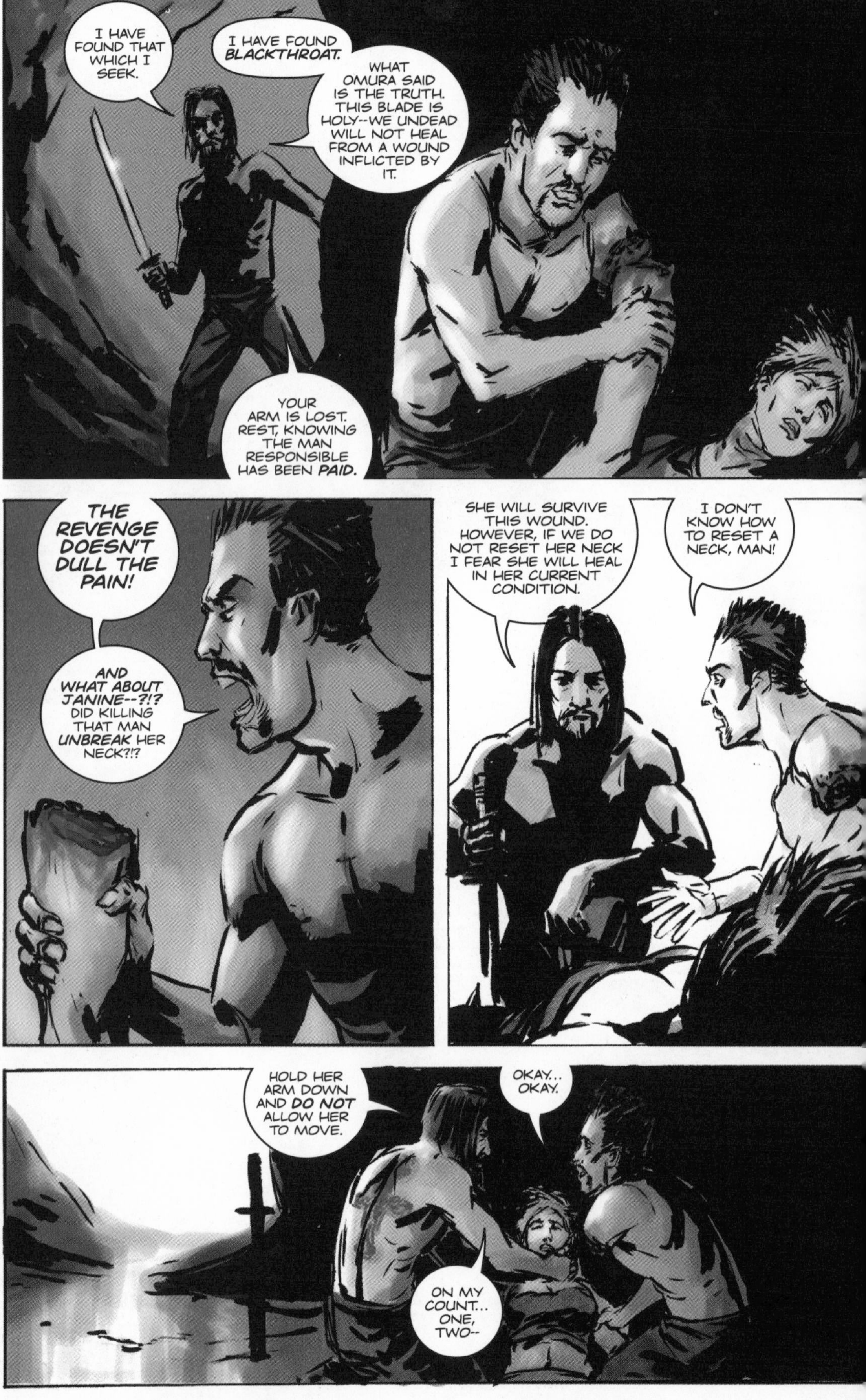
I HAVE FOUND THAT WHICH I SEEK.
I HAVE FOUND BLACKTHROAT.
WHAT OMURA SAID IS THE TRUTH. THIS BLADE IS HOLY--WE UNDEAD WILL NOT HEAL FROM A WOUND INFLICTED BY IT.
YOUR ARM IS LOST. REST, KNOWING THE MAN RESPONSIBLE HAS BEEN PAID.
THE REVENGE DOESN'T DULL THE PAIN!
AND WHAT ABOUT JANINE--?!? DID KILLING THAT MAN UNBREAK HER NECK?!?
SHE WILL SURVIVE THIS WOUND. HOWEVER, IF WE DO NOT RESET HER NECK I FEAR SHE WILL HEAL IN HER CURRENT CONDITION.
I DON'T KNOW HOW TO RESET A NECK, MAN!
HOLD HER ARM DOWN AND DO NOT ALLOW HER TO MOVE.
OKAY... OKAY.
ON MY COUNT... ONE, TWO--

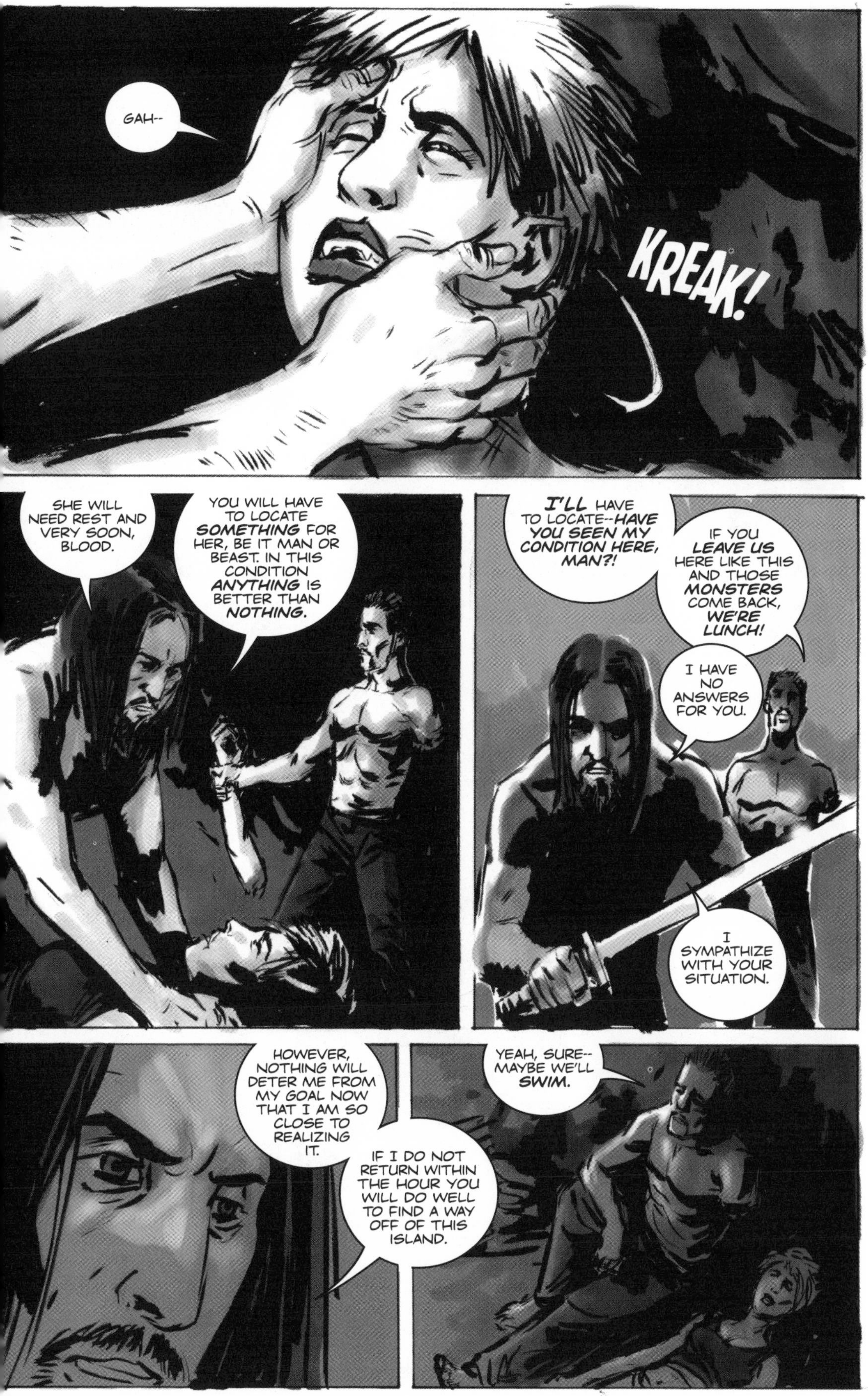
GAH--
KREAK!
SHE WILL NEED REST AND VERY SOON, BLOOD.
YOU WILL HAVE TO LOCATE SOMETHING FOR HER, BE IT MAN OR BEAST. IN THIS CONDITION ANYTHING IS BETTER THAN NOTHING.
I'LL HAVE TO LOCATE--HAVE YOU SEEN MY CONDITION HERE, MAN?!
IF YOU LEAVE US HERE LIKE THIS AND THOSE MONSTERS COME BACK, WE'RE LUNCH!
I HAVE NO ANSWERS FOR YOU.
I SYMPATHIZE WITH YOUR SITUATION.
HOWEVER, NOTHING WILL DETER ME FROM MY GOAL NOW THAT I AM SO CLOSE TO REALIZING IT.
IF I DO NOT RETURN WITHIN THE HOUR YOU WILL DO WELL TO FIND A WAY OFF OF THIS ISLAND.
YEAH, SURE--MAYBE WE'LL SWIM.

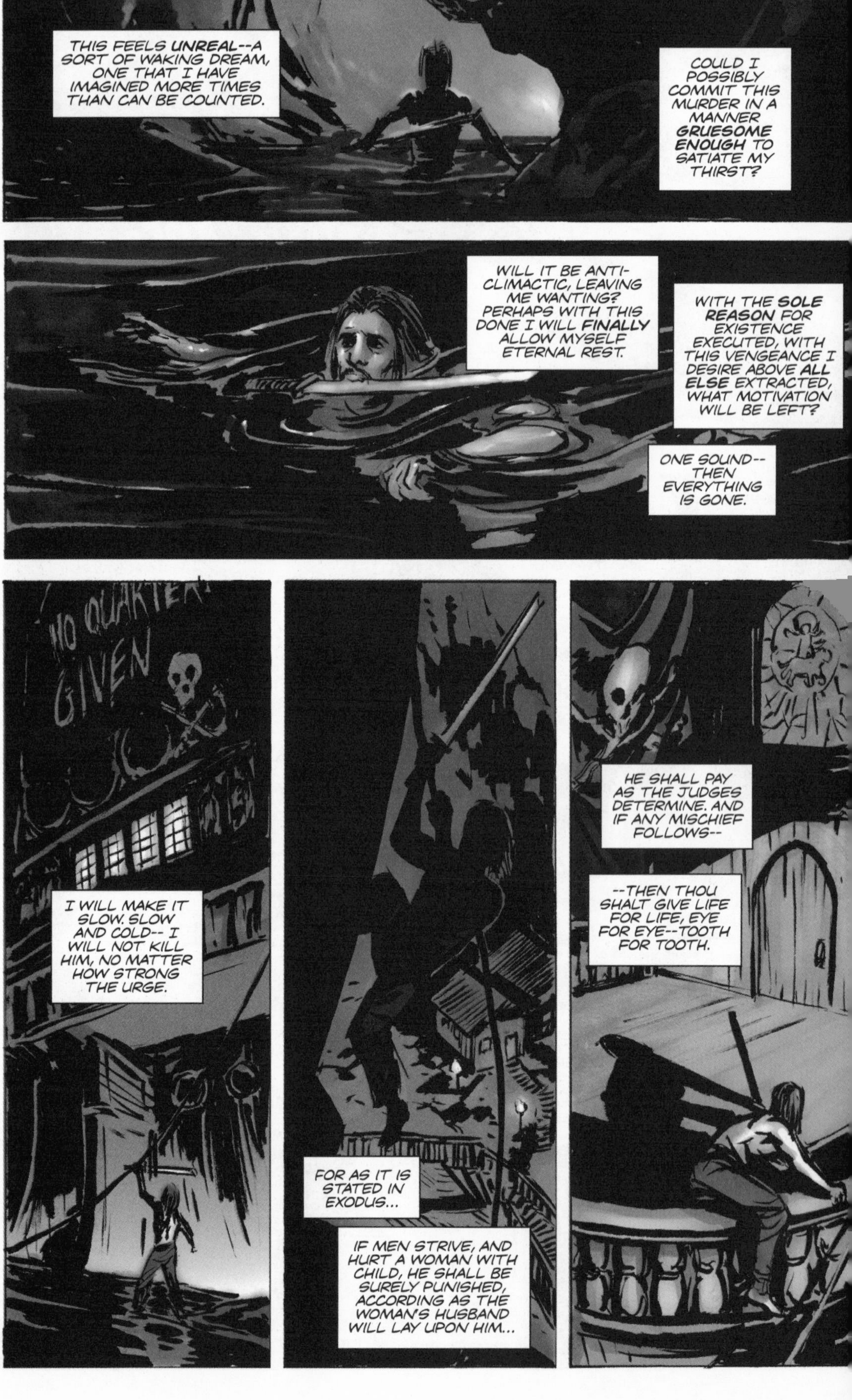
THIS FEELS UNREAL--A SORT OF WAKING DREAM, ONE THAT I HAVE IMAGINED MORE TIMES THAN CAN BE COUNTED.
COULD I POSSIBLY COMMIT THIS MURDER IN A MANNER GRUESOME ENOUGH TO SATIATE MY THIRST?
WILL IT BE ANTI-CLIMACTIC, LEAVING ME WANTING? PERHAPS WITH THIS DONE I WILL FINALLY ALLOW MYSELF ETERNAL REST.
WITH THE SOLE REASON FOR EXISTENCE EXECUTED, WITH THIS VENGEANCE I DESIRE ABOVE ALL ELSE EXTRACTED, WHAT MOTIVATION WILL BE LEFT?
ONE SOUND--THEN EVERYTHING IS GONE.
NO QUARTER GIVEN
I WILL MAKE IT SLOW. SLOW AND COLD-- I WILL NOT KILL HIM, NO MATTER HOW STRONG THE URGE.
FOR AS IT IS STATED IN EXODUS...
IF MEN STRIVE, AND HURT A WOMAN WITH CHILD, HE SHALL BE SURELY PUNISHED, ACCORDING AS THE WOMAN'S HUSBAND WILL LAY UPON HIM...
HE SHALL PAY AS THE JUDGES DETERMINE. AND IF ANY MISCHIEF FOLLOWS--
--THEN THOU SHALT GIVE LIFE FOR LIFE, EYE FOR EYE--TOOTH FOR TOOTH.

SCHOLARS SAY WE CHOOSE OUR STORIES.

DID I CHOOSE AN ETERNITY THAT LEADS ONLY TO THIS?

IF I DID CHOOSE IT OR NOT IS OF *NO CONSEQUENCE.* I AM COME, WITH *GLORIOUS PURPOSE.*

A DARK SHADOW TAKES HOLD OF ME AND FILLS MY HEART WITH DREAD.

YOU'D DO WELL TO MASK YOUR ENTHUSIASM FOR THE DIRTY WORK AT HAND.

THIS IS NOT AS I IMAGINED.

AS I CONFRONT HIM HE INSPIRES A SUDDEN AND GREAT FEAR IN ME. THE MOMENT CARRIES THE WEIGHT OF FIVE CENTURIES.

THE BLADE WEIGHS HEAVY IN MY TREMBLING HANDS.

500 YEARS-- THE MORTAL MIND IS *NARROWLY CAPABLE* OF DEALING WITH SUCH A LIFE SPAN LIVED *ABOVE THE GROUND.*

THE STATE OF YOUR MIND MUST BE *CALAMITOUS.*

IT IMMEDIATELY OCCURS TO ME--I AM *NOT THE HUNTER HERE...*

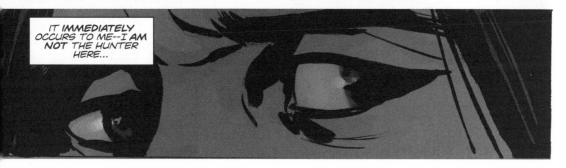

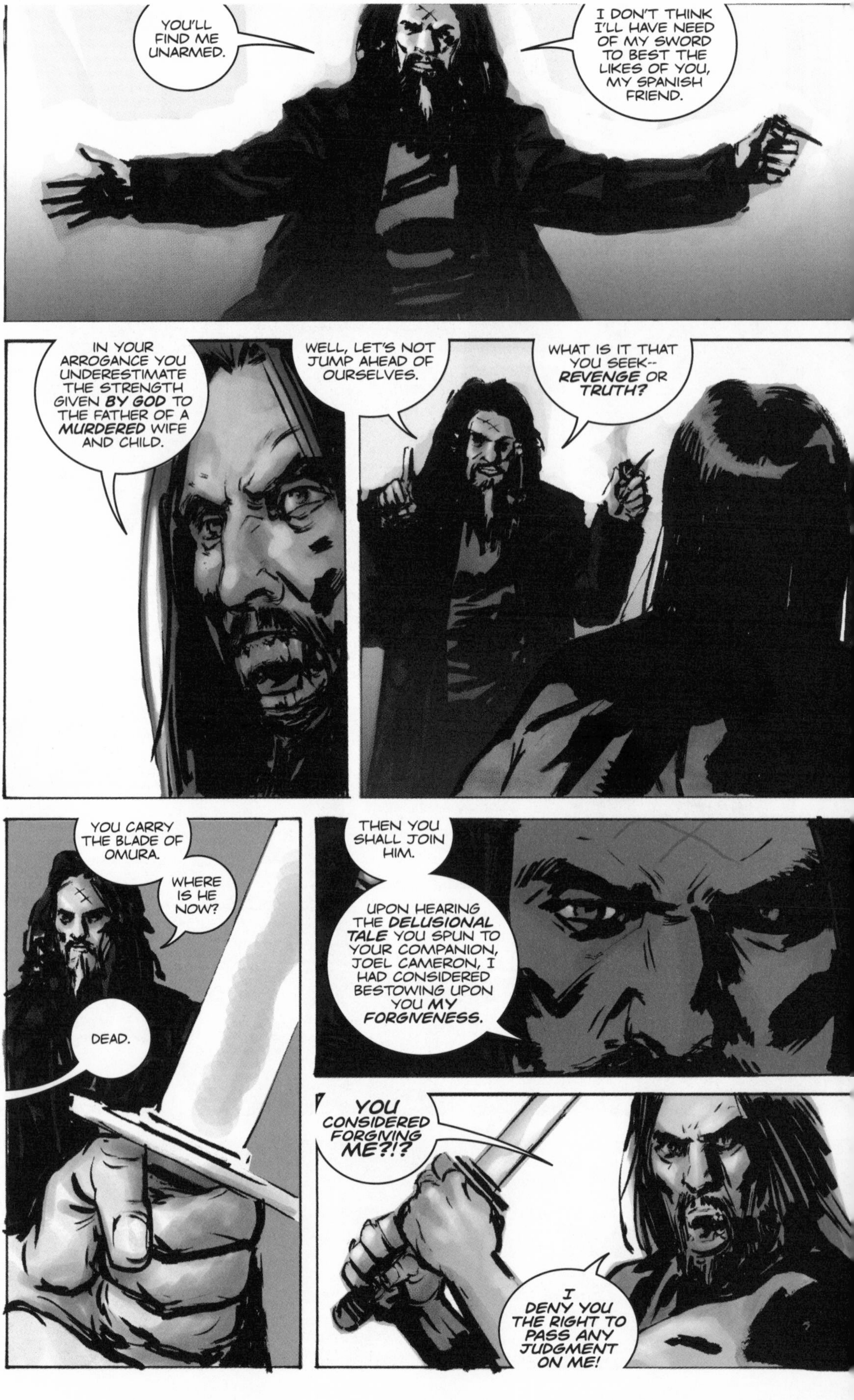
YOU'LL FIND ME UNARMED.
I DON'T THINK I'LL HAVE NEED OF MY SWORD TO BEST THE LIKES OF YOU, MY SPANISH FRIEND.
IN YOUR ARROGANCE YOU UNDERESTIMATE THE STRENGTH GIVEN BY GOD TO THE FATHER OF A MURDERED WIFE AND CHILD.
WELL, LET'S NOT JUMP AHEAD OF OURSELVES.
WHAT IS IT THAT YOU SEEK-- REVENGE OR TRUTH?
YOU CARRY THE BLADE OF OMURA.
WHERE IS HE NOW?
DEAD.
THEN YOU SHALL JOIN HIM.
UPON HEARING THE DELUSIONAL TALE YOU SPUN TO YOUR COMPANION, JOEL CAMERON, I HAD CONSIDERED BESTOWING UPON YOU MY FORGIVENESS.
YOU CONSIDERED FORGIVING ME?!?
I DENY YOU THE RIGHT TO PASS ANY JUDGMENT ON ME!

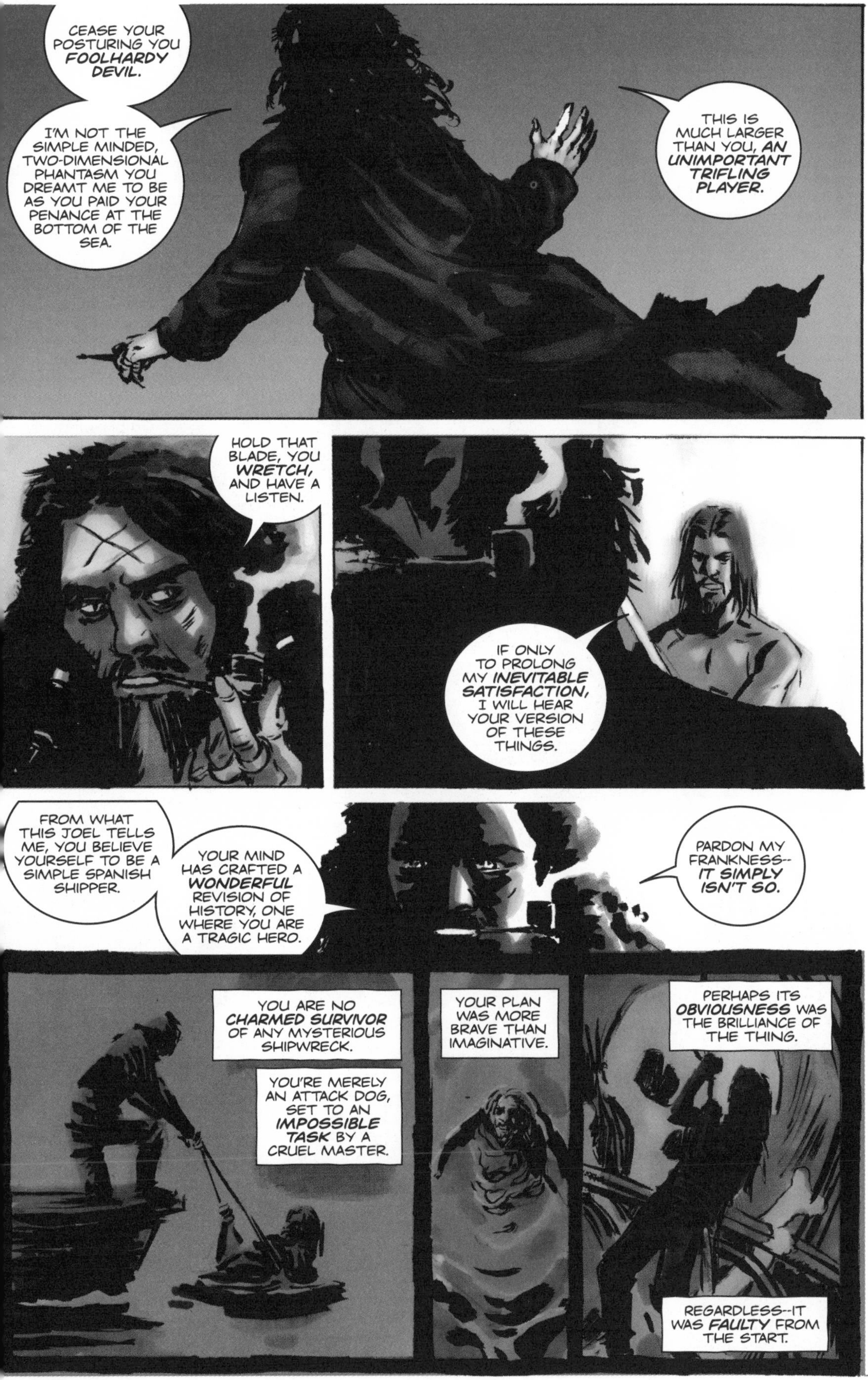
CEASE YOUR POSTURING YOU FOOLHARDY DEVIL.
I'M NOT THE SIMPLE MINDED, TWO-DIMENSIONAL PHANTASM YOU DREAMT ME TO BE AS YOU PAID YOUR PENANCE AT THE BOTTOM OF THE SEA.
THIS IS MUCH LARGER THAN YOU, AN UNIMPORTANT TRIFLING PLAYER.
HOLD THAT BLADE, YOU WRETCH, AND HAVE A LISTEN.
IF ONLY TO PROLONG MY INEVITABLE SATISFACTION, I WILL HEAR YOUR VERSION OF THESE THINGS.
FROM WHAT THIS JOEL TELLS ME, YOU BELIEVE YOURSELF TO BE A SIMPLE SPANISH SHIPPER.
YOUR MIND HAS CRAFTED A WONDERFUL REVISION OF HISTORY, ONE WHERE YOU ARE A TRAGIC HERO.
PARDON MY FRANKNESS-- IT SIMPLY ISN'T SO.
YOU ARE NO CHARMED SURVIVOR OF ANY MYSTERIOUS SHIPWRECK.
YOU'RE MERELY AN ATTACK DOG, SET TO AN IMPOSSIBLE TASK BY A CRUEL MASTER.
YOUR PLAN WAS MORE BRAVE THAN IMAGINATIVE.
PERHAPS ITS OBVIOUSNESS WAS THE BRILLIANCE OF THE THING.
REGARDLESS--IT WAS FAULTY FROM THE START.

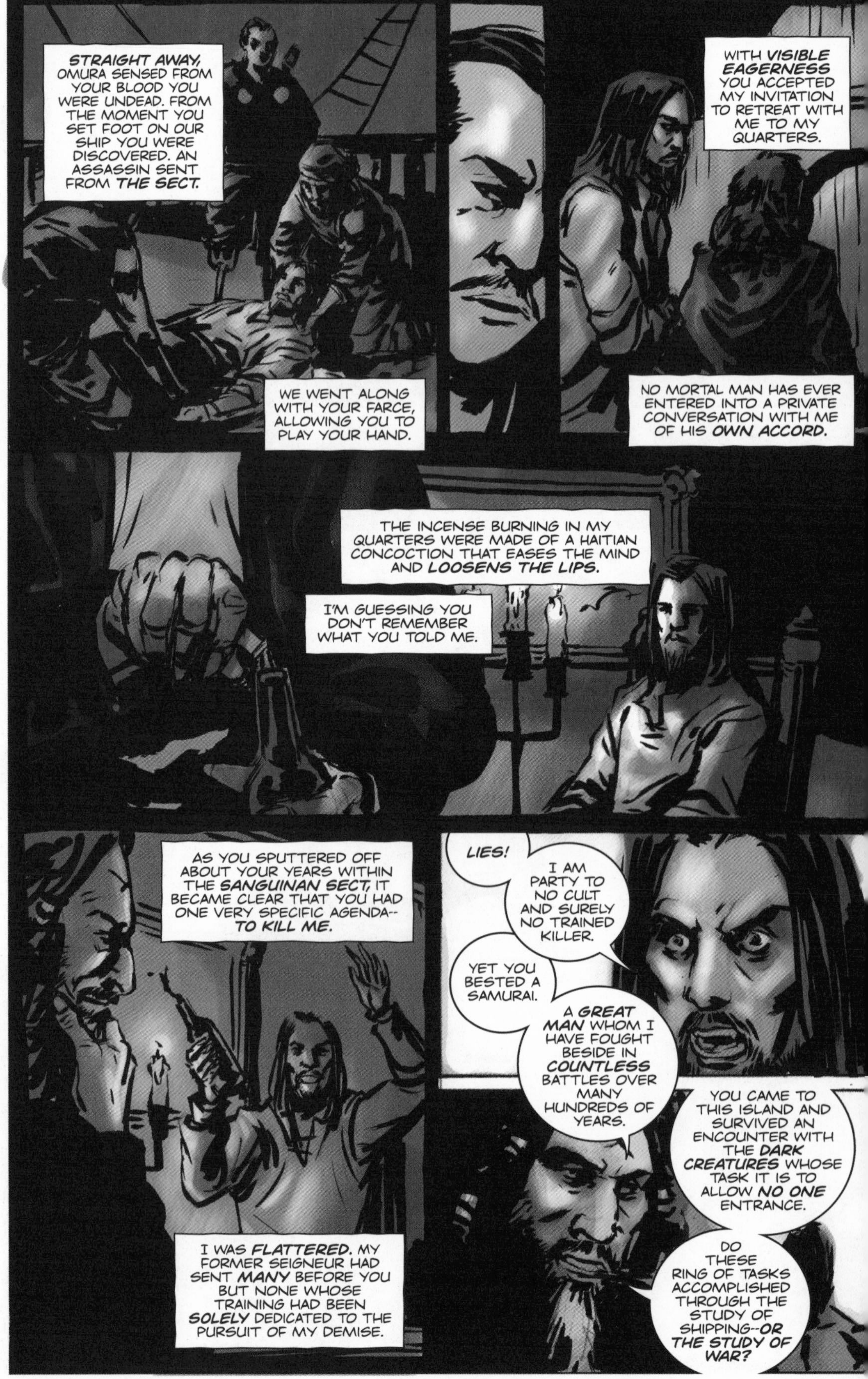
STRAIGHT AWAY, OMURA SENSED FROM YOUR BLOOD YOU WERE UNDEAD. FROM THE MOMENT YOU SET FOOT ON OUR SHIP YOU WERE DISCOVERED. AN ASSASSIN SENT FROM THE SECT.
WE WENT ALONG WITH YOUR FARCE, ALLOWING YOU TO PLAY YOUR HAND.
WITH VISIBLE EAGERNESS YOU ACCEPTED MY INVITATION TO RETREAT WITH ME TO MY QUARTERS.
NO MORTAL MAN HAS EVER ENTERED INTO A PRIVATE CONVERSATION WITH ME OF HIS OWN ACCORD.
THE INCENSE BURNING IN MY QUARTERS WERE MADE OF A HAITIAN CONCOCTION THAT EASES THE MIND AND LOOSENS THE LIPS.
I'M GUESSING YOU DON'T REMEMBER WHAT YOU TOLD ME.
AS YOU SPUTTERED OFF ABOUT YOUR YEARS WITHIN THE SANGUINAN SECT, IT BECAME CLEAR THAT YOU HAD ONE VERY SPECIFIC AGENDA-- TO KILL ME.
I WAS FLATTERED. MY FORMER SEIGNEUR HAD SENT MANY BEFORE YOU BUT NONE WHOSE TRAINING HAD BEEN SOLELY DEDICATED TO THE PURSUIT OF MY DEMISE.
LIES!
I AM PARTY TO NO CULT AND SURELY NO TRAINED KILLER.
YET YOU BESTED A SAMURAI.
A GREAT MAN WHOM I HAVE FOUGHT BESIDE IN COUNTLESS BATTLES OVER MANY HUNDREDS OF YEARS.
YOU CAME TO THIS ISLAND AND SURVIVED AN ENCOUNTER WITH THE DARK CREATURES WHOSE TASK IT IS TO ALLOW NO ONE ENTRANCE.
DO THESE RING OF TASKS ACCOMPLISHED THROUGH THE STUDY OF SHIPPING--OR THE STUDY OF WAR?

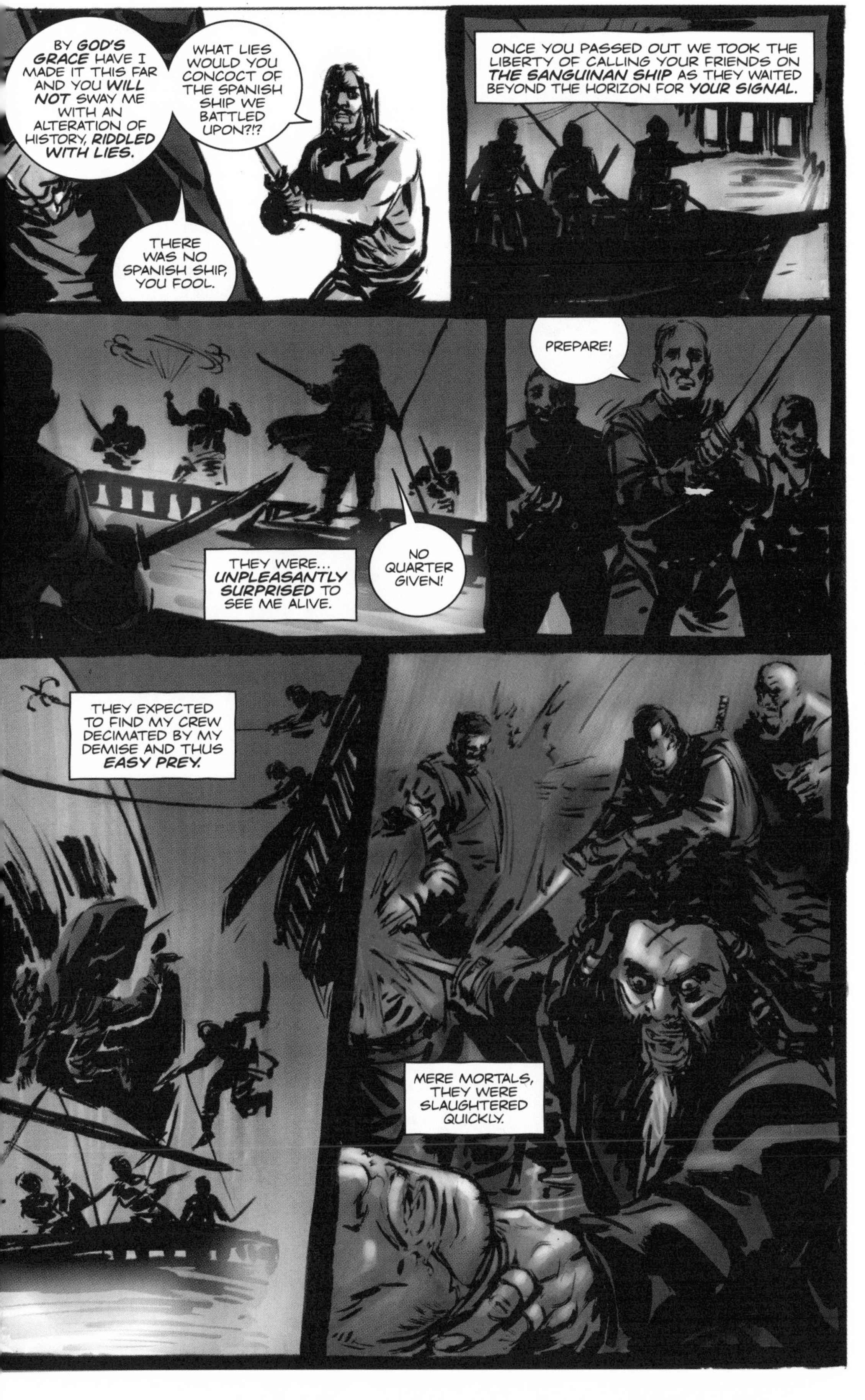
BY GOD'S GRACE HAVE I MADE IT THIS FAR AND YOU WILL NOT SWAY ME WITH AN ALTERATION OF HISTORY, RIDDLED WITH LIES.
WHAT LIES WOULD YOU CONCOCT OF THE SPANISH SHIP WE BATTLED UPON?!?
THERE WAS NO SPANISH SHIP, YOU FOOL.
ONCE YOU PASSED OUT WE TOOK THE LIBERTY OF CALLING YOUR FRIENDS ON THE SANGUINAN SHIP AS THEY WAITED BEYOND THE HORIZON FOR YOUR SIGNAL.
THEY WERE... UNPLEASANTLY SURPRISED TO SEE ME ALIVE.
NO QUARTER GIVEN!
PREPARE!
THEY EXPECTED TO FIND MY CREW DECIMATED BY MY DEMISE AND THUS EASY PREY.
MERE MORTALS, THEY WERE SLAUGHTERED QUICKLY.

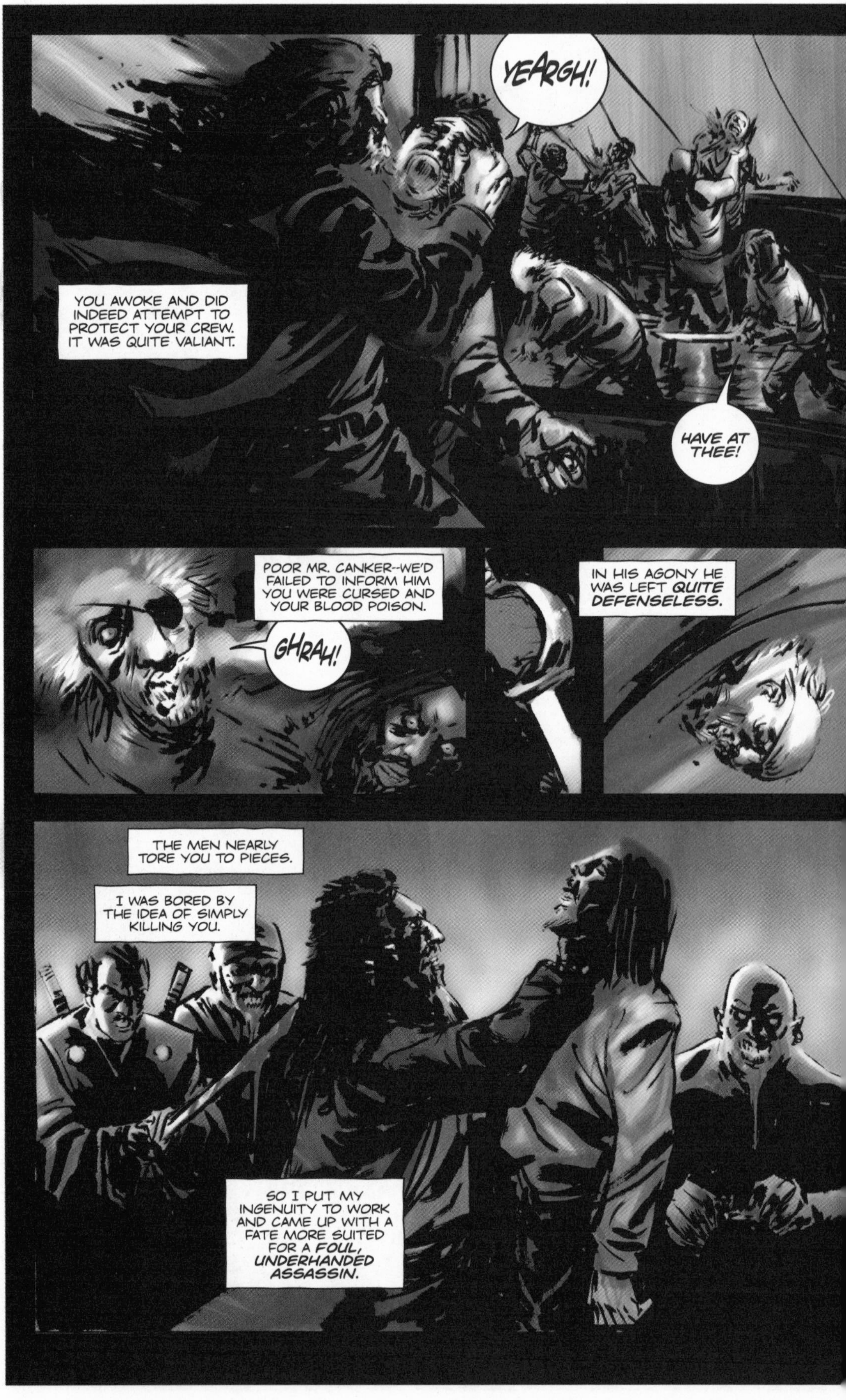
YEARGH!
YOU AWOKE AND DID INDEED ATTEMPT TO PROTECT YOUR CREW. IT WAS QUITE VALIANT.
HAVE AT THEE!
POOR MR. CANKER--WE'D FAILED TO INFORM HIM YOU WERE CURSED AND YOUR BLOOD POISON.
GHRAH!
IN HIS AGONY HE WAS LEFT QUITE DEFENSELESS.
THE MEN NEARLY TORE YOU TO PIECES.
I WAS BORED BY THE IDEA OF SIMPLY KILLING YOU.
SO I PUT MY INGENUITY TO WORK AND CAME UP WITH A FATE MORE SUITED FOR A FOUL, UNDERHANDED ASSASSIN.

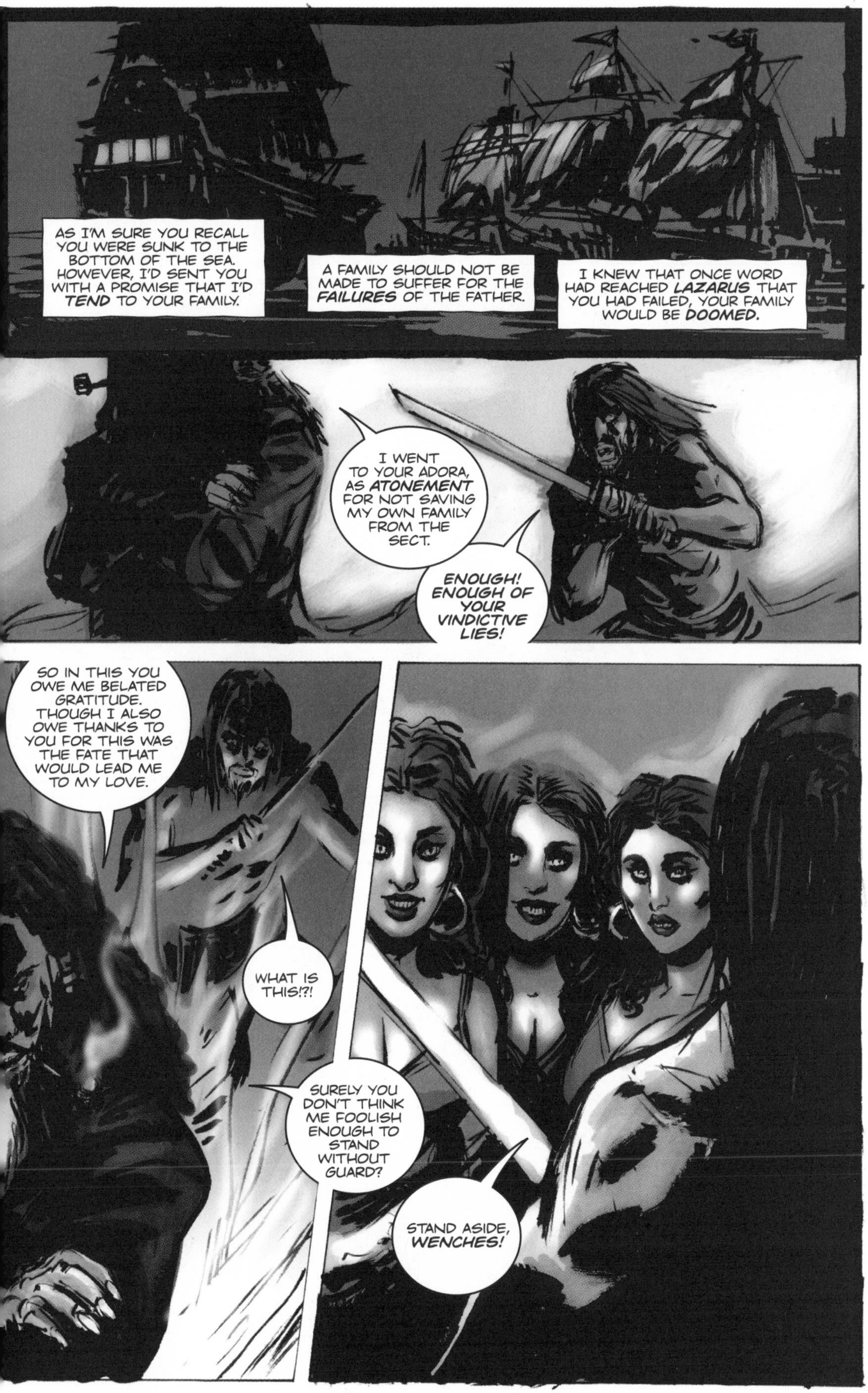

AS I'M SURE YOU RECALL YOU WERE SUNK TO THE BOTTOM OF THE SEA. HOWEVER, I'D SENT YOU WITH A PROMISE THAT I'D TEND TO YOUR FAMILY.
A FAMILY SHOULD NOT BE MADE TO SUFFER FOR THE FAILURES OF THE FATHER.
I KNEW THAT ONCE WORD HAD REACHED LAZARUS THAT YOU HAD FAILED, YOUR FAMILY WOULD BE DOOMED.
I WENT TO YOUR ADORA, AS ATONEMENT FOR NOT SAVING MY OWN FAMILY FROM THE SECT.
ENOUGH! ENOUGH OF YOUR VINDICTIVE LIES!
SO IN THIS YOU OWE ME BELATED GRATITUDE. THOUGH I ALSO OWE THANKS TO YOU FOR THIS WAS THE FATE THAT WOULD LEAD ME TO MY LOVE.
WHAT IS THIS!?!
SURELY YOU DON'T THINK ME FOOLISH ENOUGH TO STAND WITHOUT GUARD?
STAND ASIDE, WENCHES!

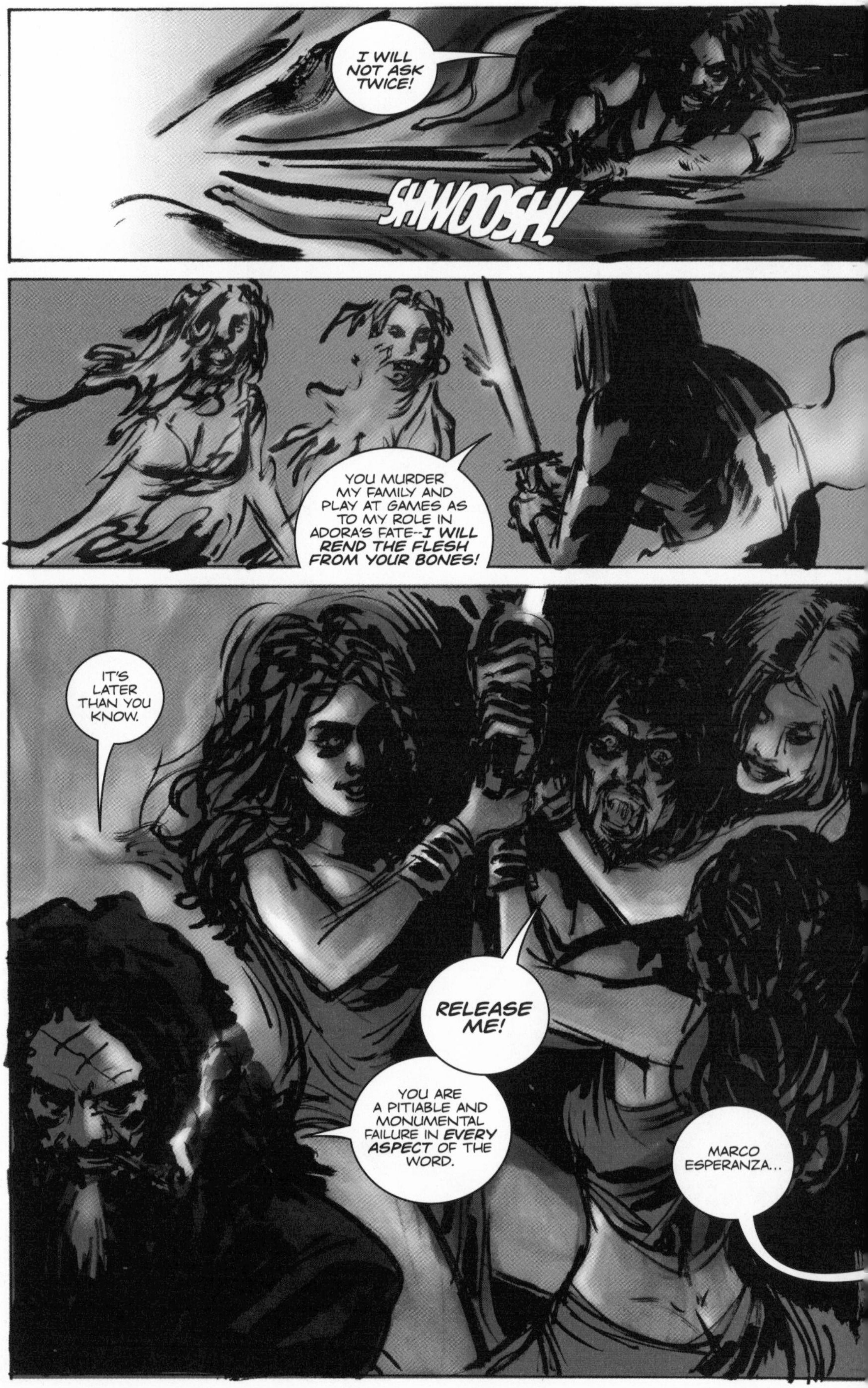
I WILL NOT ASK TWICE!
SHWOOSH!
YOU MURDER MY FAMILY AND PLAY AT GAMES AS TO MY ROLE IN ADORA'S FATE--I WILL REND THE FLESH FROM YOUR BONES!
IT'S LATER THAN YOU KNOW.
RELEASE ME!
YOU ARE A PITIABLE AND MONUMENTAL FAILURE IN EVERY ASPECT OF THE WORD.
MARCO ESPERANZA...

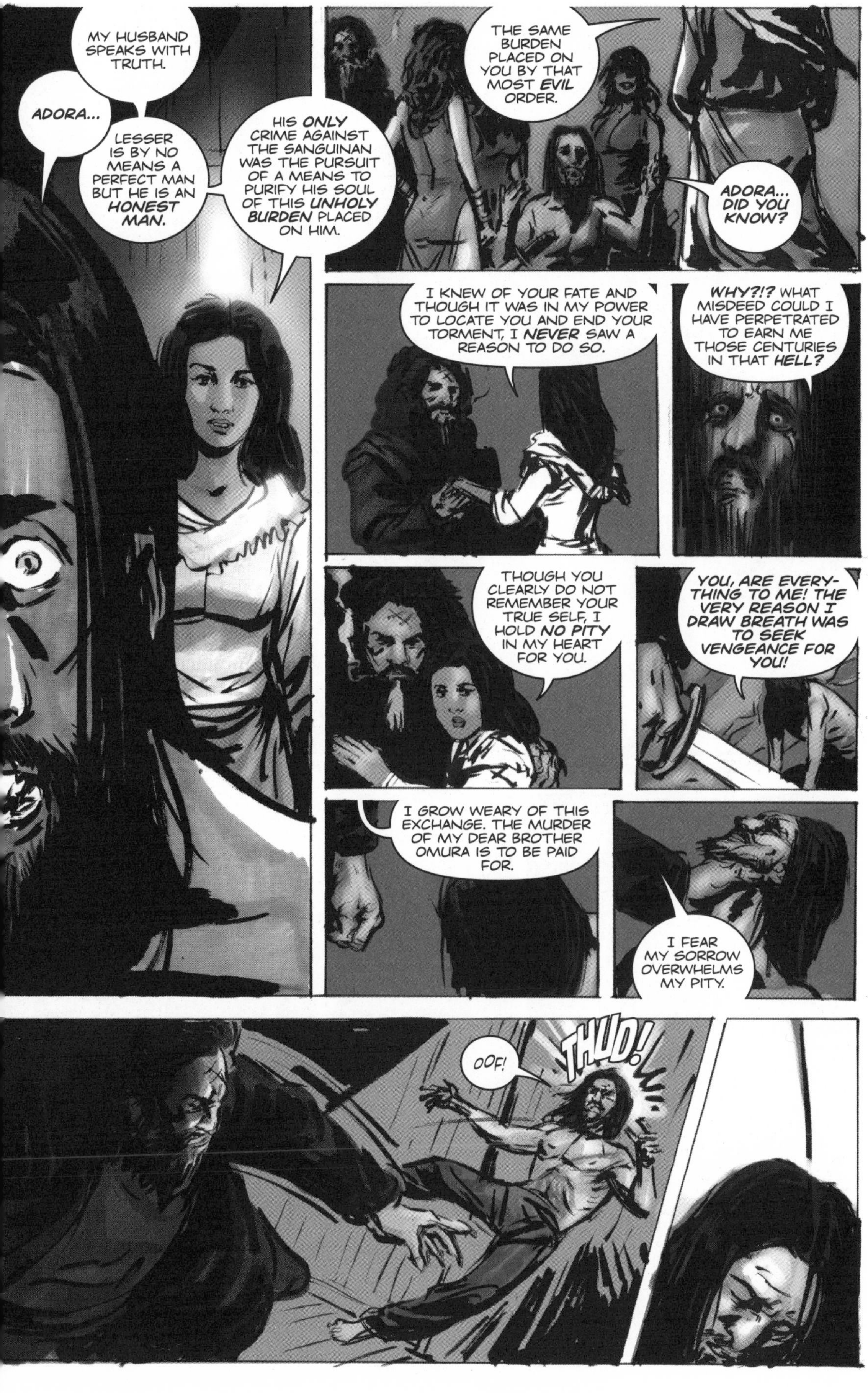
MY HUSBAND SPEAKS WITH TRUTH.
ADORA...
LESSER IS BY NO MEANS A PERFECT MAN BUT HE IS AN **HONEST MAN.**
HIS **ONLY** CRIME AGAINST THE SANGUINAN WAS THE PURSUIT OF A MEANS TO PURIFY HIS SOUL OF THIS **UNHOLY BURDEN** PLACED ON HIM.
THE SAME BURDEN PLACED ON YOU BY THAT MOST **EVIL** ORDER.
ADORA... DID YOU KNOW?
I KNEW OF YOUR FATE AND THOUGH IT WAS IN MY POWER TO LOCATE YOU AND END YOUR TORMENT, I **NEVER** SAW A REASON TO DO SO.
WHY?!? WHAT MISDEED COULD I HAVE PERPETRATED TO EARN ME THOSE CENTURIES IN THAT **HELL?**
THOUGH YOU CLEARLY DO NOT REMEMBER YOUR TRUE SELF, I HOLD **NO PITY** IN MY HEART FOR YOU.
YOU, ARE EVERYTHING TO ME! THE VERY REASON I DRAW BREATH WAS TO SEEK VENGEANCE FOR YOU!
I GROW WEARY OF THIS EXCHANGE. THE MURDER OF MY DEAR BROTHER OMURA IS TO BE PAID FOR.
I FEAR MY SORROW OVERWHELMS MY PITY.
OOF!
THUD!

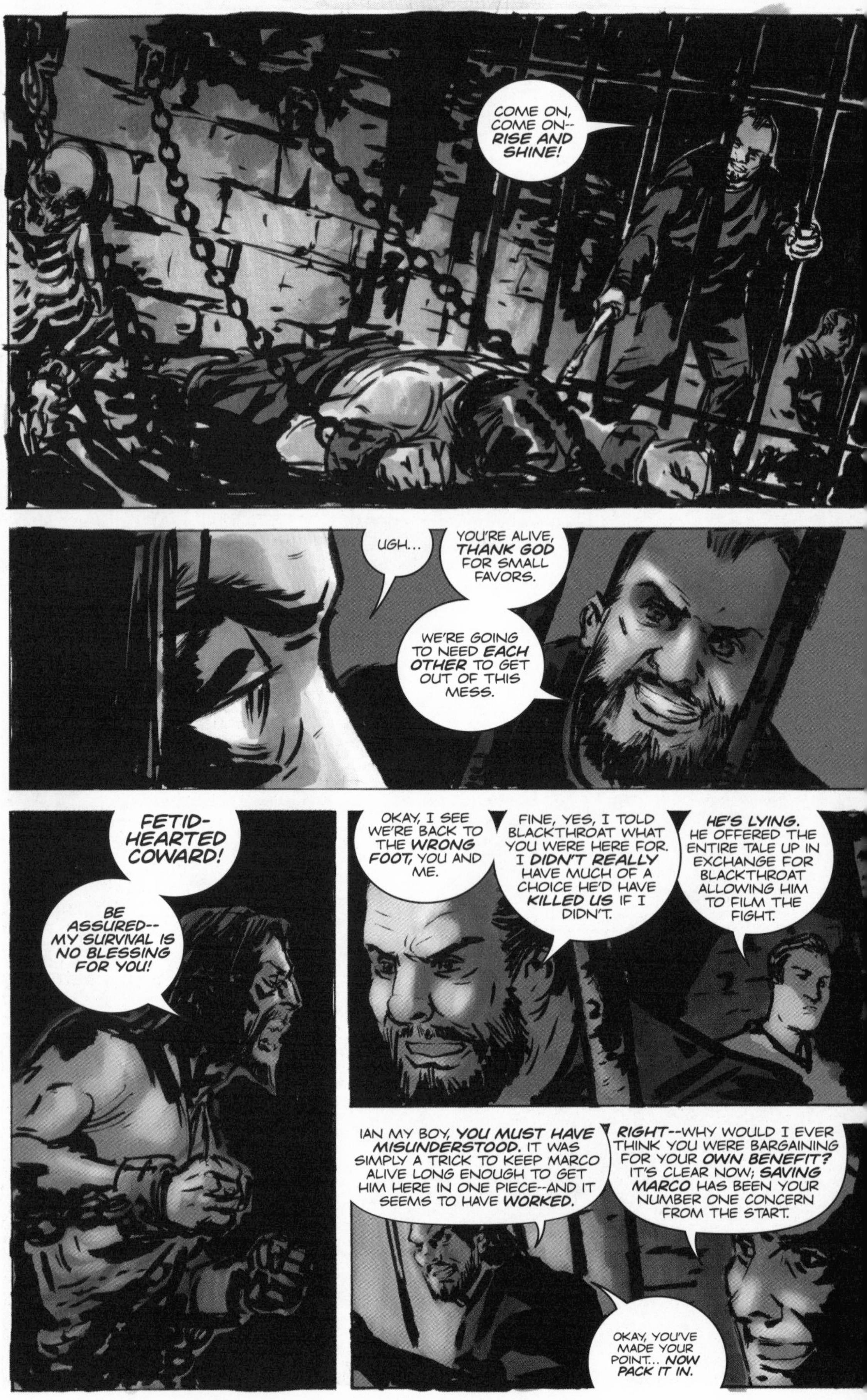
COME ON, COME ON-- RISE AND SHINE!
UGH...
YOU'RE ALIVE, THANK GOD FOR SMALL FAVORS.
WE'RE GOING TO NEED EACH OTHER TO GET OUT OF THIS MESS.
FETID-HEARTED COWARD!
BE ASSURED-- MY SURVIVAL IS NO BLESSING FOR YOU!
OKAY, I SEE WE'RE BACK TO THE WRONG FOOT, YOU AND ME.
FINE, YES, I TOLD BLACKTHROAT WHAT YOU WERE HERE FOR. I DIDN'T REALLY HAVE MUCH OF A CHOICE HE'D HAVE KILLED US IF I DIDN'T.
HE'S LYING. HE OFFERED THE ENTIRE TALE UP IN EXCHANGE FOR BLACKTHROAT ALLOWING HIM TO FILM THE FIGHT.
IAN MY BOY, YOU MUST HAVE MISUNDERSTOOD. IT WAS SIMPLY A TRICK TO KEEP MARCO ALIVE LONG ENOUGH TO GET HIM HERE IN ONE PIECE--AND IT SEEMS TO HAVE WORKED.
RIGHT--WHY WOULD I EVER THINK YOU WERE BARGAINING FOR YOUR OWN BENEFIT? IT'S CLEAR NOW; SAVING MARCO HAS BEEN YOUR NUMBER ONE CONCERN FROM THE START.
OKAY, YOU'VE MADE YOUR POINT... NOW PACK IT IN.

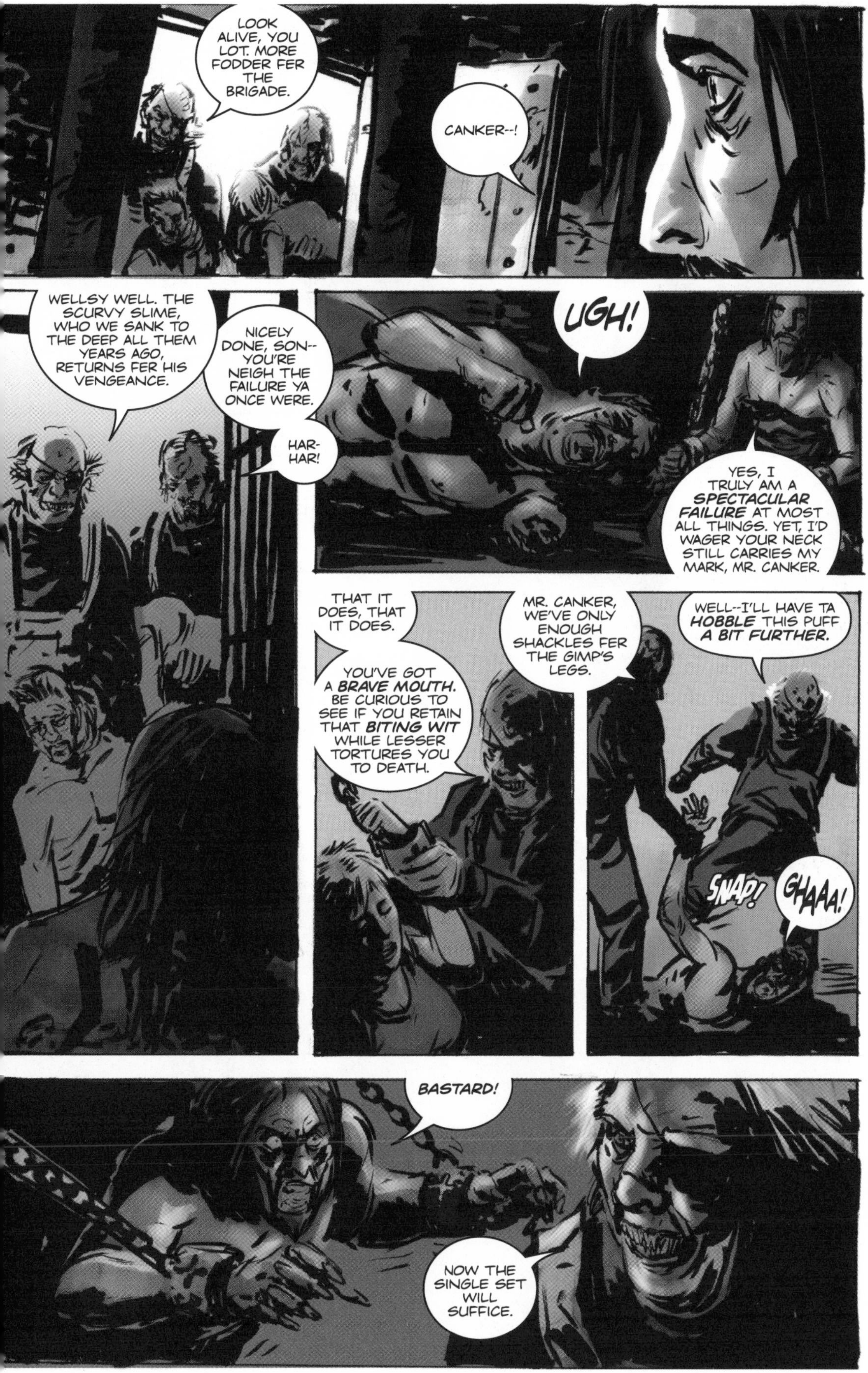
LOOK ALIVE, YOU LOT. MORE FODDER FER THE BRIGADE.
CANKER--!
WELLSY WELL. THE SCURVY SLIME, WHO WE SANK TO THE DEEP ALL THEM YEARS AGO, RETURNS FER HIS VENGEANCE.
NICELY DONE, SON--YOU'RE NEIGH THE FAILURE YA ONCE WERE.
HAR-HAR!
UGH!
YES, I TRULY AM A **SPECTACULAR FAILURE** AT MOST ALL THINGS. YET, I'D WAGER YOUR NECK STILL CARRIES MY MARK, MR. CANKER.
THAT IT DOES, THAT IT DOES.
YOU'VE GOT A **BRAVE MOUTH.** BE CURIOUS TO SEE IF YOU RETAIN THAT **BITING WIT** WHILE LESSER TORTURES YOU TO DEATH.
MR. CANKER, WE'VE ONLY ENOUGH SHACKLES FER THE GIMP'S LEGS.
WELL--I'LL HAVE TA **HOBBLE** THIS PUFF **A BIT FURTHER.**
SNAP!
GHAAA!
BASTARD!
NOW THE SINGLE SET WILL SUFFICE.

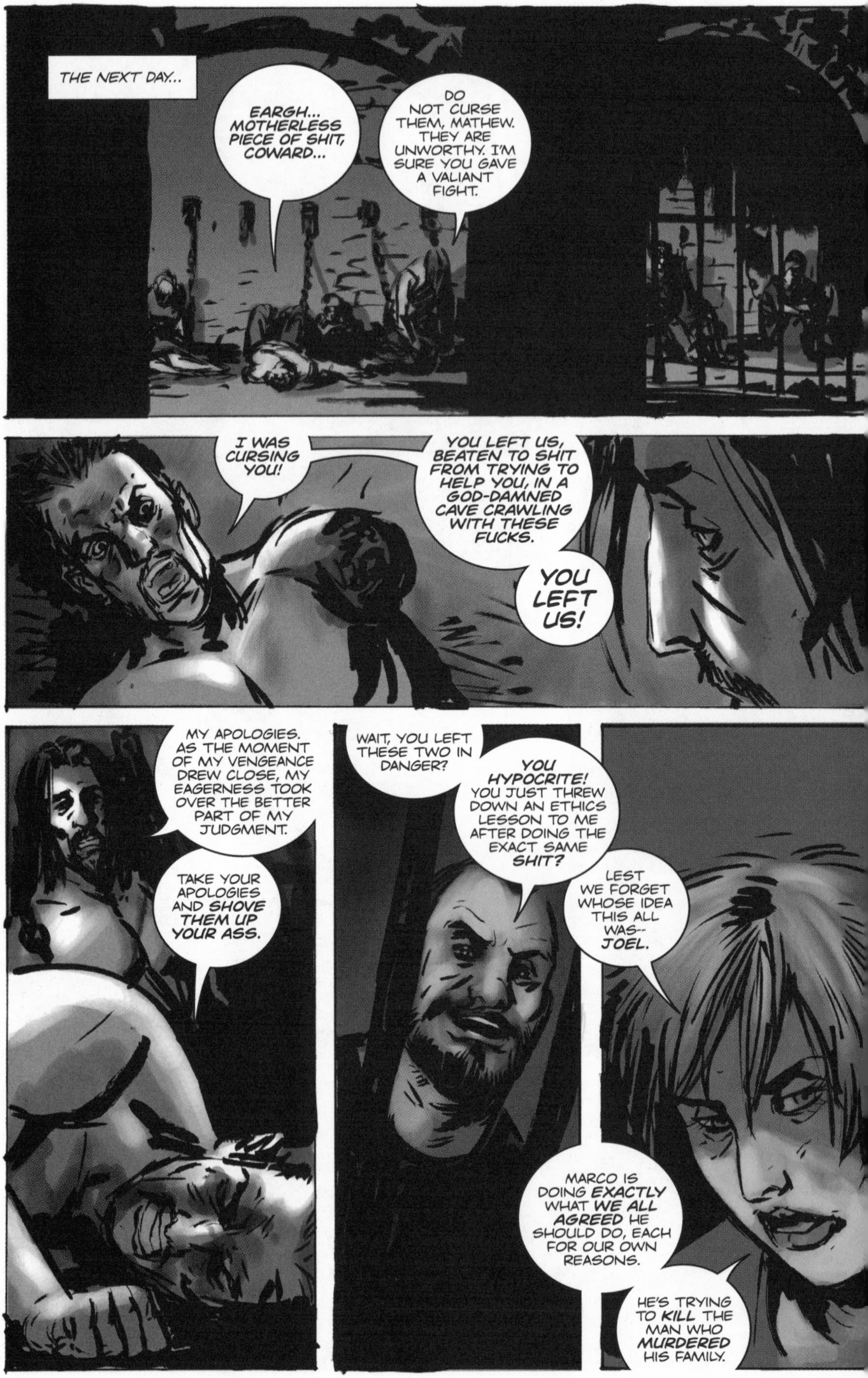
THE NEXT DAY...
EARGH... MOTHERLESS PIECE OF SHIT, COWARD...
DO NOT CURSE THEM, MATHEW. THEY ARE UNWORTHY. I'M SURE YOU GAVE A VALIANT FIGHT.
I WAS CURSING YOU!
YOU LEFT US, BEATEN TO SHIT FROM TRYING TO HELP YOU, IN A GOD-DAMNED CAVE CRAWLING WITH THESE FUCKS.
YOU LEFT US!
MY APOLOGIES. AS THE MOMENT OF MY VENGEANCE DREW CLOSE, MY EAGERNESS TOOK OVER THE BETTER PART OF MY JUDGMENT.
TAKE YOUR APOLOGIES AND SHOVE THEM UP YOUR ASS.
WAIT, YOU LEFT THESE TWO IN DANGER?
YOU HYPOCRITE! YOU JUST THREW DOWN AN ETHICS LESSON TO ME AFTER DOING THE EXACT SAME SHIT?
LEST WE FORGET WHOSE IDEA THIS ALL WAS-- JOEL.
MARCO IS DOING EXACTLY WHAT WE ALL AGREED HE SHOULD DO, EACH FOR OUR OWN REASONS.
HE'S TRYING TO KILL THE MAN WHO MURDERED HIS FAMILY.

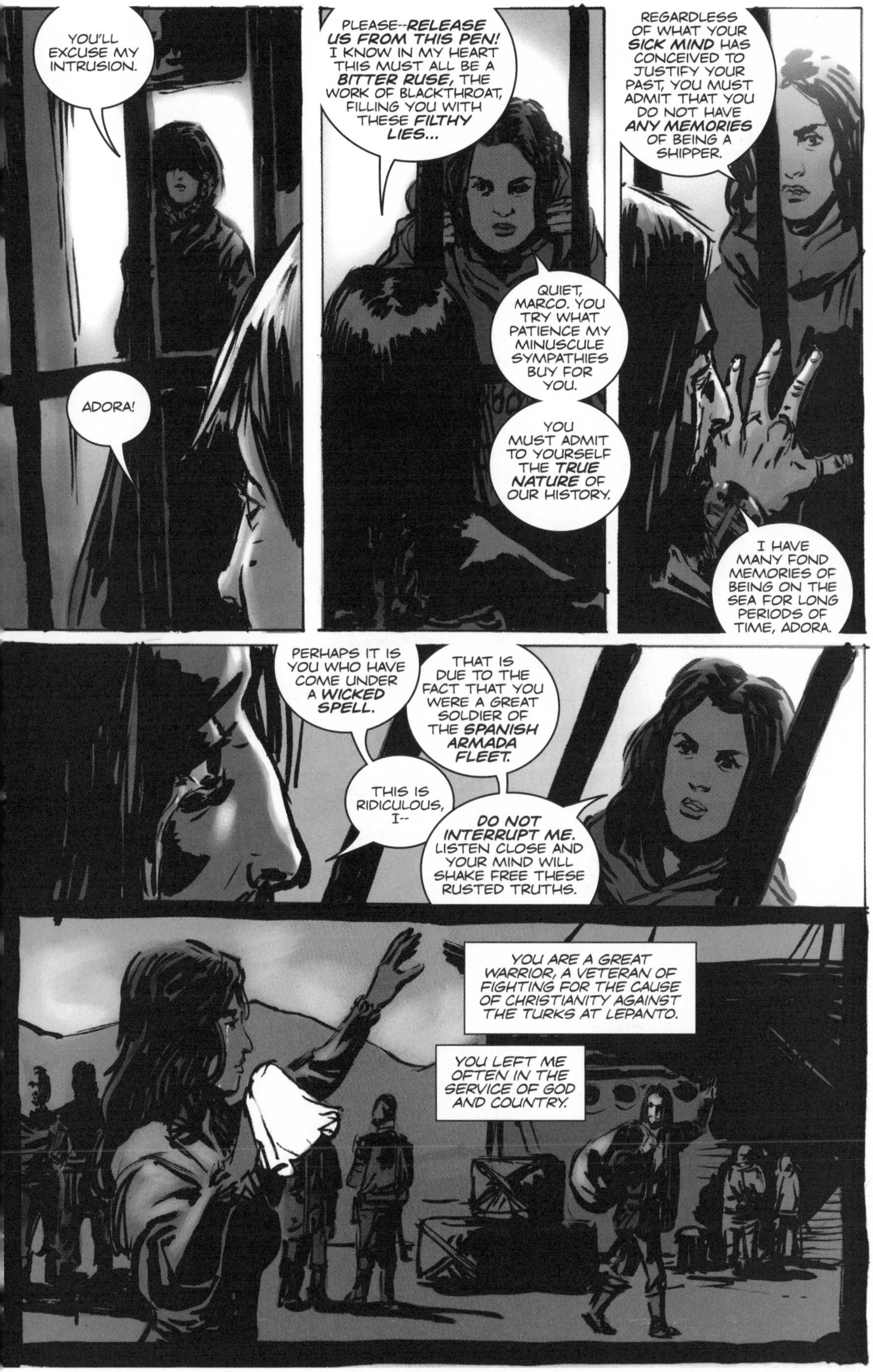
YOU'LL EXCUSE MY INTRUSION.
ADORA!
PLEASE--RELEASE US FROM THIS PEN! I KNOW IN MY HEART THIS MUST ALL BE A BITTER RUSE, THE WORK OF BLACKTHROAT, FILLING YOU WITH THESE FILTHY LIES...
QUIET, MARCO. YOU TRY WHAT PATIENCE MY MINUSCULE SYMPATHIES BUY FOR YOU.
YOU MUST ADMIT TO YOURSELF THE TRUE NATURE OF OUR HISTORY.
REGARDLESS OF WHAT YOUR SICK MIND HAS CONCEIVED TO JUSTIFY YOUR PAST, YOU MUST ADMIT THAT YOU DO NOT HAVE ANY MEMORIES OF BEING A SHIPPER.
I HAVE MANY FOND MEMORIES OF BEING ON THE SEA FOR LONG PERIODS OF TIME, ADORA.
PERHAPS IT IS YOU WHO HAVE COME UNDER A WICKED SPELL.
THAT IS DUE TO THE FACT THAT YOU WERE A GREAT SOLDIER OF THE SPANISH ARMADA FLEET.
THIS IS RIDICULOUS, I--
DO NOT INTERRUPT ME. LISTEN CLOSE AND YOUR MIND WILL SHAKE FREE THESE RUSTED TRUTHS.
YOU ARE A GREAT WARRIOR, A VETERAN OF FIGHTING FOR THE CAUSE OF CHRISTIANITY AGAINST THE TURKS AT LEPANTO.
YOU LEFT ME OFTEN IN THE SERVICE OF GOD AND COUNTRY.

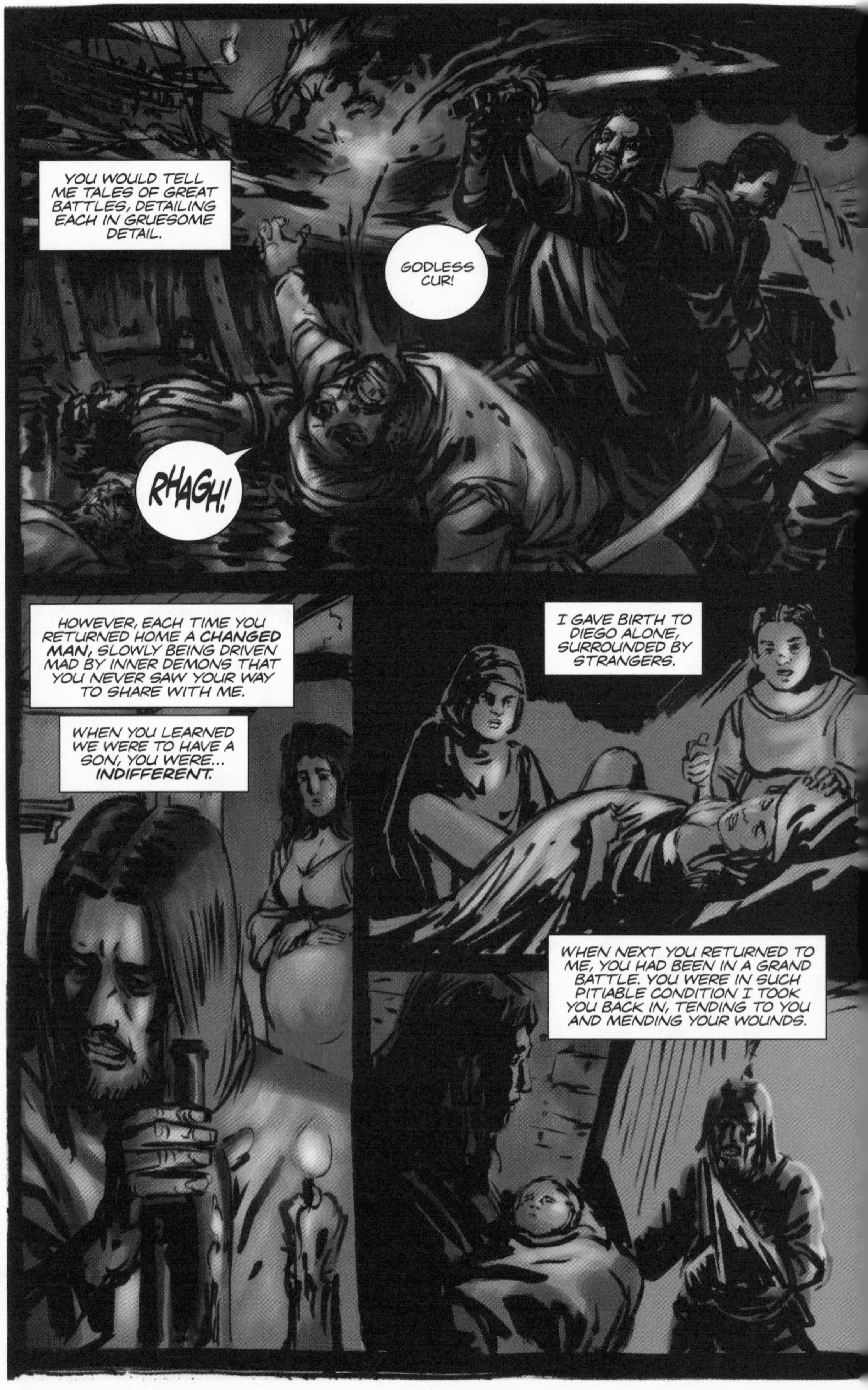
YOU WOULD TELL ME TALES OF GREAT BATTLES, DETAILING EACH IN GRUESOME DETAIL.
GODLESS CUR!
RHAGH!
HOWEVER, EACH TIME YOU RETURNED HOME A **CHANGED MAN,** SLOWLY BEING DRIVEN MAD BY INNER DEMONS THAT YOU NEVER SAW YOUR WAY TO SHARE WITH ME.
WHEN YOU LEARNED WE WERE TO HAVE A SON, YOU WERE... **INDIFFERENT.**
I GAVE BIRTH TO DIEGO ALONE, SURROUNDED BY STRANGERS.
WHEN NEXT YOU RETURNED TO ME, YOU HAD BEEN IN A GRAND BATTLE. YOU WERE IN SUCH PITIABLE CONDITION I TOOK YOU BACK IN, TENDING TO YOU AND MENDING YOUR WOUNDS.

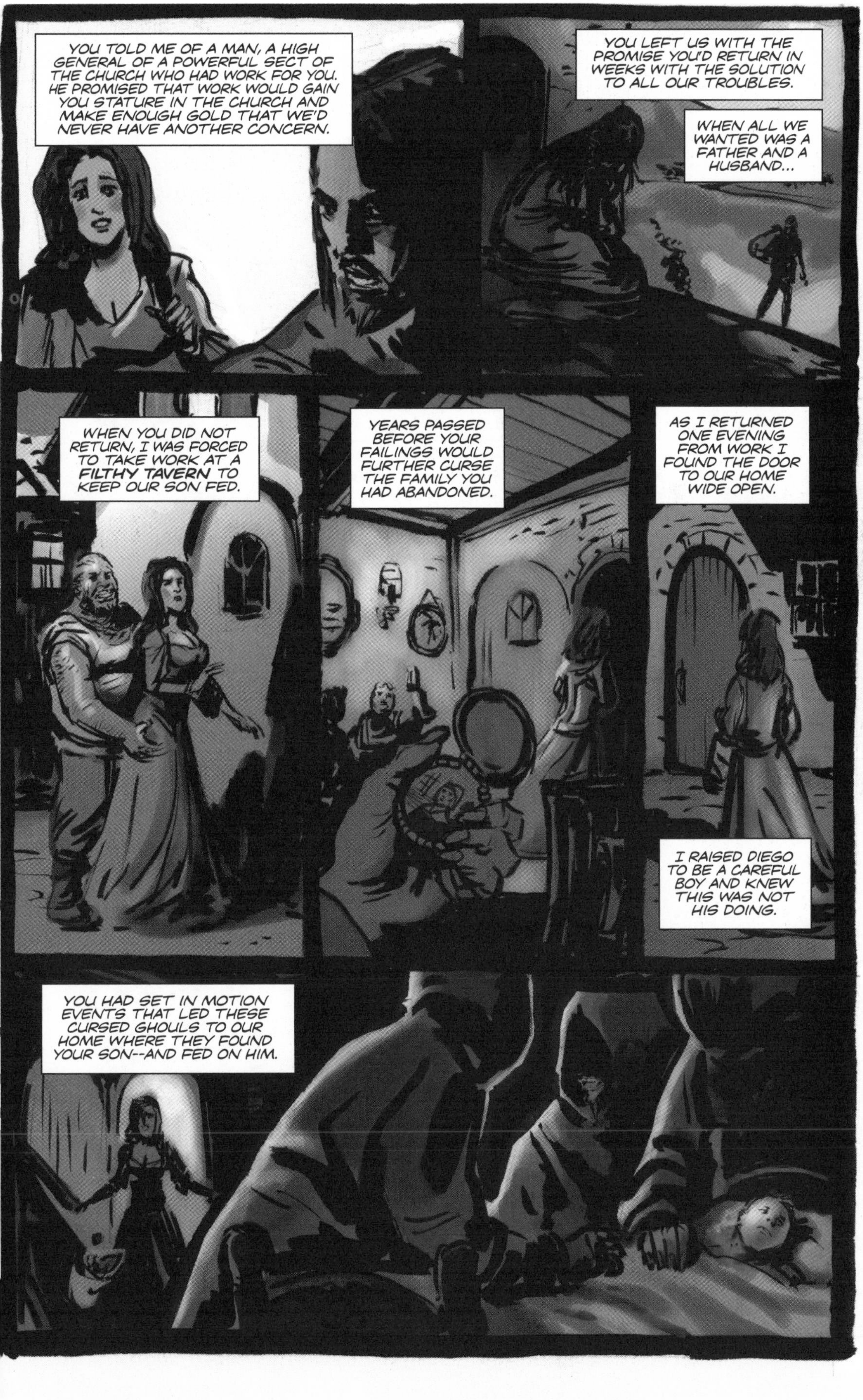
YOU TOLD ME OF A MAN, A HIGH GENERAL OF A POWERFUL SECT OF THE CHURCH WHO HAD WORK FOR YOU. HE PROMISED THAT WORK WOULD GAIN YOU STATURE IN THE CHURCH AND MAKE ENOUGH GOLD THAT WE'D NEVER HAVE ANOTHER CONCERN.
YOU LEFT US WITH THE PROMISE YOU'D RETURN IN WEEKS WITH THE SOLUTION TO ALL OUR TROUBLES.
WHEN ALL WE WANTED WAS A FATHER AND A HUSBAND...
WHEN YOU DID NOT RETURN, I WAS FORCED TO TAKE WORK AT A **FILTHY TAVERN** TO KEEP OUR SON FED.
YEARS PASSED BEFORE YOUR FAILINGS WOULD FURTHER CURSE THE FAMILY YOU HAD ABANDONED.
AS I RETURNED ONE EVENING FROM WORK I FOUND THE DOOR TO OUR HOME WIDE OPEN.
I RAISED DIEGO TO BE A CAREFUL BOY AND KNEW THIS WAS NOT HIS DOING.
YOU HAD SET IN MOTION EVENTS THAT LED THESE CURSED GHOULS TO OUR HOME WHERE THEY FOUND YOUR SON--AND FED ON HIM.

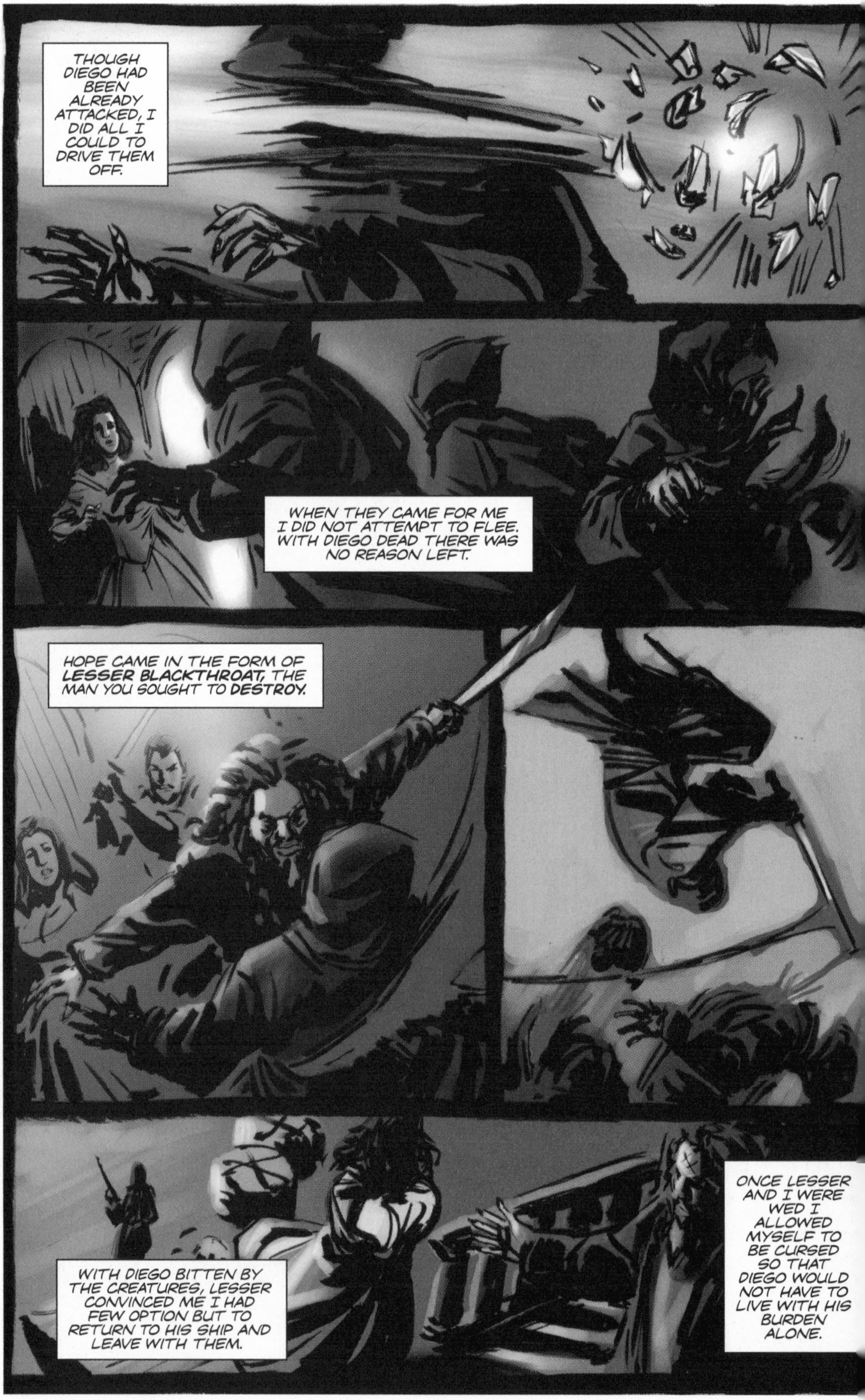
THOUGH DIEGO HAD BEEN ALREADY ATTACKED, I DID ALL I COULD TO DRIVE THEM OFF.
WHEN THEY CAME FOR ME I DID NOT ATTEMPT TO FLEE. WITH DIEGO DEAD THERE WAS NO REASON LEFT.
HOPE CAME IN THE FORM OF LESSER BLACKTHROAT, THE MAN YOU SOUGHT TO DESTROY.
WITH DIEGO BITTEN BY THE CREATURES, LESSER CONVINCED ME I HAD FEW OPTION BUT TO RETURN TO HIS SHIP AND LEAVE WITH THEM.
ONCE LESSER AND I WERE WED I ALLOWED MYSELF TO BE CURSED SO THAT DIEGO WOULD NOT HAVE TO LIVE WITH HIS BURDEN ALONE.

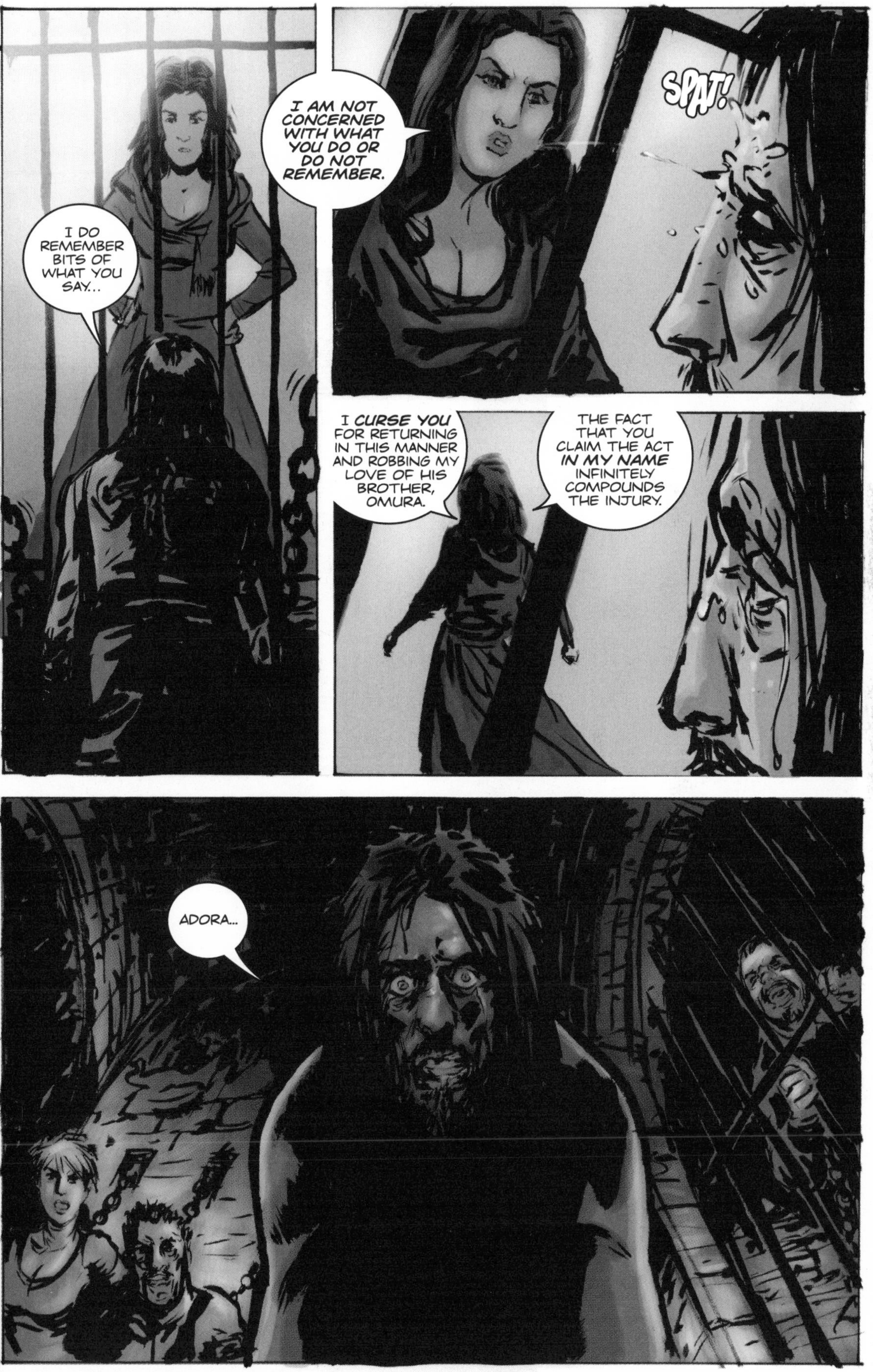
I DO REMEMBER BITS OF WHAT YOU SAY...
I AM NOT CONCERNED WITH WHAT YOU DO OR DO NOT REMEMBER.
SPAT!
I CURSE YOU FOR RETURNING IN THIS MANNER AND ROBBING MY LOVE OF HIS BROTHER, OMURA.
THE FACT THAT YOU CLAIM THE ACT IN MY NAME INFINITELY COMPOUNDS THE INJURY.
ADORA...

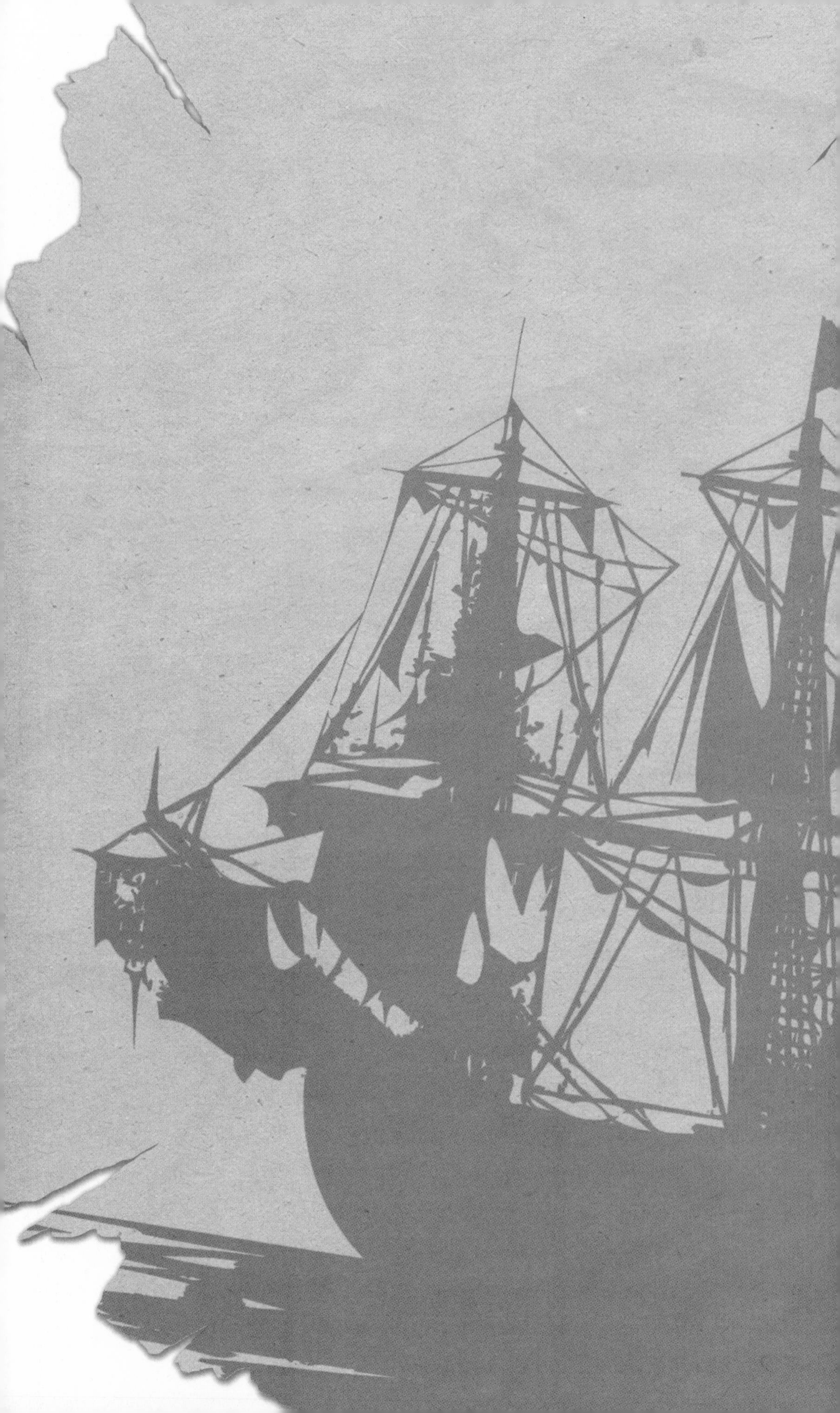

Seven

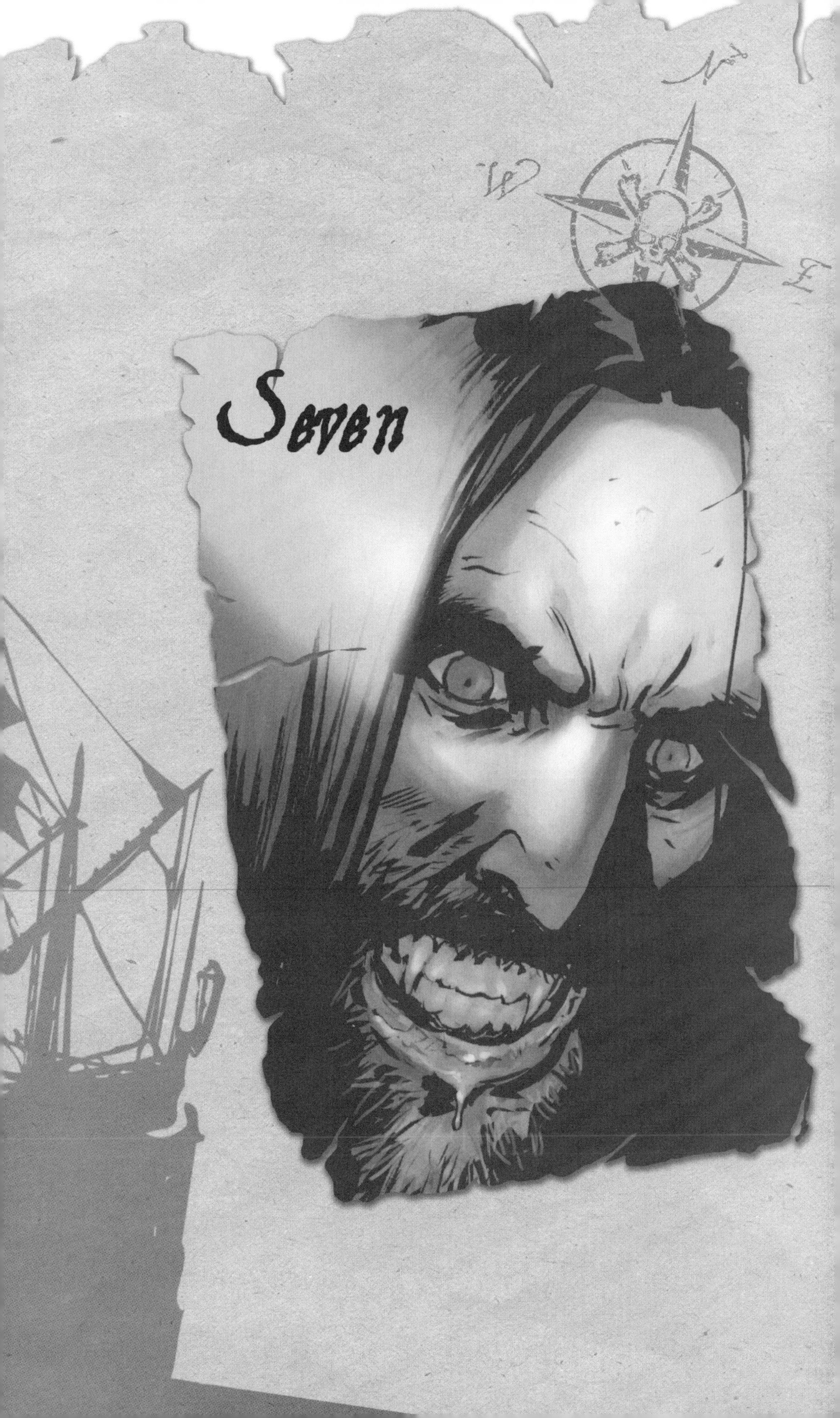

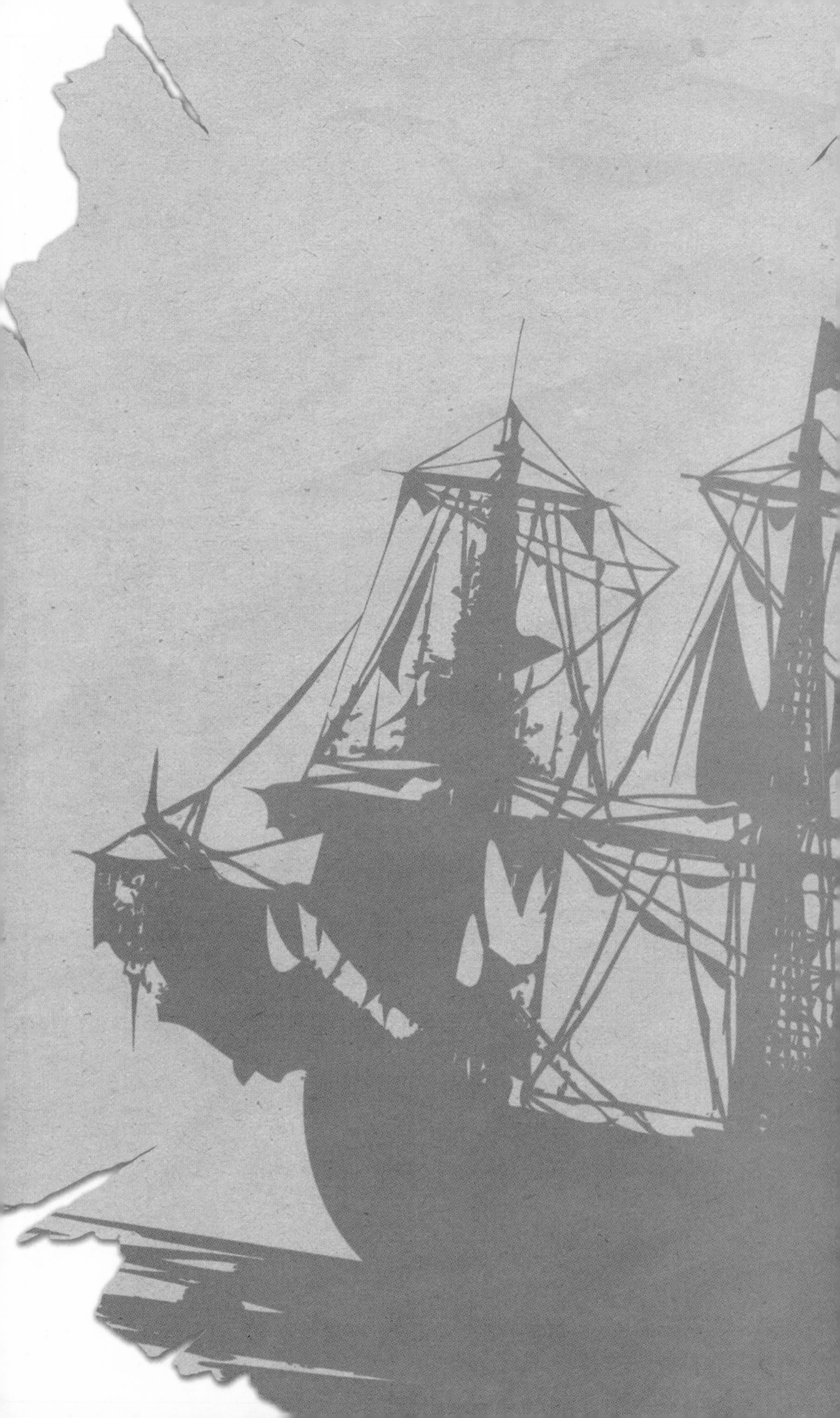

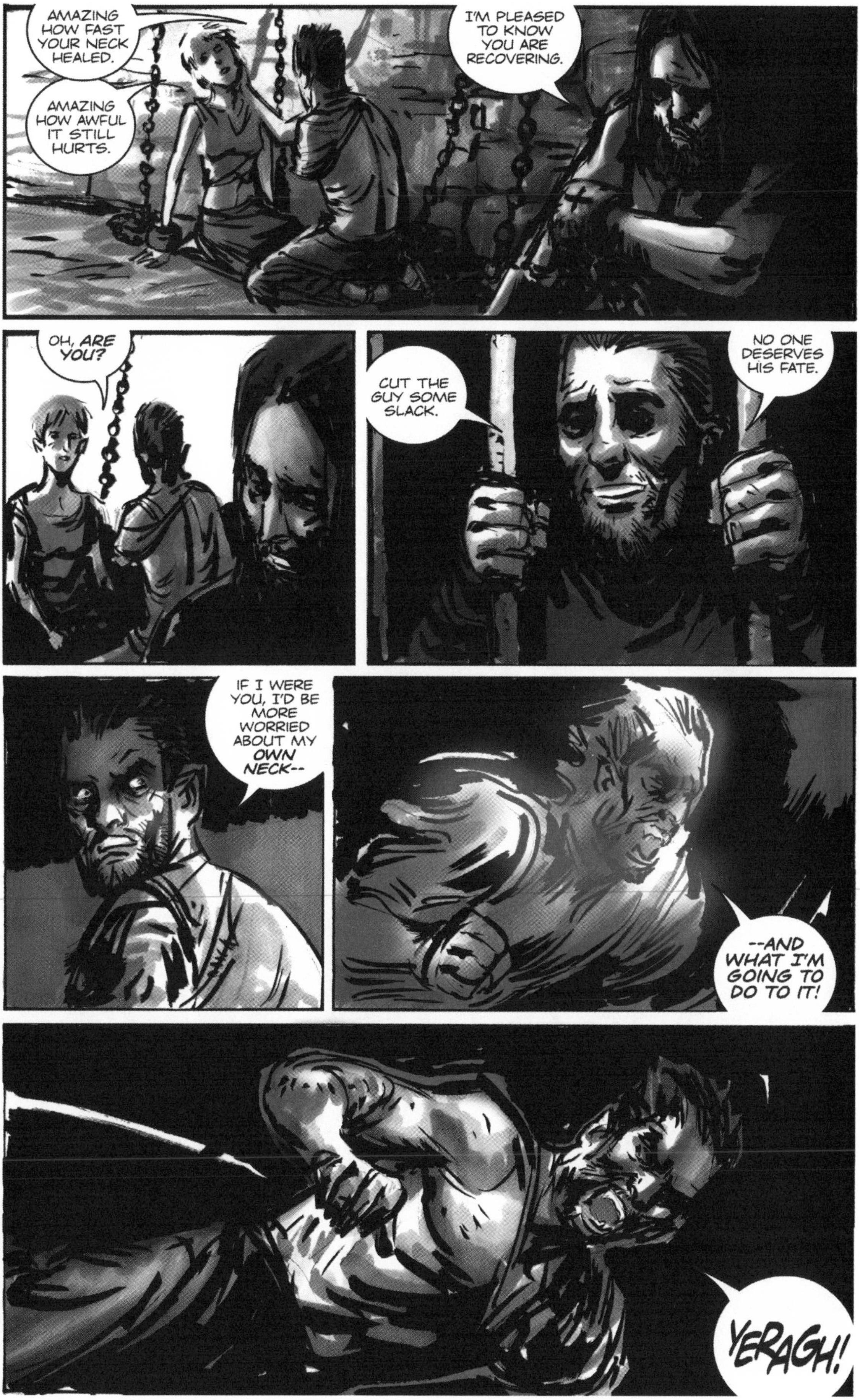
AMAZING HOW FAST YOUR NECK HEALED.
AMAZING HOW AWFUL IT STILL HURTS.
I'M PLEASED TO KNOW YOU ARE RECOVERING.
OH, ARE YOU?
CUT THE GUY SOME SLACK.
NO ONE DESERVES HIS FATE.
IF I WERE YOU, I'D BE MORE WORRIED ABOUT MY OWN NECK--
--AND WHAT I'M GOING TO DO TO IT!
YERAGH!

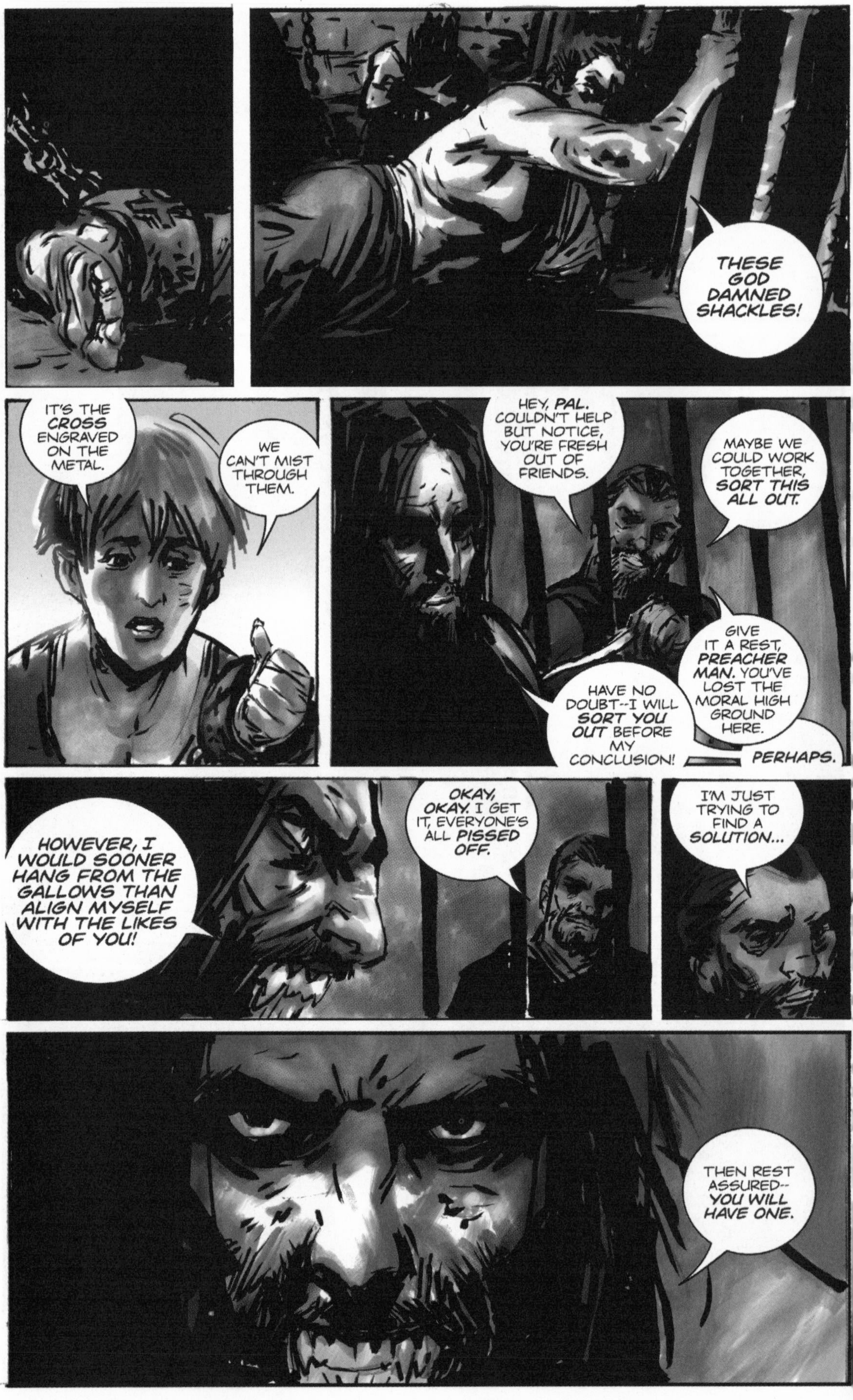
THESE GOD DAMNED SHACKLES!
IT'S THE CROSS ENGRAVED ON THE METAL.
WE CAN'T MIST THROUGH THEM.
HEY, PAL. COULDN'T HELP BUT NOTICE, YOU'RE FRESH OUT OF FRIENDS.
MAYBE WE COULD WORK TOGETHER, SORT THIS ALL OUT.
HAVE NO DOUBT--I WILL SORT YOU OUT BEFORE MY CONCLUSION!
GIVE IT A REST, PREACHER MAN. YOU'VE LOST THE MORAL HIGH GROUND HERE.
PERHAPS.
HOWEVER, I WOULD SOONER HANG FROM THE GALLOWS THAN ALIGN MYSELF WITH THE LIKES OF YOU!
OKAY, OKAY. I GET IT, EVERYONE'S ALL PISSED OFF.
I'M JUST TRYING TO FIND A SOLUTION...
THEN REST ASSURED--YOU WILL HAVE ONE.

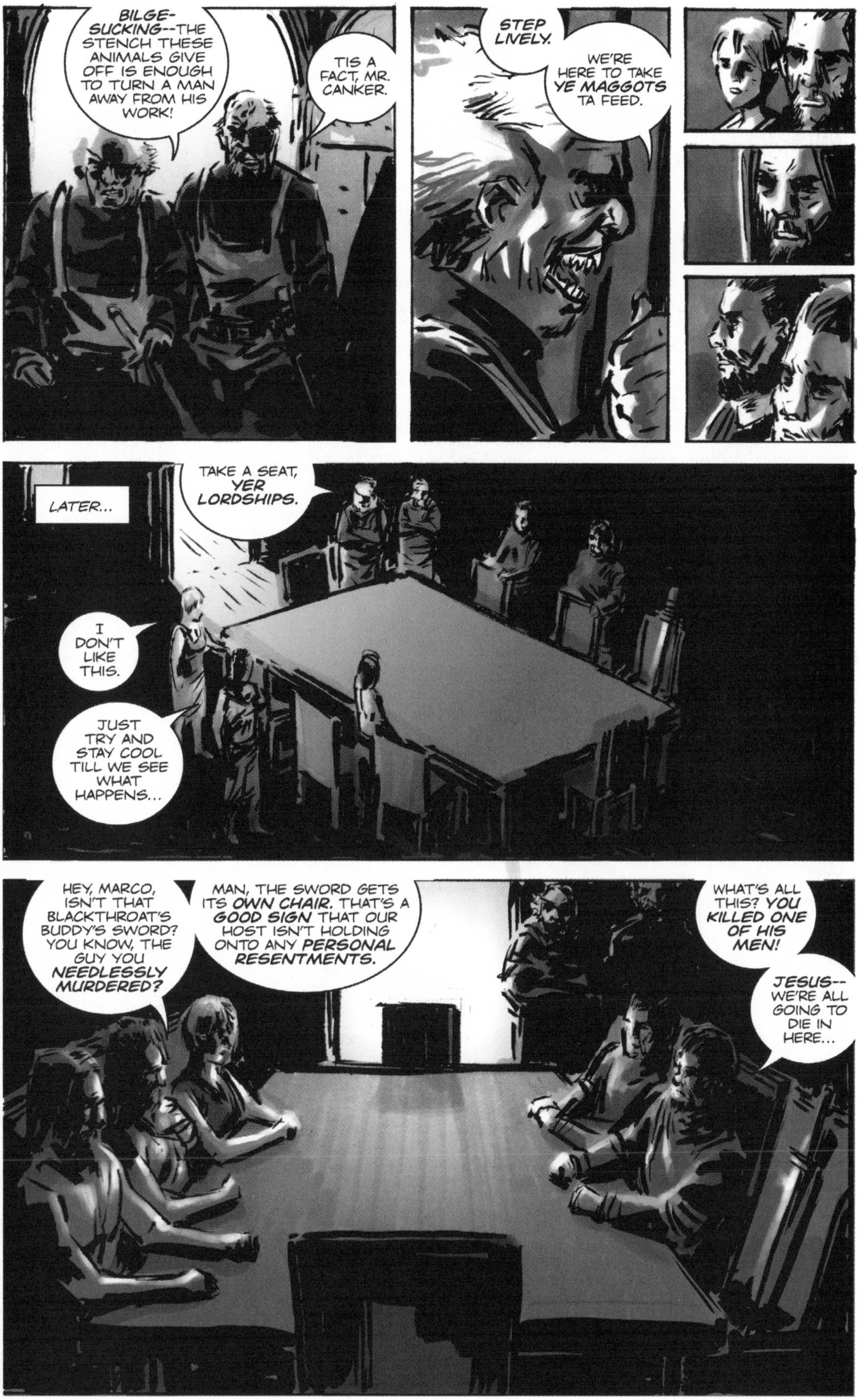
BILGE-SUCKING--THE STENCH THESE ANIMALS GIVE OFF IS ENOUGH TO TURN A MAN AWAY FROM HIS WORK!
TIS A FACT, MR. CANKER.
STEP LIVELY.
WE'RE HERE TO TAKE YE MAGGOTS TA FEED.
LATER...
TAKE A SEAT, YER LORDSHIPS.
I DON'T LIKE THIS.
JUST TRY AND STAY COOL TILL WE SEE WHAT HAPPENS...
HEY, MARCO, ISN'T THAT BLACKTHROAT'S BUDDY'S SWORD? YOU KNOW, THE GUY YOU NEEDLESSLY MURDERED?
MAN, THE SWORD GETS ITS OWN CHAIR. THAT'S A GOOD SIGN THAT OUR HOST ISN'T HOLDING ONTO ANY PERSONAL RESENTMENTS.
WHAT'S ALL THIS? YOU KILLED ONE OF HIS MEN!
JESUS-- WE'RE ALL GOING TO DIE IN HERE...

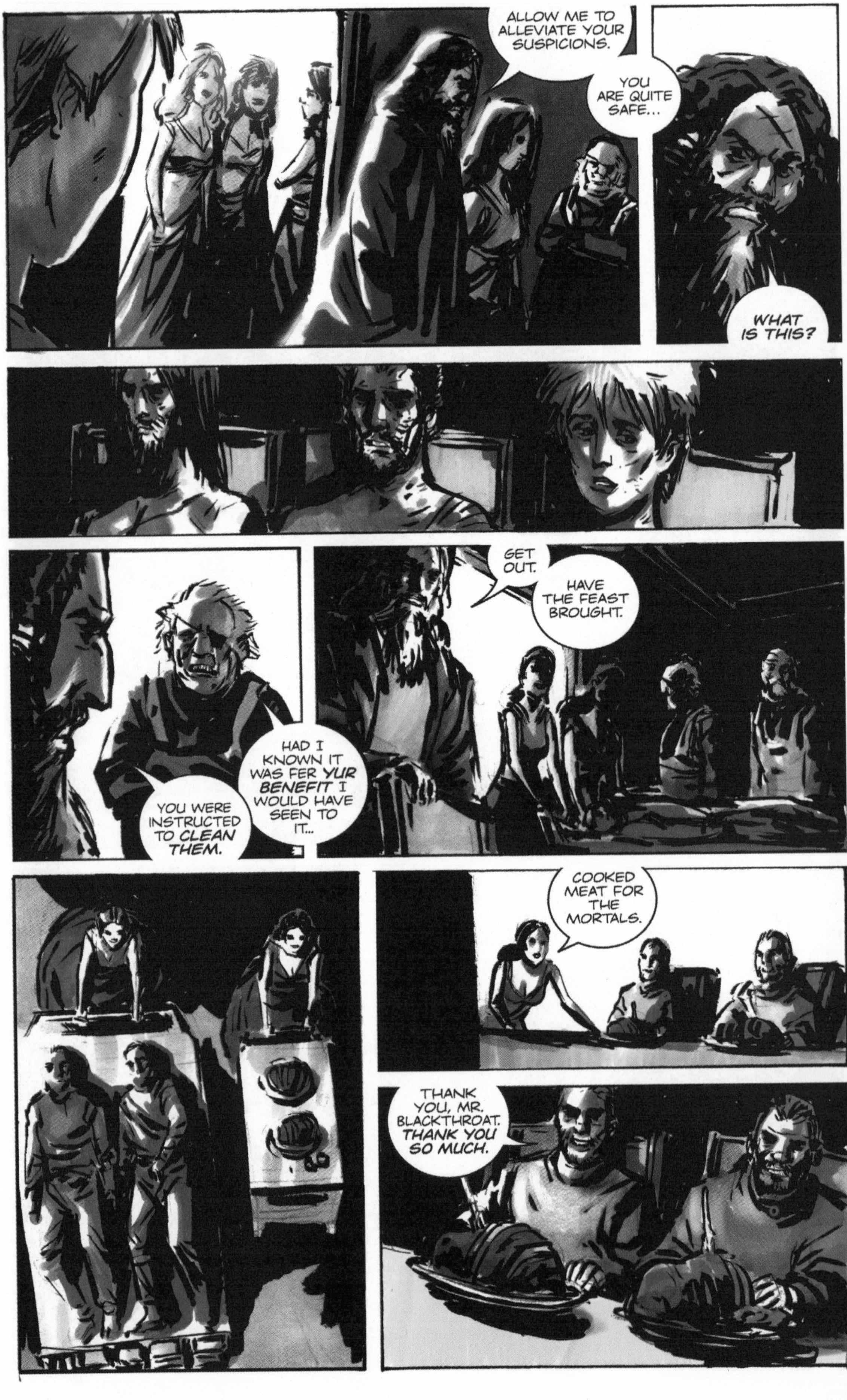

ALLOW ME TO ALLEVIATE YOUR SUSPICIONS.
YOU ARE QUITE SAFE...
WHAT IS THIS?
YOU WERE INSTRUCTED TO CLEAN THEM.
HAD I KNOWN IT WAS FER YUR BENEFIT I WOULD HAVE SEEN TO IT...
GET OUT.
HAVE THE FEAST BROUGHT.
COOKED MEAT FOR THE MORTALS.
THANK YOU, MR. BLACKTHROAT. THANK YOU SO MUCH.

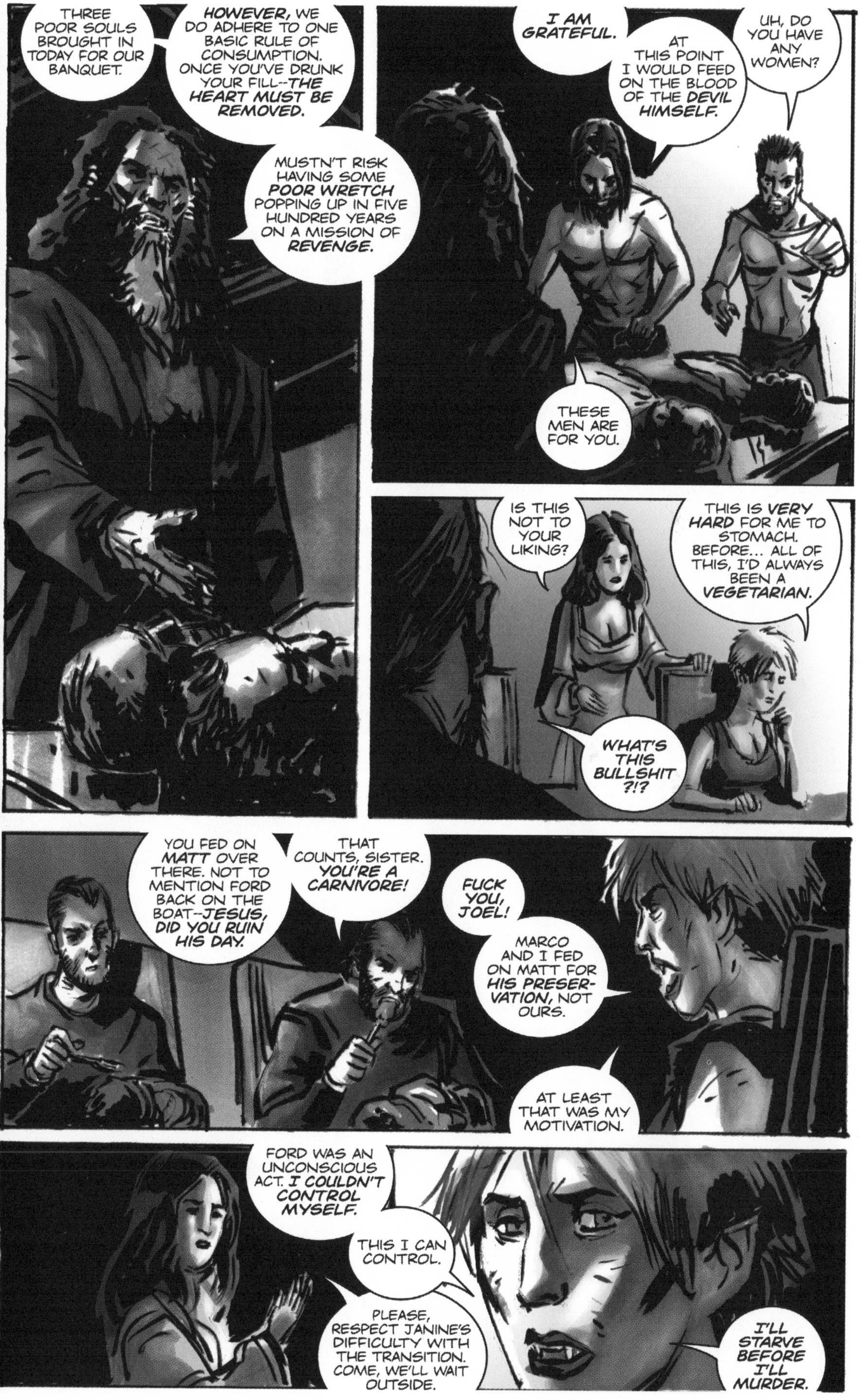
THREE POOR SOULS BROUGHT IN TODAY FOR OUR BANQUET.
HOWEVER, WE DO ADHERE TO ONE BASIC RULE OF CONSUMPTION. ONCE YOU'VE DRUNK YOUR FILL--THE HEART MUST BE REMOVED.
MUSTN'T RISK HAVING SOME POOR WRETCH POPPING UP IN FIVE HUNDRED YEARS ON A MISSION OF REVENGE.
I AM GRATEFUL.
AT THIS POINT I WOULD FEED ON THE BLOOD OF THE DEVIL HIMSELF.
UH, DO YOU HAVE ANY WOMEN?
THESE MEN ARE FOR YOU.
IS THIS NOT TO YOUR LIKING?
THIS IS VERY HARD FOR ME TO STOMACH. BEFORE... ALL OF THIS, I'D ALWAYS BEEN A VEGETARIAN.
WHAT'S THIS BULLSHIT ?!?
YOU FED ON MATT OVER THERE. NOT TO MENTION FORD BACK ON THE BOAT--JESUS, DID YOU RUIN HIS DAY.
THAT COUNTS, SISTER. YOU'RE A CARNIVORE!
FUCK YOU, JOEL!
MARCO AND I FED ON MATT FOR HIS PRESER-VATION, NOT OURS.
AT LEAST THAT WAS MY MOTIVATION.
FORD WAS AN UNCONSCIOUS ACT. I COULDN'T CONTROL MYSELF.
THIS I CAN CONTROL.
PLEASE, RESPECT JANINE'S DIFFICULTY WITH THE TRANSITION. COME, WE'LL WAIT OUTSIDE.
I'LL STARVE BEFORE I'LL MURDER.

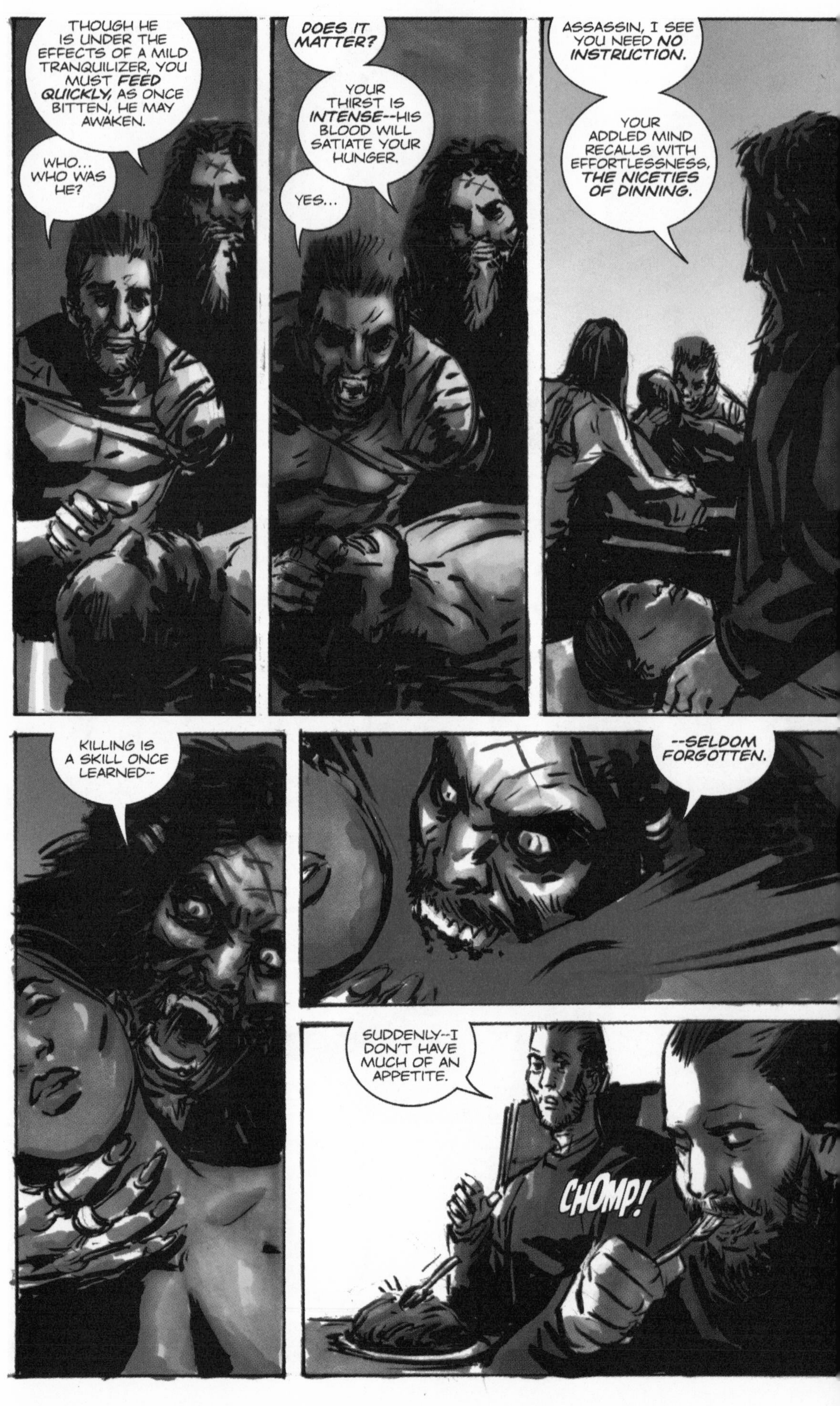
THOUGH HE IS UNDER THE EFFECTS OF A MILD TRANQUILIZER, YOU MUST FEED QUICKLY, AS ONCE BITTEN, HE MAY AWAKEN.
WHO... WHO WAS HE?
DOES IT MATTER?
YOUR THIRST IS INTENSE--HIS BLOOD WILL SATIATE YOUR HUNGER.
YES...
ASSASSIN, I SEE YOU NEED NO INSTRUCTION.
YOUR ADDLED MIND RECALLS WITH EFFORTLESSNESS, THE NICETIES OF DINNING.
KILLING IS A SKILL ONCE LEARNED--
--SELDOM FORGOTTEN.
SUDDENLY--I DON'T HAVE MUCH OF AN APPETITE.
CHOMP!

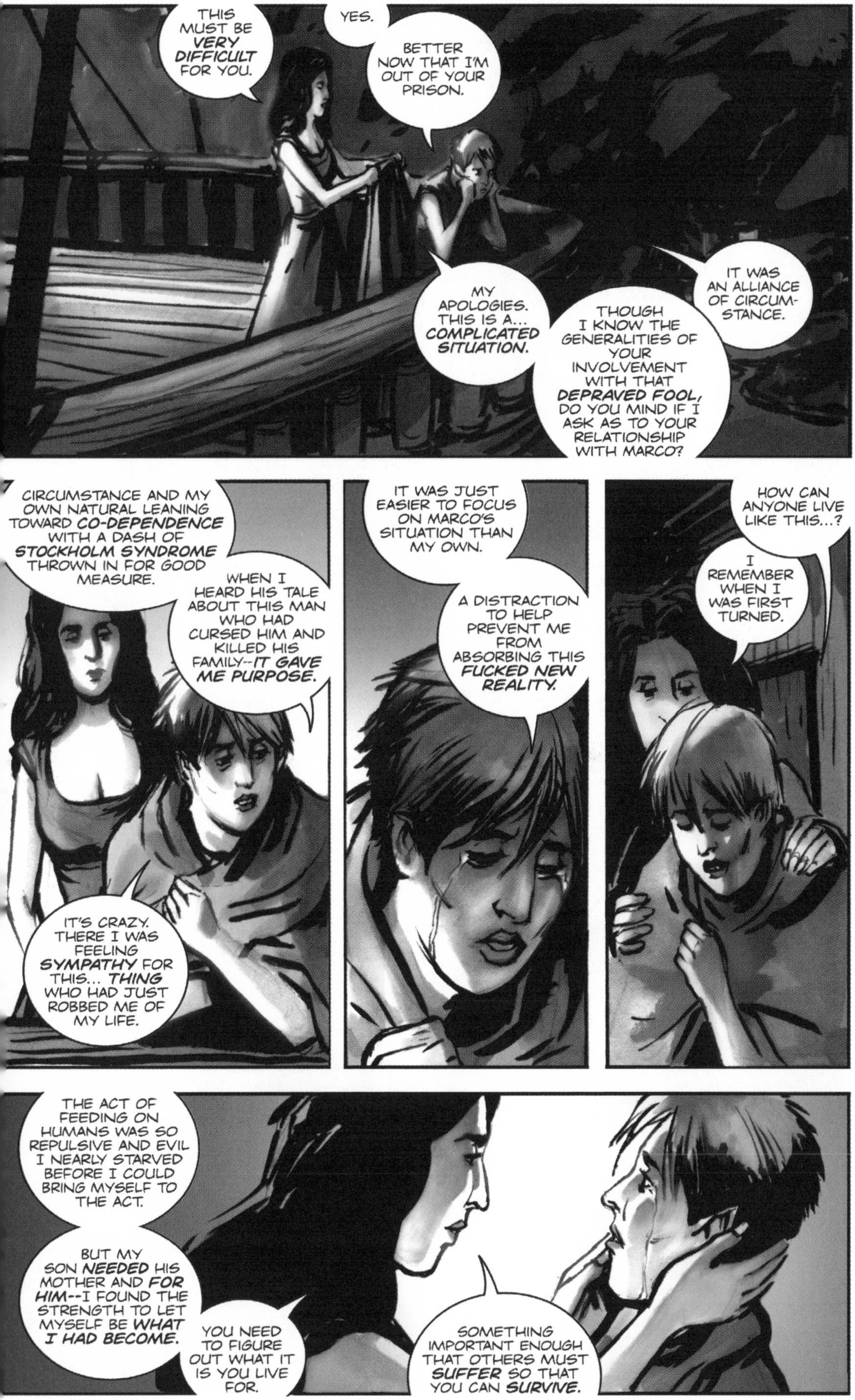

THIS MUST BE VERY DIFFICULT FOR YOU.
YES.
BETTER NOW THAT I'M OUT OF YOUR PRISON.
MY APOLOGIES. THIS IS A... COMPLICATED SITUATION.
THOUGH I KNOW THE GENERALITIES OF YOUR INVOLVEMENT WITH THAT DEPRAVED FOOL, DO YOU MIND IF I ASK AS TO YOUR RELATIONSHIP WITH MARCO?
IT WAS AN ALLIANCE OF CIRCUM-STANCE.
CIRCUMSTANCE AND MY OWN NATURAL LEANING TOWARD CO-DEPENDENCE WITH A DASH OF STOCKHOLM SYNDROME THROWN IN FOR GOOD MEASURE.
WHEN I HEARD HIS TALE ABOUT THIS MAN WHO HAD CURSED HIM AND KILLED HIS FAMILY--IT GAVE ME PURPOSE.
IT'S CRAZY. THERE I WAS FEELING SYMPATHY FOR THIS... THING WHO HAD JUST ROBBED ME OF MY LIFE.
IT WAS JUST EASIER TO FOCUS ON MARCO'S SITUATION THAN MY OWN.
A DISTRACTION TO HELP PREVENT ME FROM ABSORBING THIS FUCKED NEW REALITY.
HOW CAN ANYONE LIVE LIKE THIS...?
I REMEMBER WHEN I WAS FIRST TURNED.
THE ACT OF FEEDING ON HUMANS WAS SO REPULSIVE AND EVIL I NEARLY STARVED BEFORE I COULD BRING MYSELF TO THE ACT.
BUT MY SON NEEDED HIS MOTHER AND FOR HIM--I FOUND THE STRENGTH TO LET MYSELF BE WHAT I HAD BECOME.
YOU NEED TO FIGURE OUT WHAT IT IS YOU LIVE FOR.
SOMETHING IMPORTANT ENOUGH THAT OTHERS MUST SUFFER SO THAT YOU CAN SURVIVE.

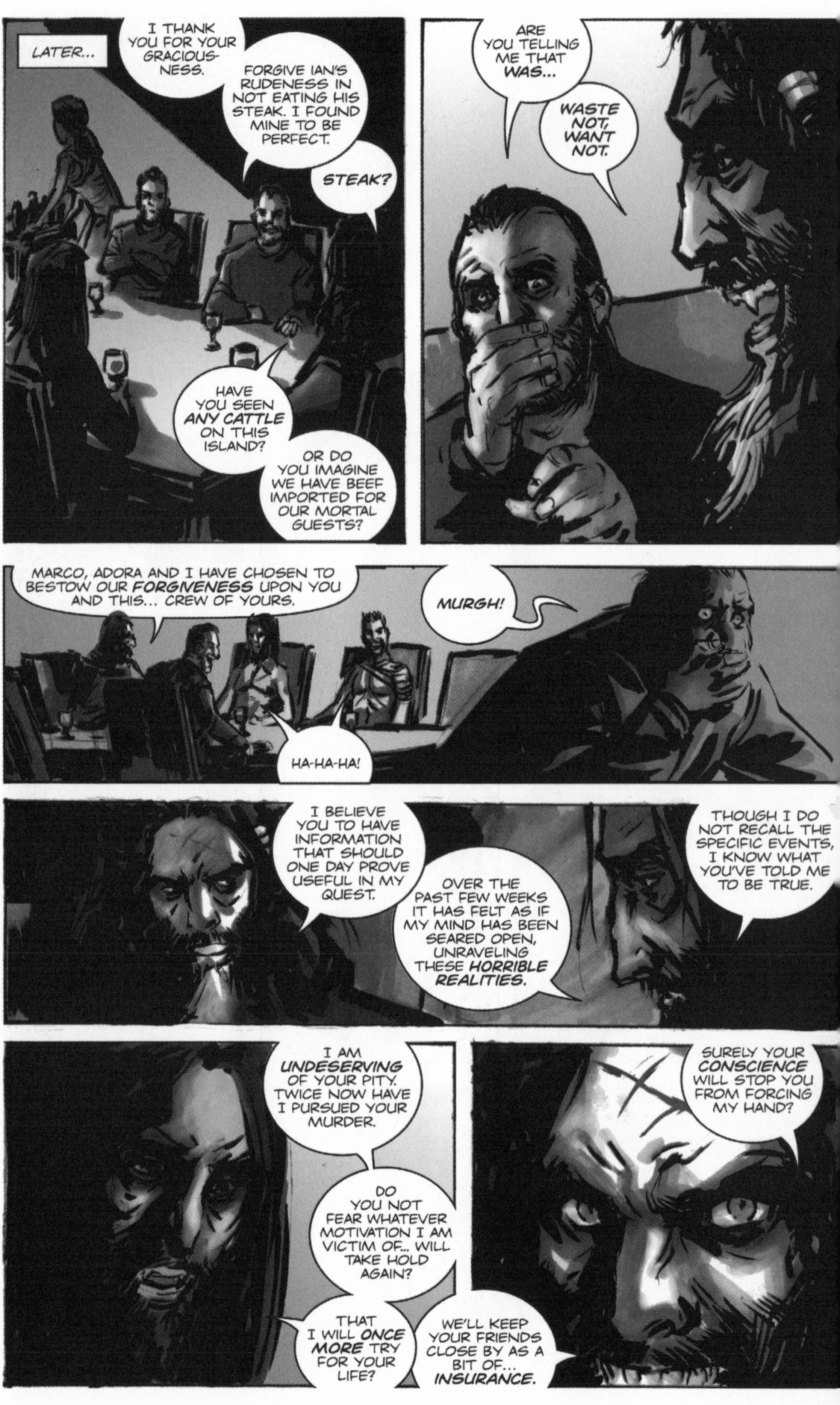
LATER...
I THANK YOU FOR YOUR GRACIOUS-NESS.
FORGIVE IAN'S RUDENESS IN NOT EATING HIS STEAK. I FOUND MINE TO BE PERFECT.
STEAK?
HAVE YOU SEEN ANY CATTLE ON THIS ISLAND?
OR DO YOU IMAGINE WE HAVE BEEF IMPORTED FOR OUR MORTAL GUESTS?
ARE YOU TELLING ME THAT WAS...
WASTE NOT, WANT NOT.
MARCO, ADORA AND I HAVE CHOSEN TO BESTOW OUR FORGIVENESS UPON YOU AND THIS... CREW OF YOURS.
MURGH!
HA-HA-HA!
I BELIEVE YOU TO HAVE INFORMATION THAT SHOULD ONE DAY PROVE USEFUL IN MY QUEST.
OVER THE PAST FEW WEEKS IT HAS FELT AS IF MY MIND HAS BEEN SEARED OPEN, UNRAVELING THESE HORRIBLE REALITIES.
THOUGH I DO NOT RECALL THE SPECIFIC EVENTS, I KNOW WHAT YOU'VE TOLD ME TO BE TRUE.
I AM UNDESERVING OF YOUR PITY. TWICE NOW HAVE I PURSUED YOUR MURDER.
DO YOU NOT FEAR WHATEVER MOTIVATION I AM VICTIM OF... WILL TAKE HOLD AGAIN?
THAT I WILL ONCE MORE TRY FOR YOUR LIFE?
SURELY YOUR CONSCIENCE WILL STOP YOU FROM FORCING MY HAND?
WE'LL KEEP YOUR FRIENDS CLOSE BY AS A BIT OF... INSURANCE.

UPON LEARNING THE TRUTH OF MY TALE, THEY HOLD ME IN CONTEMPT.

REGARDLESS, FOR THEIR ROLL IN MY RESCUE I AM HELD FOREVER IN THEIR DEBT.

I SENSE YOUR FONDNESS FOR THEM, ESPECIALLY THE GIRL.

THIS ARRANGEMENT WILL SUFFICE.

LISTEN MAN, YES--I *FUCKED UP.* THERE ISN'T ANYTHING ELSE I CAN SAY.

I PANICKED AND I'M SO USED TO TAKING DIRECTIONS FROM JOEL, I DIDN'T EVEN THINK ABOUT WHAT IT WAS HE WAS TELLING ME TO DO.

FUCK.

YOU'RE JUST ANOTHER EXCESSIVELY DRIVEN, STATUS HUNGRY, HOLLYWOOD FAGGOT!

YOU'LL NEVER STAND UP AND BE COUNTED FOR *ANYTHING* OTHER THAN *YOUR CAREER!*

YOU WERE GOING TO LET US DIE!

I'M SORRY...

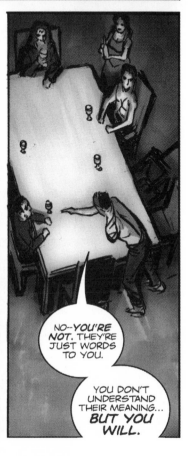

NO--*YOU'RE NOT.* THEY'RE JUST WORDS TO YOU.

YOU DON'T UNDERSTAND THEIR MEANING... *BUT YOU WILL.*

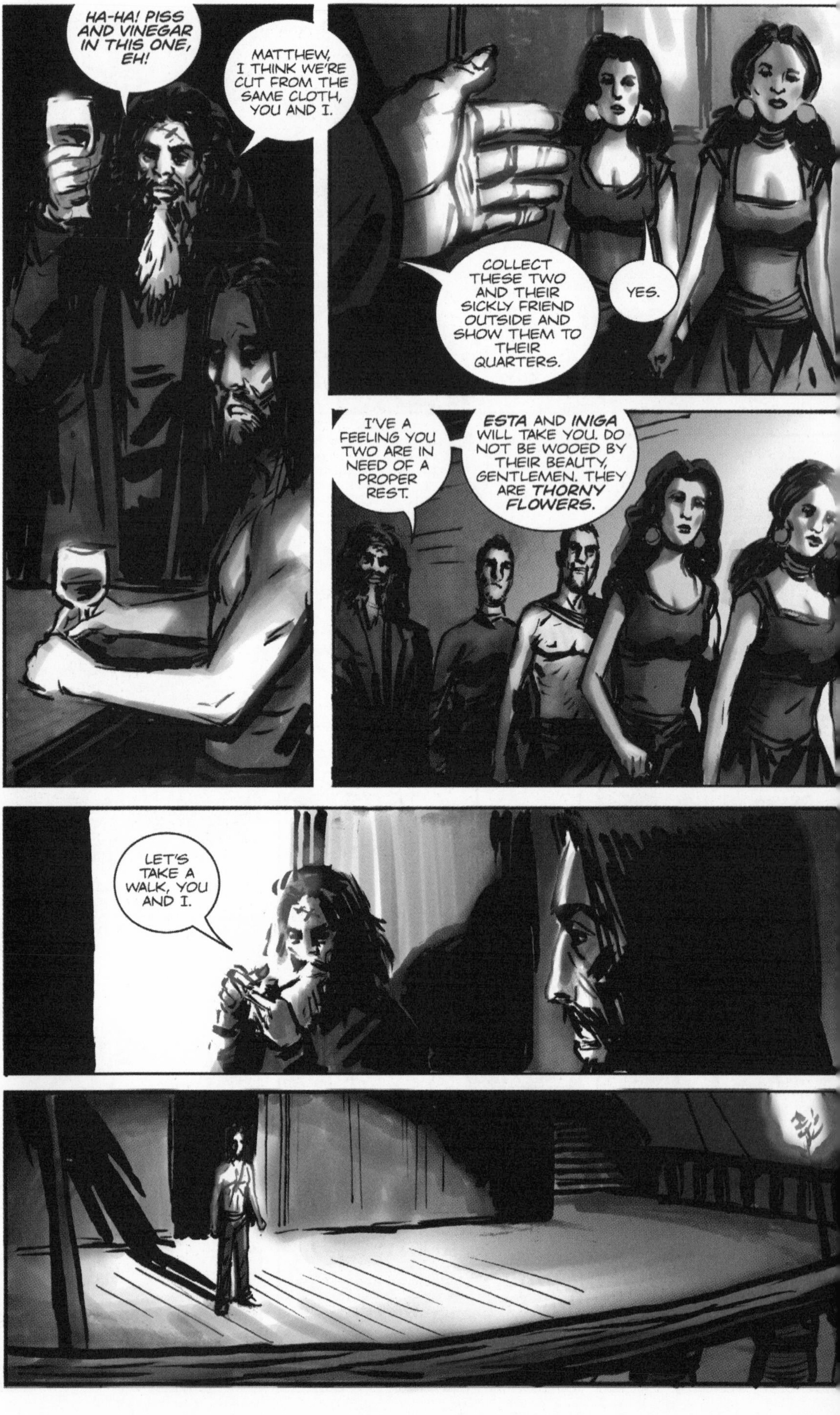
HA-HA! PISS AND VINEGAR IN THIS ONE, EH!
MATTHEW, I THINK WE'RE CUT FROM THE SAME CLOTH, YOU AND I.
COLLECT THESE TWO AND THEIR SICKLY FRIEND OUTSIDE AND SHOW THEM TO THEIR QUARTERS.
YES.
I'VE A FEELING YOU TWO ARE IN NEED OF A PROPER REST.
ESTA AND INIGA WILL TAKE YOU. DO NOT BE WOOED BY THEIR BEAUTY, GENTLEMEN. THEY ARE THORNY FLOWERS.
LET'S TAKE A WALK, YOU AND I.

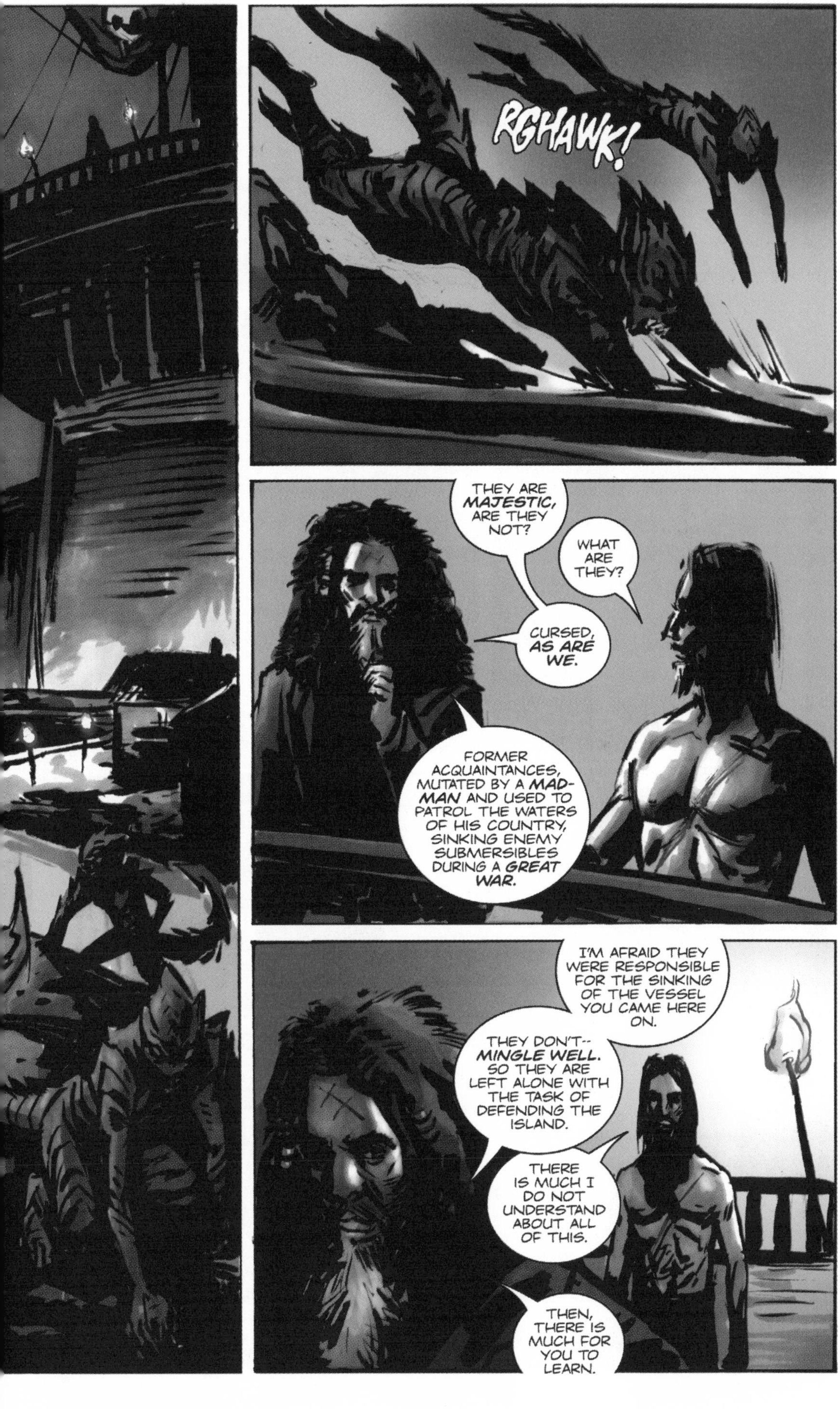
RGHAWK!
THEY ARE MAJESTIC, ARE THEY NOT?
WHAT ARE THEY?
CURSED, AS ARE WE.
FORMER ACQUAINTANCES, MUTATED BY A MAD-MAN AND USED TO PATROL THE WATERS OF HIS COUNTRY, SINKING ENEMY SUBMERSIBLES DURING A GREAT WAR.
I'M AFRAID THEY WERE RESPONSIBLE FOR THE SINKING OF THE VESSEL YOU CAME HERE ON.
THEY DON'T-- MINGLE WELL. SO THEY ARE LEFT ALONE WITH THE TASK OF DEFENDING THE ISLAND.
THERE IS MUCH I DO NOT UNDERSTAND ABOUT ALL OF THIS.
THEN, THERE IS MUCH FOR YOU TO LEARN.

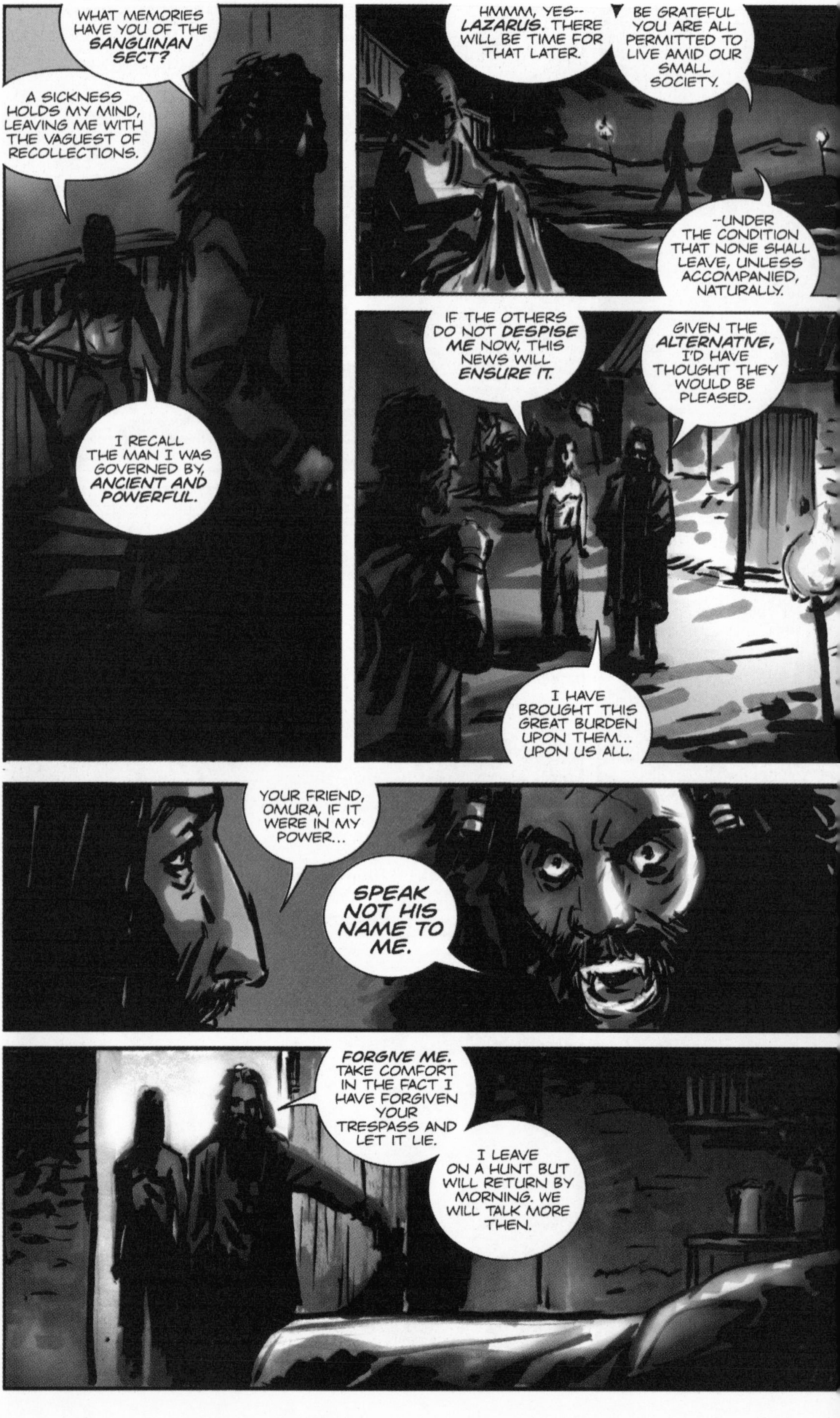
WHAT MEMORIES HAVE YOU OF THE SANGUINAN SECT?
A SICKNESS HOLDS MY MIND, LEAVING ME WITH THE VAGUEST OF RECOLLECTIONS.
I RECALL THE MAN I WAS GOVERNED BY, ANCIENT AND POWERFUL.
HMMM, YES-- LAZARUS. THERE WILL BE TIME FOR THAT LATER.
BE GRATEFUL YOU ARE ALL PERMITTED TO LIVE AMID OUR SMALL SOCIETY.
--UNDER THE CONDITION THAT NONE SHALL LEAVE, UNLESS ACCOMPANIED, NATURALLY.
IF THE OTHERS DO NOT DESPISE ME NOW, THIS NEWS WILL ENSURE IT.
GIVEN THE ALTERNATIVE, I'D HAVE THOUGHT THEY WOULD BE PLEASED.
I HAVE BROUGHT THIS GREAT BURDEN UPON THEM... UPON US ALL.
YOUR FRIEND, OMURA, IF IT WERE IN MY POWER...
SPEAK NOT HIS NAME TO ME.
FORGIVE ME. TAKE COMFORT IN THE FACT I HAVE FORGIVEN YOUR TRESPASS AND LET IT LIE.
I LEAVE ON A HUNT BUT WILL RETURN BY MORNING. WE WILL TALK MORE THEN.

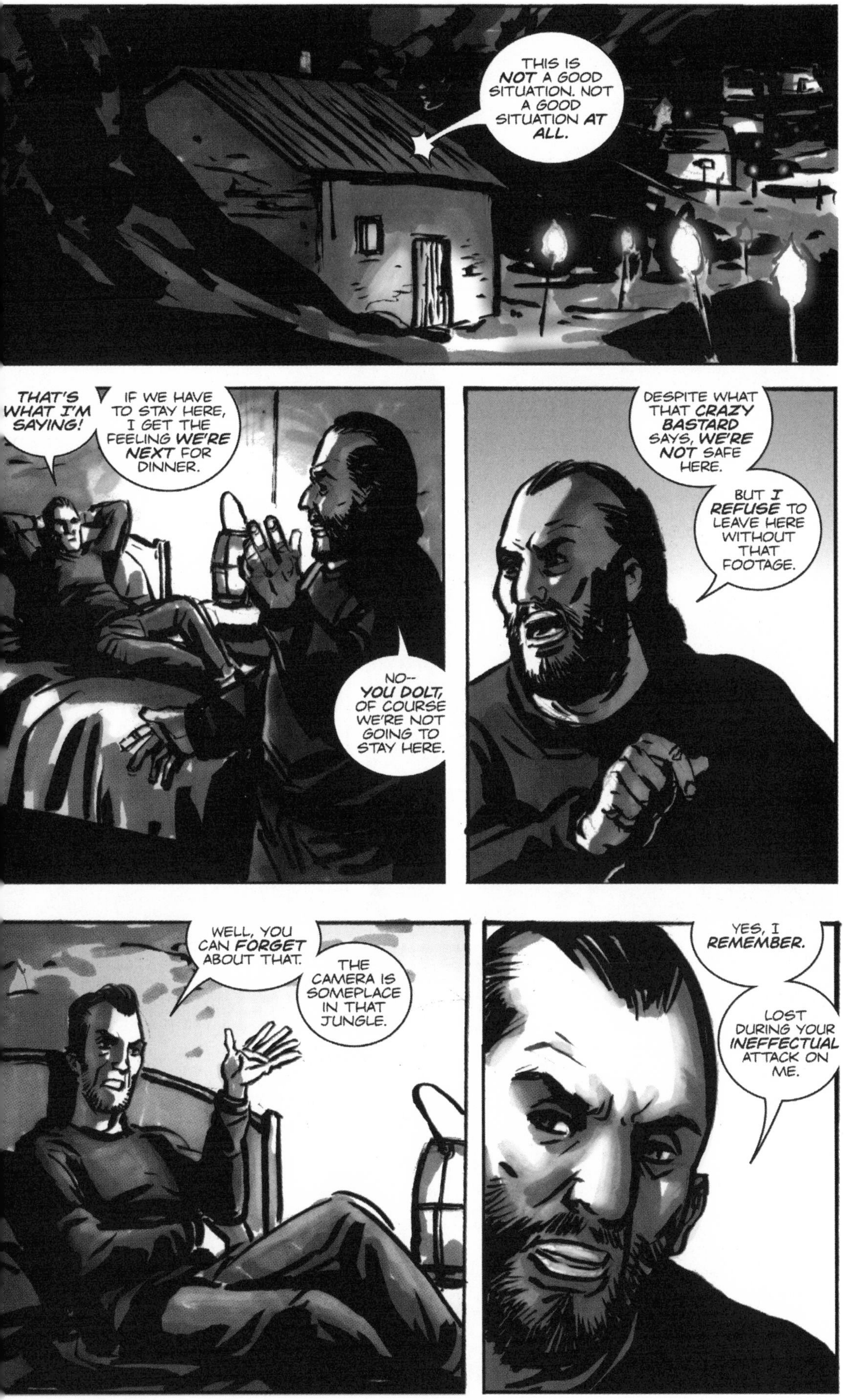
THIS IS NOT A GOOD SITUATION. NOT A GOOD SITUATION AT ALL.
THAT'S WHAT I'M SAYING!
IF WE HAVE TO STAY HERE, I GET THE FEELING WE'RE NEXT FOR DINNER.
NO-- YOU DOLT, OF COURSE WE'RE NOT GOING TO STAY HERE.
DESPITE WHAT THAT CRAZY BASTARD SAYS, WE'RE NOT SAFE HERE.
BUT I REFUSE TO LEAVE HERE WITHOUT THAT FOOTAGE.
WELL, YOU CAN FORGET ABOUT THAT.
THE CAMERA IS SOMEPLACE IN THAT JUNGLE.
YES, I REMEMBER.
LOST DURING YOUR INEFFECTUAL ATTACK ON ME.

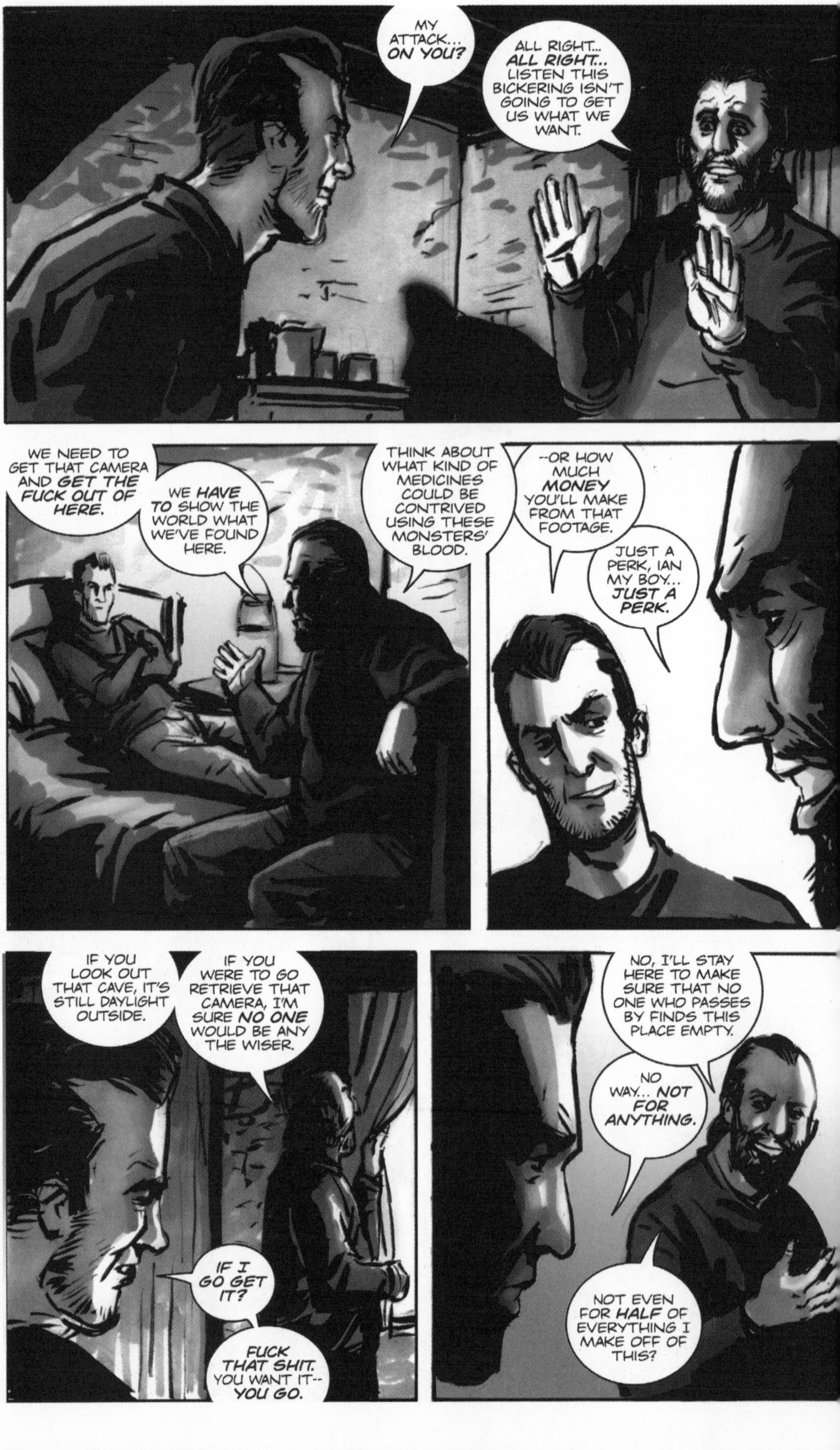
MY ATTACK... ON YOU?
ALL RIGHT... ALL RIGHT... LISTEN THIS BICKERING ISN'T GOING TO GET US WHAT WE WANT.
WE NEED TO GET THAT CAMERA AND GET THE FUCK OUT OF HERE.
WE HAVE TO SHOW THE WORLD WHAT WE'VE FOUND HERE.
THINK ABOUT WHAT KIND OF MEDICINES COULD BE CONTRIVED USING THESE MONSTERS' BLOOD.
--OR HOW MUCH MONEY YOU'LL MAKE FROM THAT FOOTAGE.
JUST A PERK, IAN MY BOY... JUST A PERK.
IF YOU LOOK OUT THAT CAVE, IT'S STILL DAYLIGHT OUTSIDE.
IF YOU WERE TO GO RETRIEVE THAT CAMERA, I'M SURE NO ONE WOULD BE ANY THE WISER.
IF I GO GET IT?
FUCK THAT SHIT. YOU WANT IT-- YOU GO.
NO, I'LL STAY HERE TO MAKE SURE THAT NO ONE WHO PASSES BY FINDS THIS PLACE EMPTY.
NO WAY... NOT FOR ANYTHING.
NOT EVEN FOR HALF OF EVERYTHING I MAKE OFF OF THIS?

I CAN'T FUCKING BELIEVE THIS. I GET TO LIVE FOREVER BUT AS A GIMP WHO HAS TO EAT PEOPLE.

YOU HAVE TO FOCUS SO MUCH ON THE BRIGHT SIDE ALL THE TIME?

YEAH YOU'RE RIGHT-- THIS MIGHT ACTUALLY BE KINDA COOL. MAYBE I'LL GET A ROBOT ARM OR I CAN ATTACH A CHAINSAW.

SORRY SWEETIE, DONE TO DEATH, ON BOTH COUNTS.

JUST BE HAPPY THAT NASTY BREAK HEALED AS QUICKLY AS IT DID.

YEAH, THE HEALING FAST THING IS PRETTY WICKED-- WE'RE LIKE WOLVERINE.

I'M TELLING YOU IF I JUST GET MYSELF A ROBOT ARM WITH SOME CLAWS I COULD REALLY PULL THIS OFF.

CRIPPLED VAMPIRE ROBOT CLAW ARM!

I'LL GET THAT SHIT COPY WRITTEN AND BE AS RICH AS THOSE GUYS WHO CREATED SUPERMAN!

HAHAHA!

MAY I SPEAK WITH YOU?

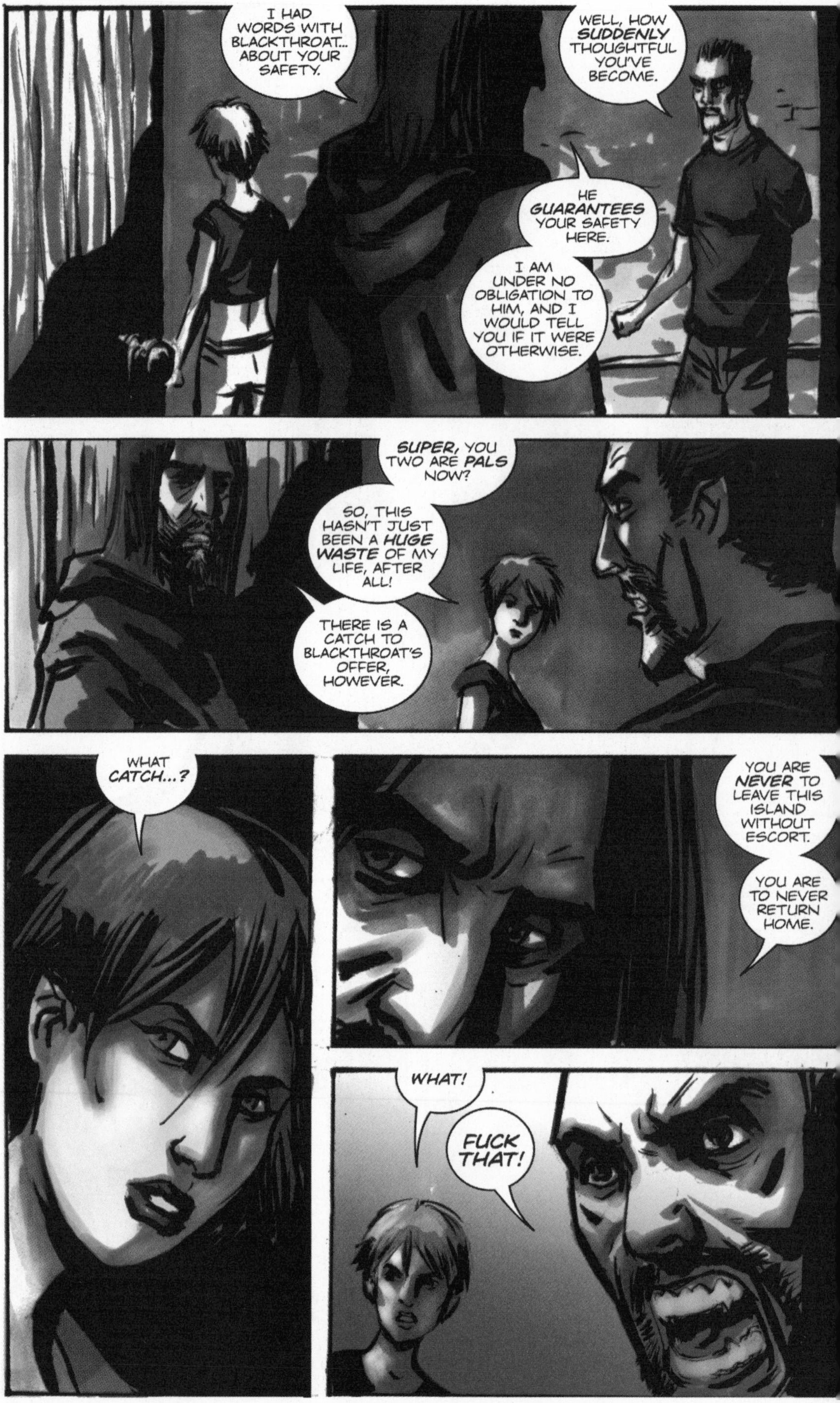
I HAD WORDS WITH BLACKTHROAT... ABOUT YOUR SAFETY.
WELL, HOW SUDDENLY THOUGHTFUL YOU'VE BECOME.
HE GUARANTEES YOUR SAFETY HERE.
I AM UNDER NO OBLIGATION TO HIM, AND I WOULD TELL YOU IF IT WERE OTHERWISE.
SUPER, YOU TWO ARE PALS NOW?
SO, THIS HASN'T JUST BEEN A HUGE WASTE OF MY LIFE, AFTER ALL!
THERE IS A CATCH TO BLACKTHROAT'S OFFER, HOWEVER.
WHAT CATCH...?
YOU ARE NEVER TO LEAVE THIS ISLAND WITHOUT ESCORT.
YOU ARE TO NEVER RETURN HOME.
WHAT!
FUCK THAT!

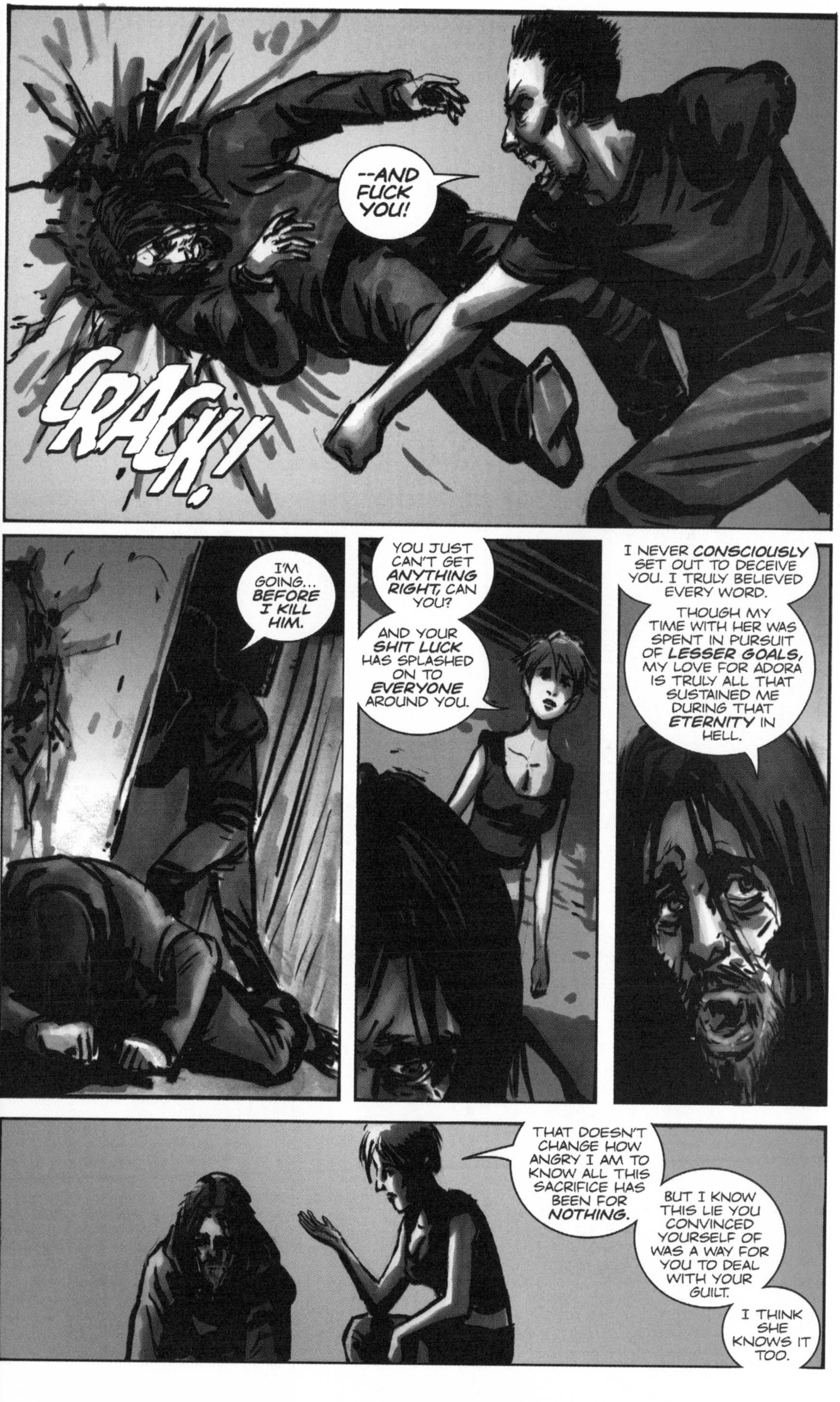
--AND FUCK YOU!
CRACK!!
I'M GOING... BEFORE I KILL HIM.
YOU JUST CAN'T GET ANYTHING RIGHT, CAN YOU?
AND YOUR SHIT LUCK HAS SPLASHED ON TO EVERYONE AROUND YOU.
I NEVER CONSCIOUSLY SET OUT TO DECEIVE YOU. I TRULY BELIEVED EVERY WORD.
THOUGH MY TIME WITH HER WAS SPENT IN PURSUIT OF LESSER GOALS, MY LOVE FOR ADORA IS TRULY ALL THAT SUSTAINED ME DURING THAT ETERNITY IN HELL.
THAT DOESN'T CHANGE HOW ANGRY I AM TO KNOW ALL THIS SACRIFICE HAS BEEN FOR NOTHING.
BUT I KNOW THIS LIE YOU CONVINCED YOURSELF OF WAS A WAY FOR YOU TO DEAL WITH YOUR GUILT.
I THINK SHE KNOWS IT TOO.

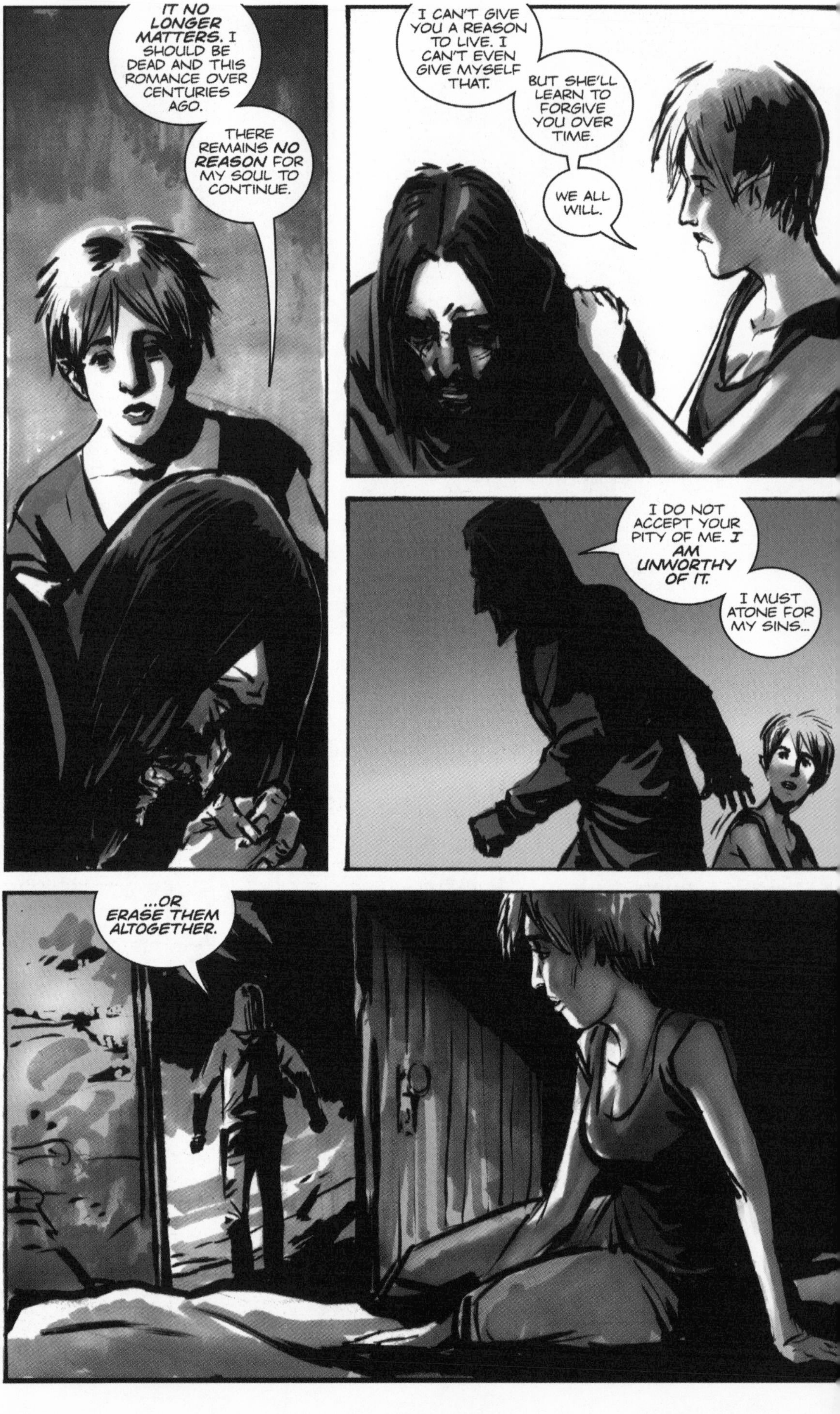
IT NO LONGER MATTERS. I SHOULD BE DEAD AND THIS ROMANCE OVER CENTURIES AGO.
THERE REMAINS NO REASON FOR MY SOUL TO CONTINUE.
I CAN'T GIVE YOU A REASON TO LIVE. I CAN'T EVEN GIVE MYSELF THAT.
BUT SHE'LL LEARN TO FORGIVE YOU OVER TIME.
WE ALL WILL.
I DO NOT ACCEPT YOUR PITY OF ME. I AM UNWORTHY OF IT.
I MUST ATONE FOR MY SINS...
...OR ERASE THEM ALTOGETHER.

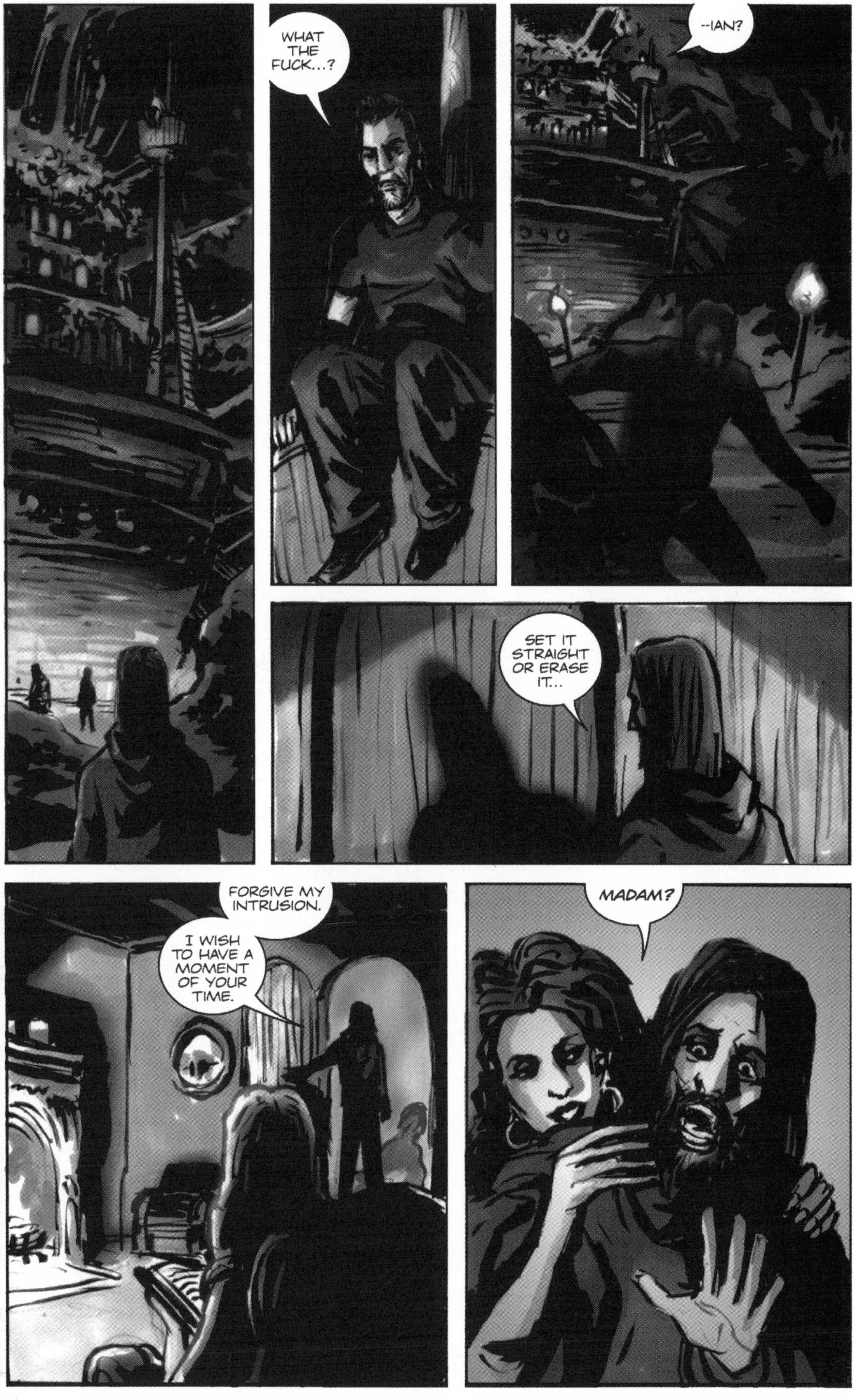
WHAT THE FUCK...?
--IAN?
SET IT STRAIGHT OR ERASE IT...
FORGIVE MY INTRUSION.
I WISH TO HAVE A MOMENT OF YOUR TIME.
MADAM?

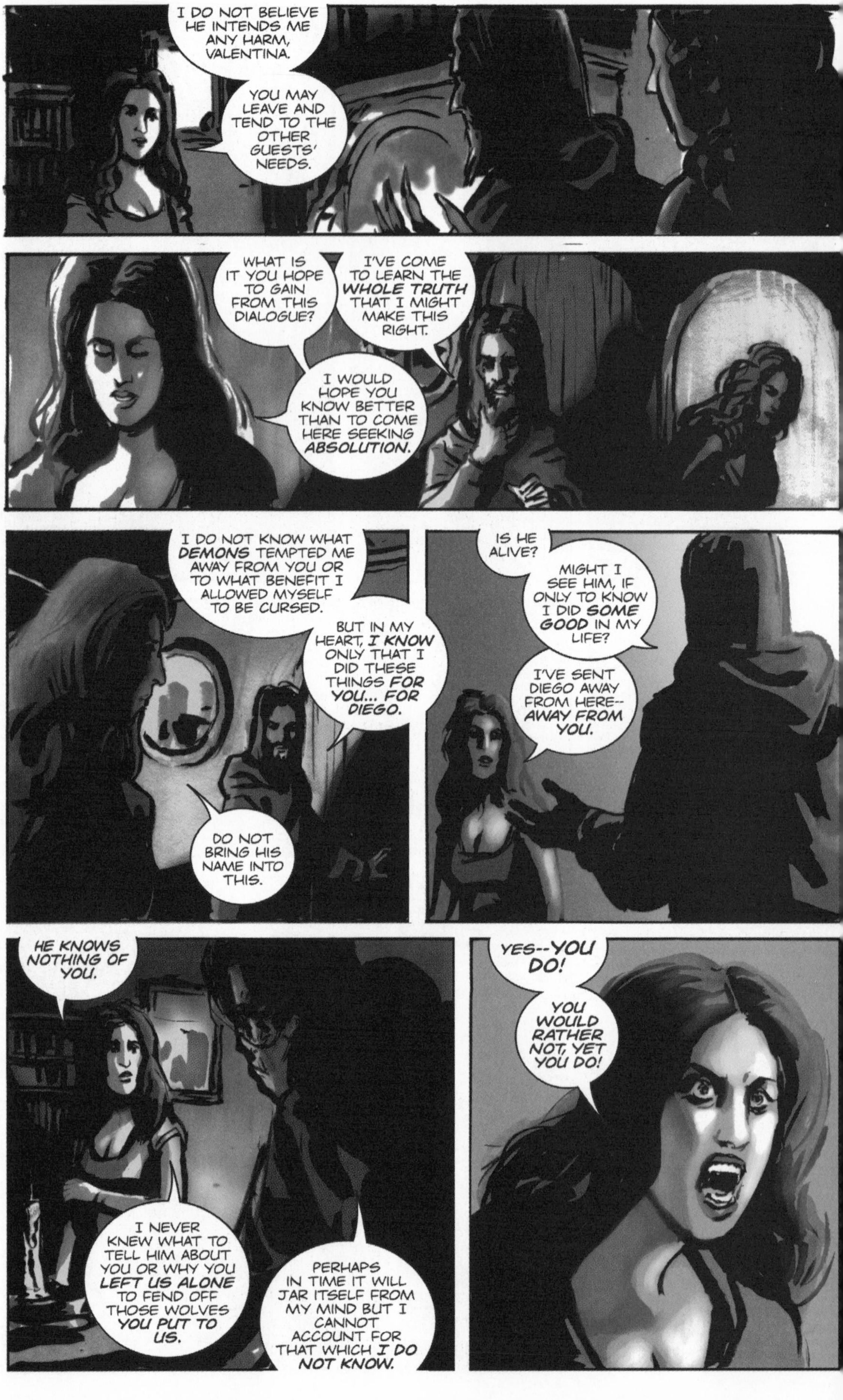
I DO NOT BELIEVE HE INTENDS ME ANY HARM, VALENTINA.
YOU MAY LEAVE AND TEND TO THE OTHER GUESTS' NEEDS.
WHAT IS IT YOU HOPE TO GAIN FROM THIS DIALOGUE?
I'VE COME TO LEARN THE WHOLE TRUTH THAT I MIGHT MAKE THIS RIGHT.
I WOULD HOPE YOU KNOW BETTER THAN TO COME HERE SEEKING ABSOLUTION.
I DO NOT KNOW WHAT DEMONS TEMPTED ME AWAY FROM YOU OR TO WHAT BENEFIT I ALLOWED MYSELF TO BE CURSED.
BUT IN MY HEART, I KNOW ONLY THAT I DID THESE THINGS FOR YOU... FOR DIEGO.
DO NOT BRING HIS NAME INTO THIS.
IS HE ALIVE?
MIGHT I SEE HIM, IF ONLY TO KNOW I DID SOME GOOD IN MY LIFE?
I'VE SENT DIEGO AWAY FROM HERE-- AWAY FROM YOU.
HE KNOWS NOTHING OF YOU.
I NEVER KNEW WHAT TO TELL HIM ABOUT YOU OR WHY YOU LEFT US ALONE TO FEND OFF THOSE WOLVES YOU PUT TO US.
PERHAPS IN TIME IT WILL JAR ITSELF FROM MY MIND BUT I CANNOT ACCOUNT FOR THAT WHICH I DO NOT KNOW.
YES--YOU DO!
YOU WOULD RATHER NOT, YET YOU DO!

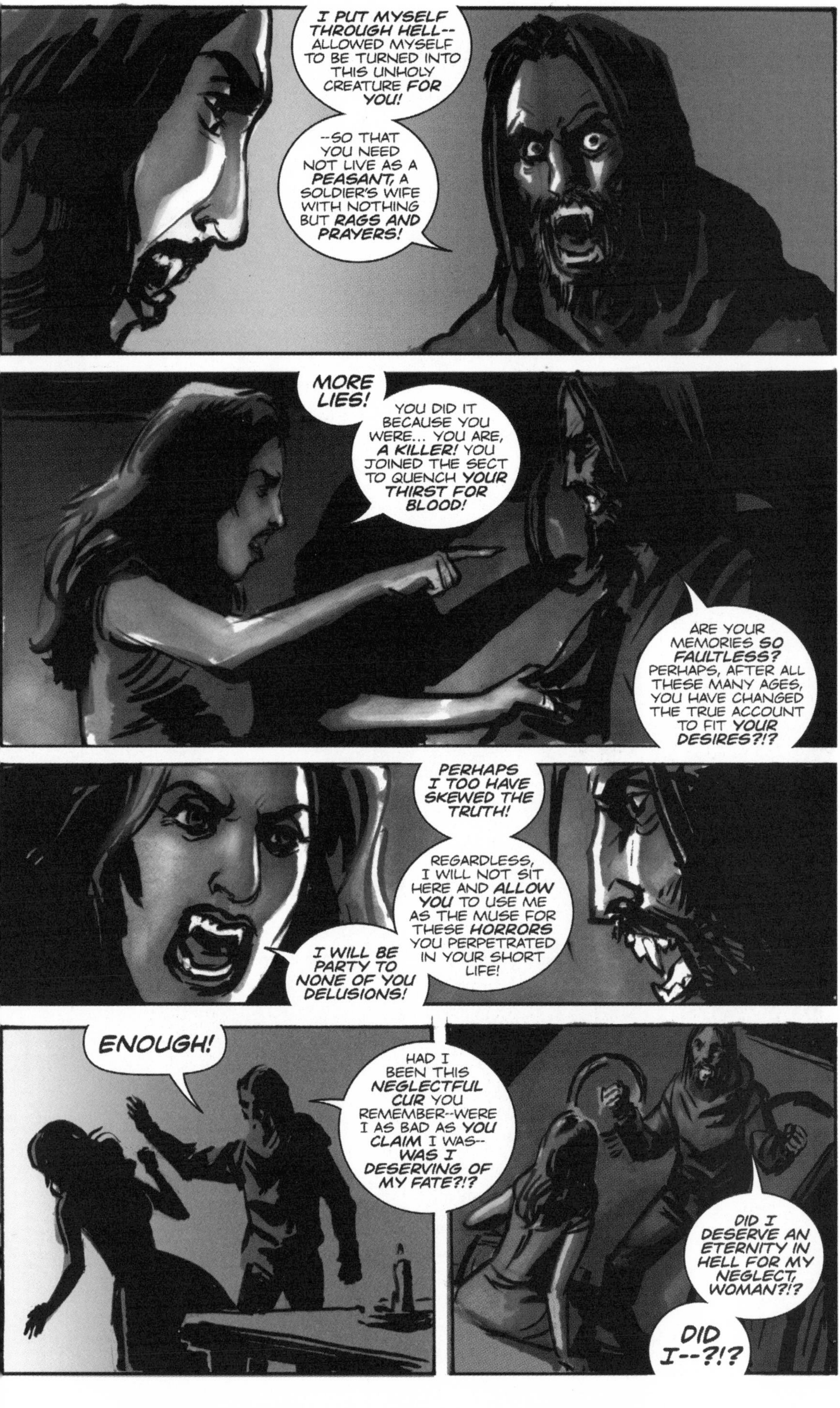
I PUT MYSELF THROUGH HELL-- ALLOWED MYSELF TO BE TURNED INTO THIS UNHOLY CREATURE FOR YOU!
--SO THAT YOU NEED NOT LIVE AS A PEASANT, A SOLDIER'S WIFE WITH NOTHING BUT RAGS AND PRAYERS!
MORE LIES!
YOU DID IT BECAUSE YOU WERE... YOU ARE, A KILLER! YOU JOINED THE SECT TO QUENCH YOUR THIRST FOR BLOOD!
ARE YOUR MEMORIES SO FAULTLESS? PERHAPS, AFTER ALL THESE MANY AGES, YOU HAVE CHANGED THE TRUE ACCOUNT TO FIT YOUR DESIRES?!?
PERHAPS I TOO HAVE SKEWED THE TRUTH!
REGARDLESS, I WILL NOT SIT HERE AND ALLOW YOU TO USE ME AS THE MUSE FOR THESE HORRORS YOU PERPETRATED IN YOUR SHORT LIFE!
I WILL BE PARTY TO NONE OF YOU DELUSIONS!
ENOUGH!
HAD I BEEN THIS NEGLECTFUL CUR YOU REMEMBER--WERE I AS BAD AS YOU CLAIM I WAS-- WAS I DESERVING OF MY FATE?!?
DID I DESERVE AN ETERNITY IN HELL FOR MY NEGLECT, WOMAN?!?
DID I--?!?

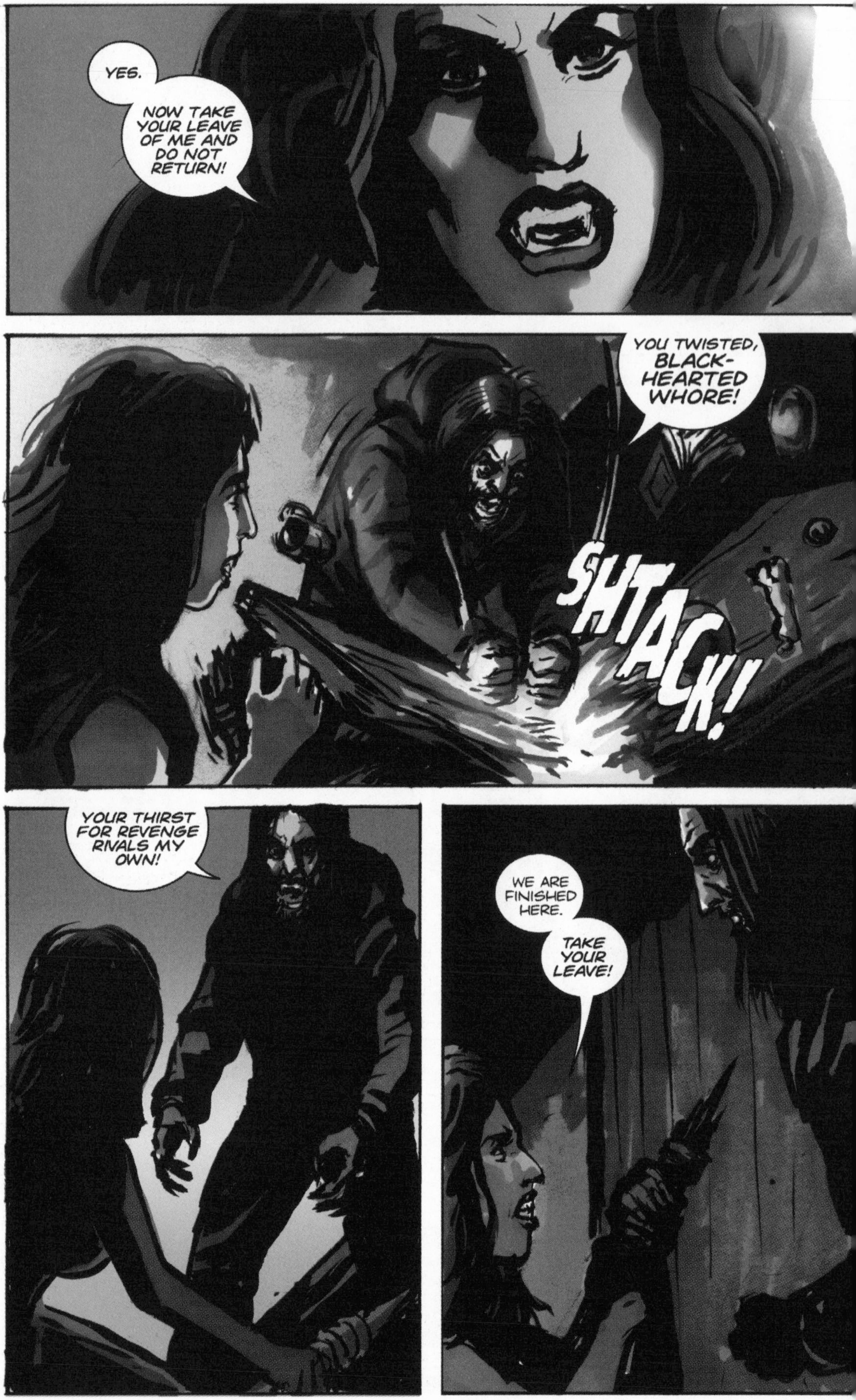
YES.
NOW TAKE YOUR LEAVE OF ME AND DO NOT RETURN!
YOU TWISTED, BLACK-HEARTED WHORE!
SHTACK!
YOUR THIRST FOR REVENGE RIVALS MY OWN!
WE ARE FINISHED HERE.
TAKE YOUR LEAVE!

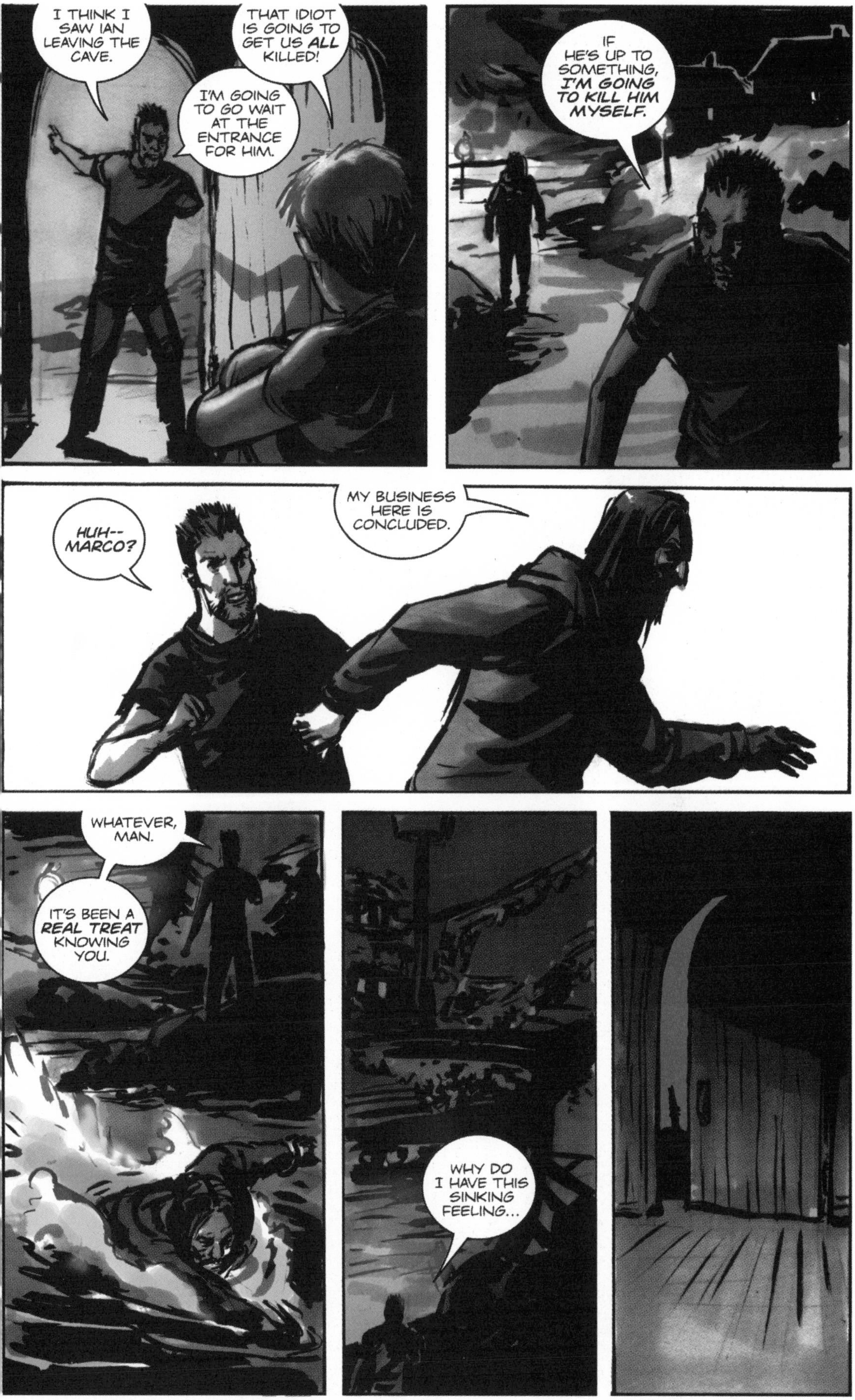
I THINK I SAW IAN LEAVING THE CAVE.
THAT IDIOT IS GOING TO GET US **ALL** KILLED!
I'M GOING TO GO WAIT AT THE ENTRANCE FOR HIM.
IF HE'S UP TO SOMETHING, ***I'M GOING TO KILL HIM MYSELF.***
HUH-- MARCO?
MY BUSINESS HERE IS CONCLUDED.
WHATEVER, MAN.
IT'S BEEN A ***REAL TREAT*** KNOWING YOU.
WHY DO I HAVE THIS SINKING FEELING...

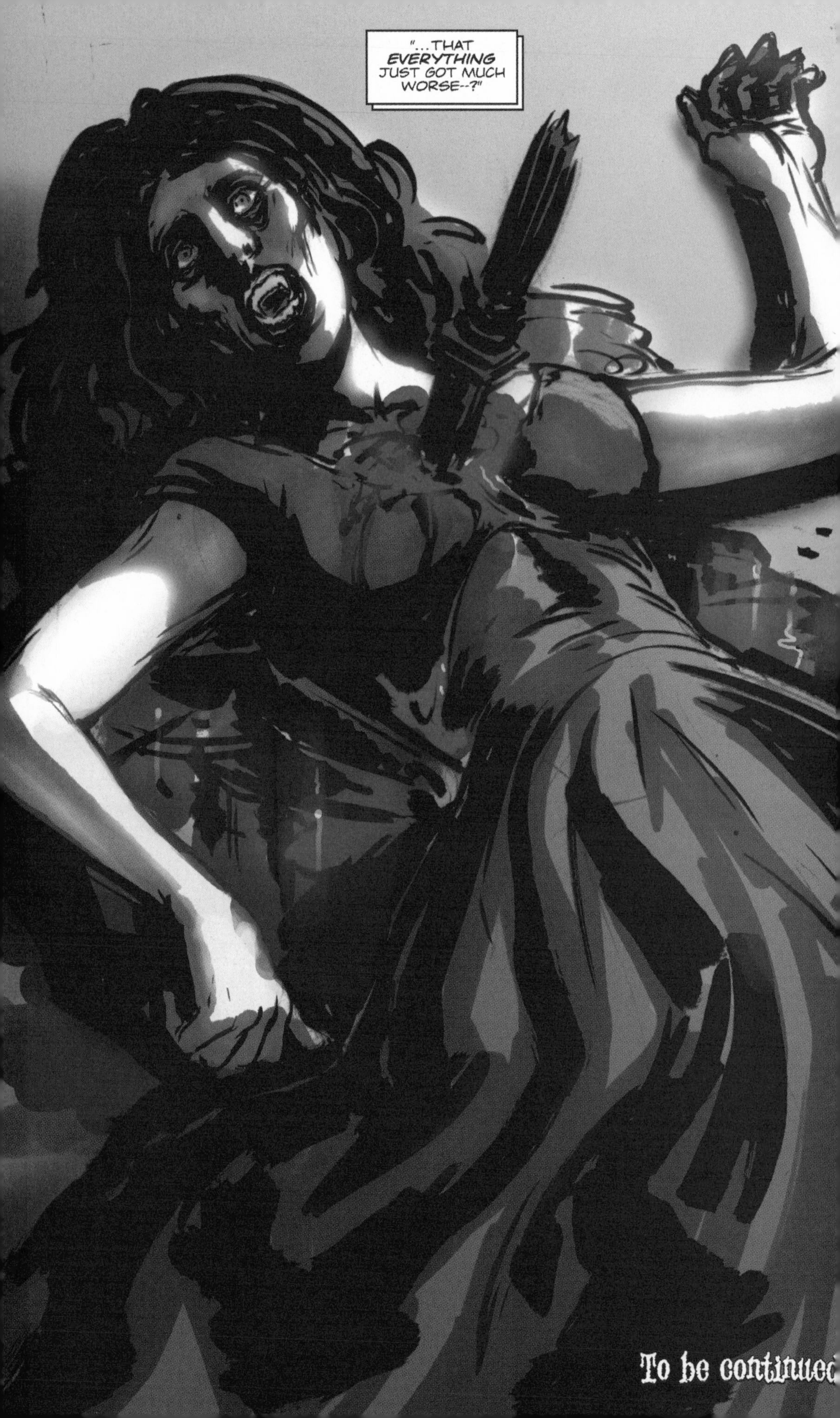
"...THAT *EVERYTHING* JUST GOT MUCH WORSE--?"
To be continued

Eight

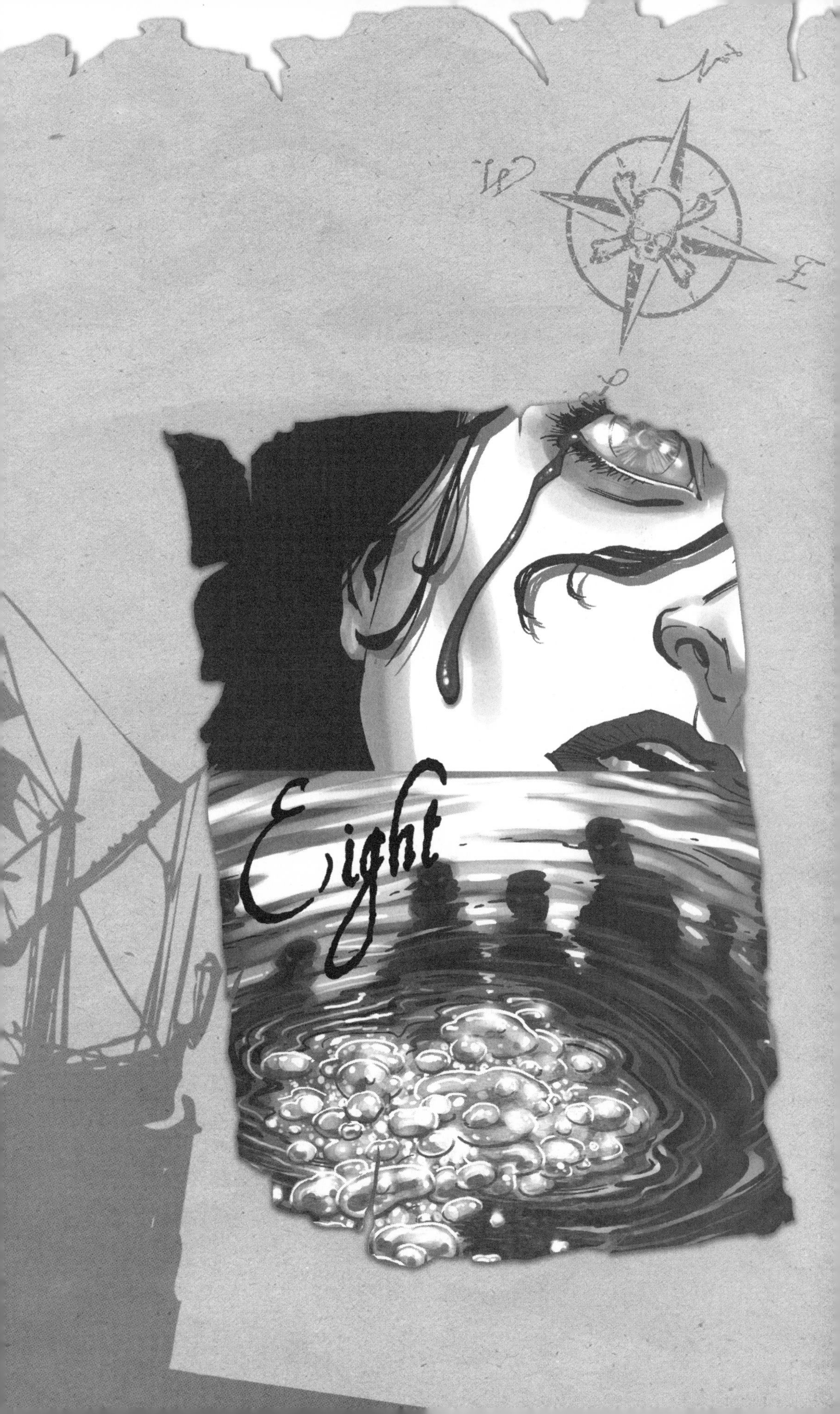

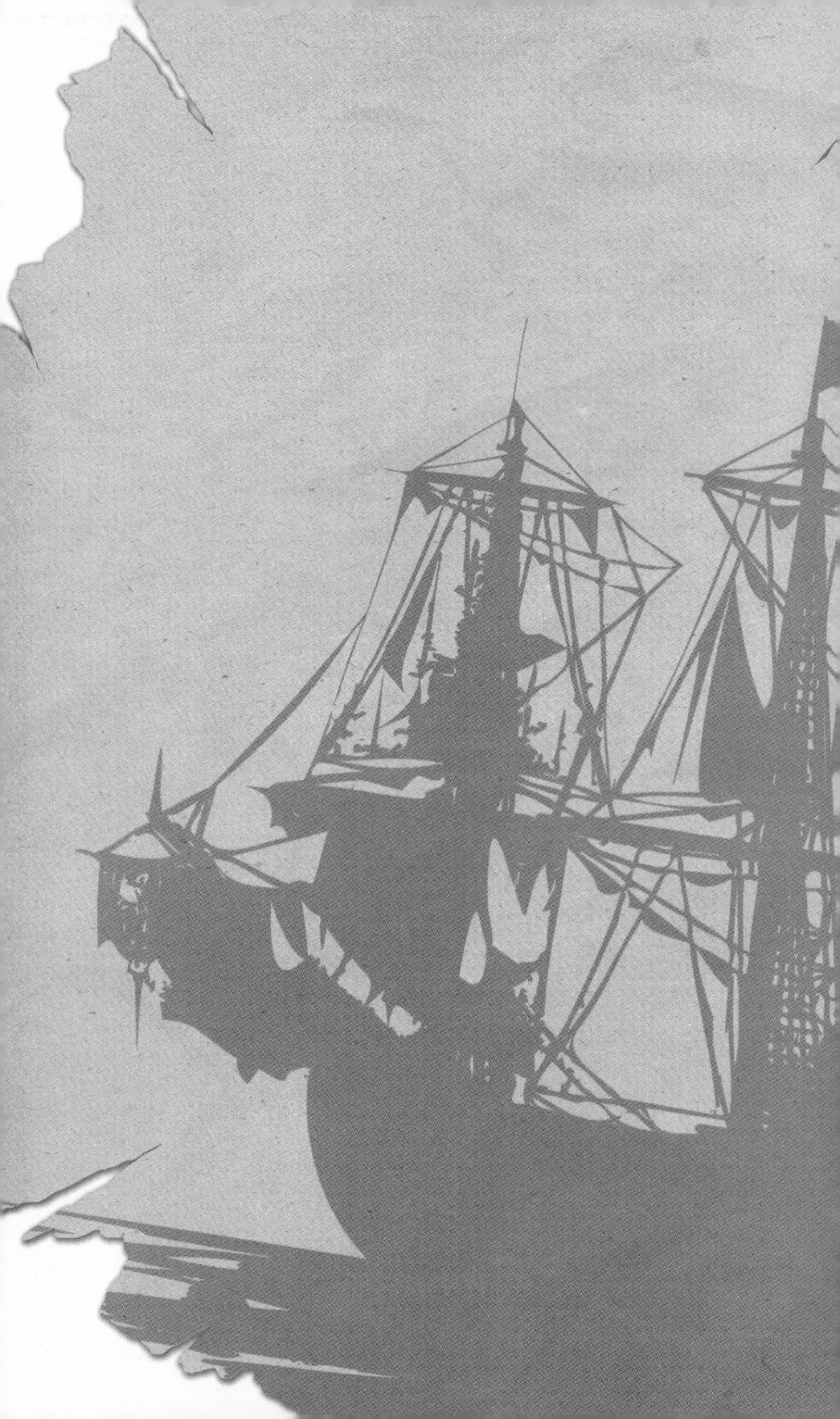

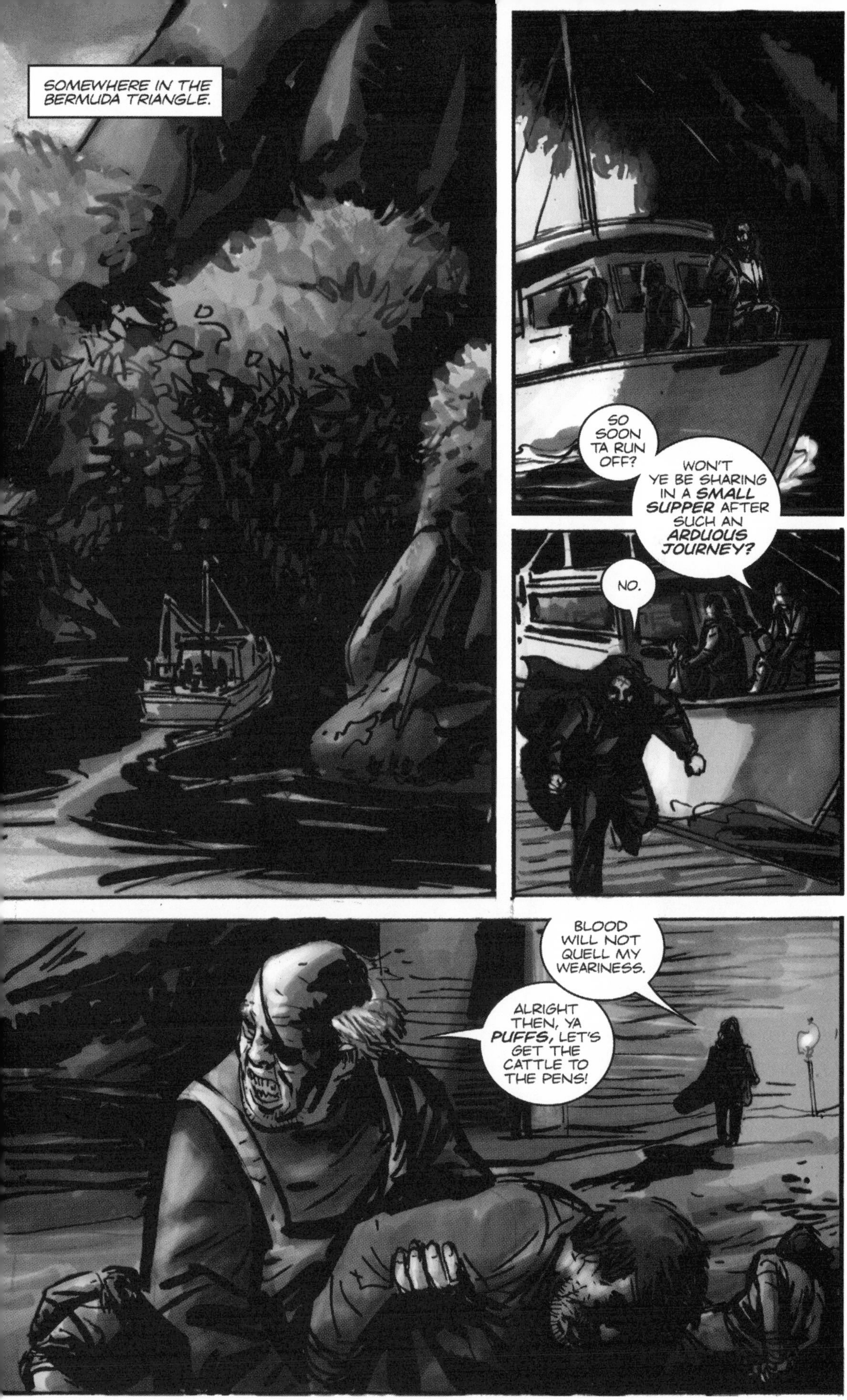
SOMEWHERE IN THE BERMUDA TRIANGLE.
SO SOON TA RUN OFF?
WON'T YE BE SHARING IN A SMALL SUPPER AFTER SUCH AN ARDUOUS JOURNEY?
NO.
BLOOD WILL NOT QUELL MY WEARINESS.
ALRIGHT THEN, YA PUFFS, LET'S GET THE CATTLE TO THE PENS!

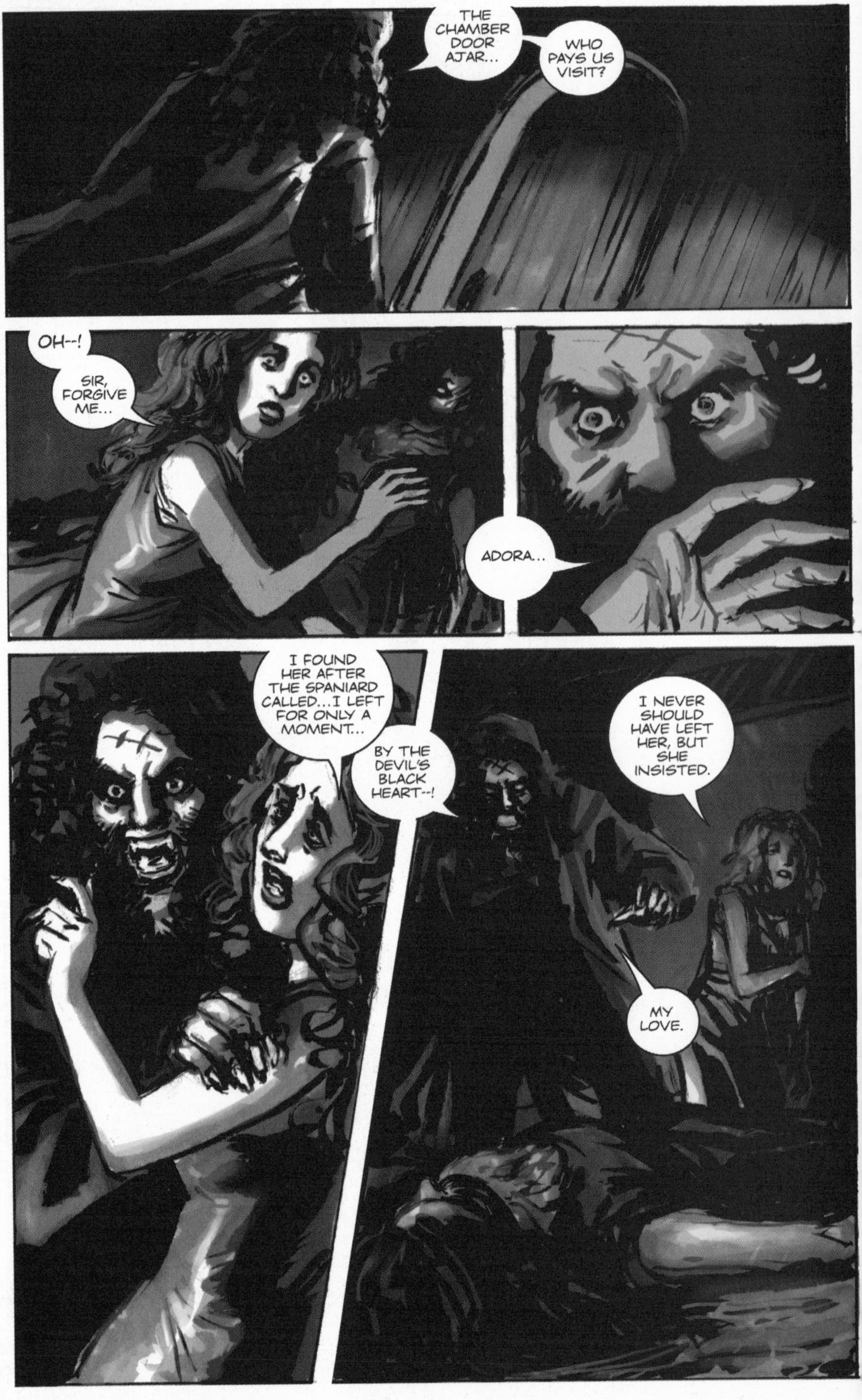
THE CHAMBER DOOR AJAR...
WHO PAYS US VISIT?
OH--!
SIR, FORGIVE ME...
ADORA...
I FOUND HER AFTER THE SPANIARD CALLED...I LEFT FOR ONLY A MOMENT...
BY THE DEVIL'S BLACK HEART--!
I NEVER SHOULD HAVE LEFT HER, BUT SHE INSISTED.
MY LOVE.

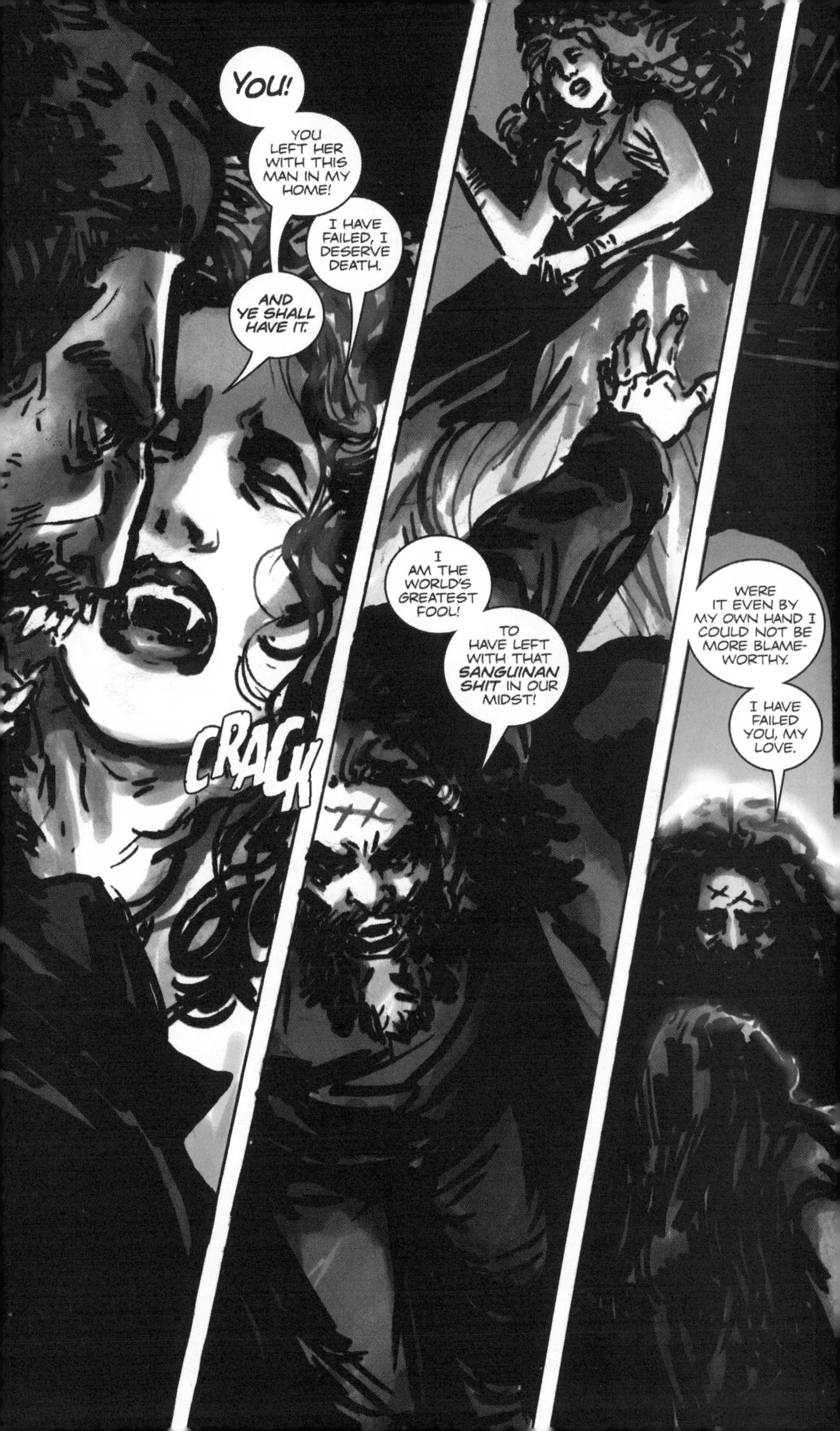
YOU!
YOU LEFT HER WITH THIS MAN IN MY HOME!
I HAVE FAILED, I DESERVE DEATH.
AND YE SHALL HAVE IT.
CRACK
I AM THE WORLD'S GREATEST FOOL!
TO HAVE LEFT WITH THAT SANGUINAN SHIT IN OUR MIDST!
WERE IT EVEN BY MY OWN HAND I COULD NOT BE MORE BLAME-WORTHY.
I HAVE FAILED YOU, MY LOVE.

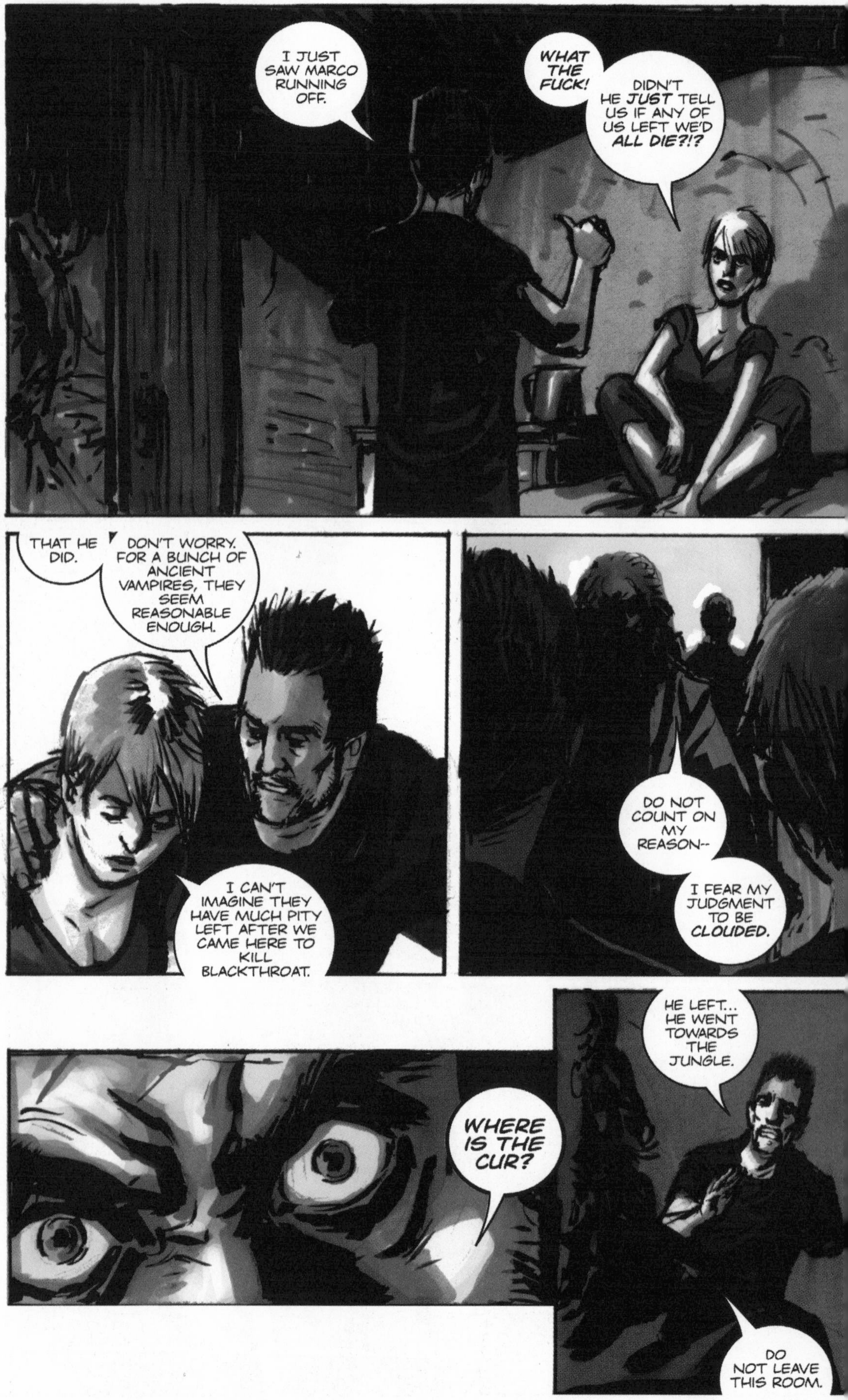
I JUST SAW MARCO RUNNING OFF.
WHAT THE FUCK!
DIDN'T HE JUST TELL US IF ANY OF US LEFT WE'D ALL DIE?!?
THAT HE DID.
DON'T WORRY. FOR A BUNCH OF ANCIENT VAMPIRES, THEY SEEM REASONABLE ENOUGH.
I CAN'T IMAGINE THEY HAVE MUCH PITY LEFT AFTER WE CAME HERE TO KILL BLACKTHROAT.
DO NOT COUNT ON MY REASON--
I FEAR MY JUDGMENT TO BE CLOUDED.
WHERE IS THE CUR?
HE LEFT... HE WENT TOWARDS THE JUNGLE.
DO NOT LEAVE THIS ROOM.

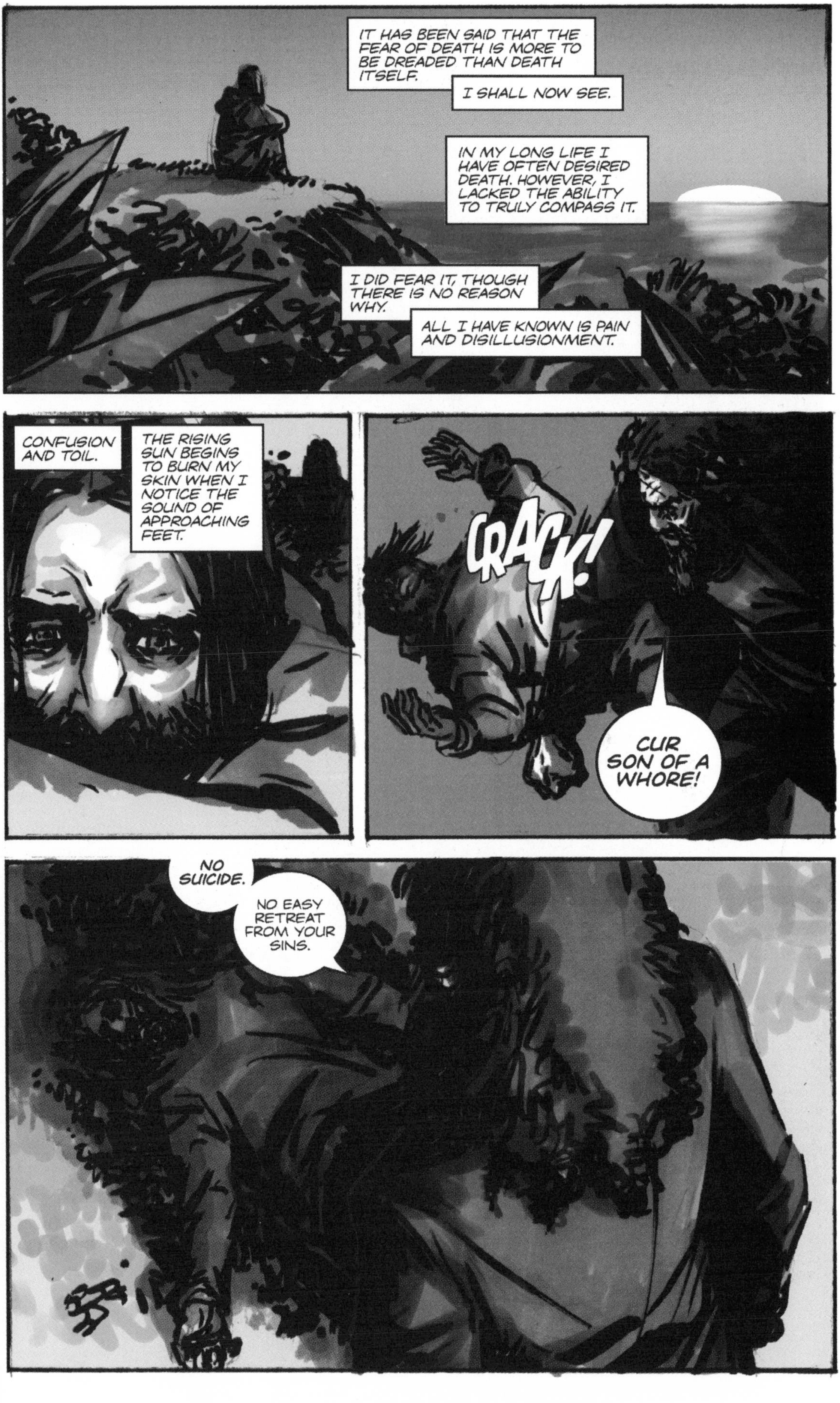
IT HAS BEEN SAID THAT THE FEAR OF DEATH IS MORE TO BE DREADED THAN DEATH ITSELF.
I SHALL NOW SEE.
IN MY LONG LIFE I HAVE OFTEN DESIRED DEATH. HOWEVER, I LACKED THE ABILITY TO TRULY COMPASS IT.
I DID FEAR IT, THOUGH THERE IS NO REASON WHY.
ALL I HAVE KNOWN IS PAIN AND DISILLUSIONMENT.
CONFUSION AND TOIL.
THE RISING SUN BEGINS TO BURN MY SKIN WHEN I NOTICE THE SOUND OF APPROACHING FEET.
CRACK!
CUR SON OF A WHORE!
NO SUICIDE.
NO EASY RETREAT FROM YOUR SINS.

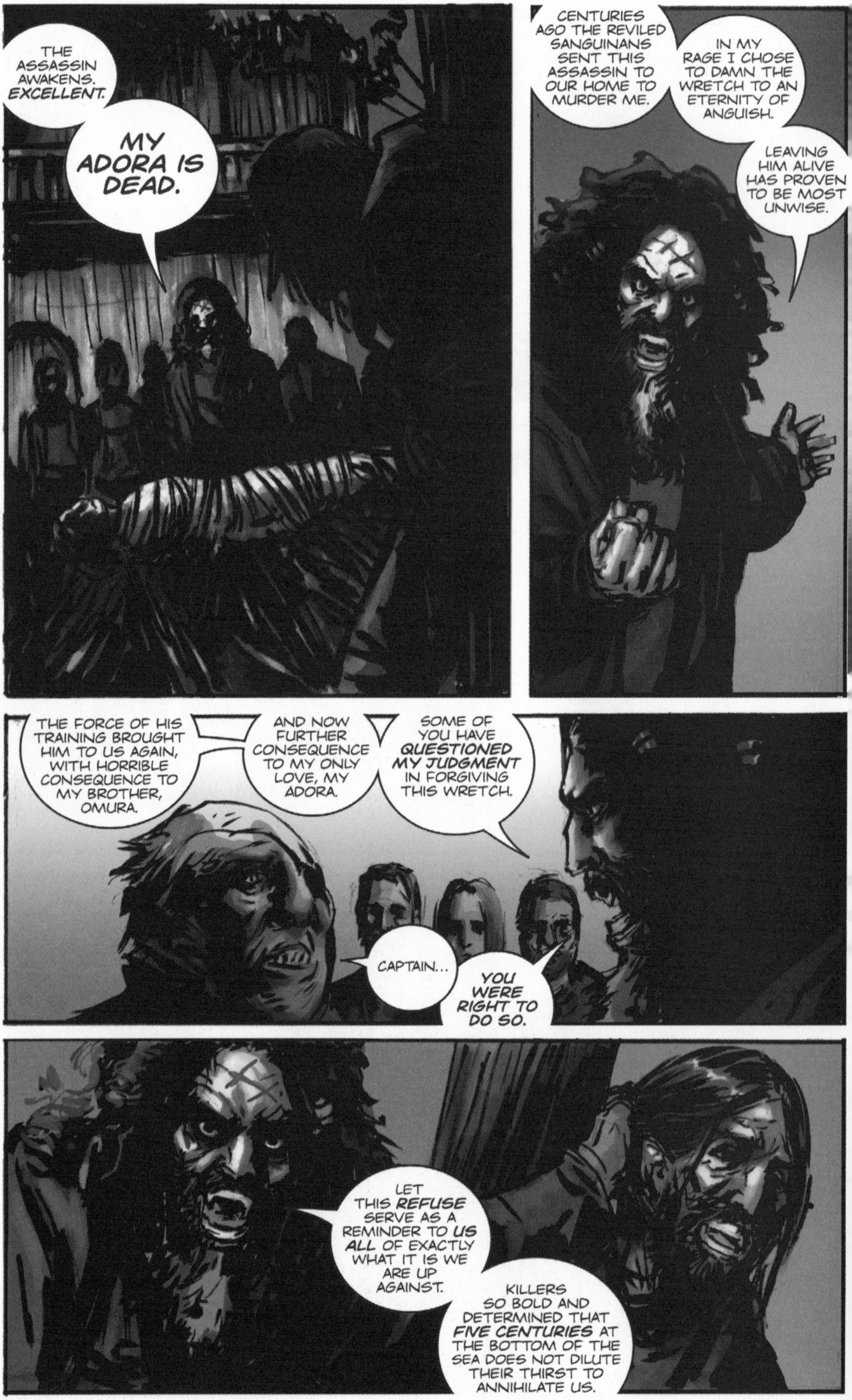
THE ASSASSIN AWAKENS. EXCELLENT.
MY ADORA IS DEAD.
CENTURIES AGO THE REVILED SANGUINANS SENT THIS ASSASSIN TO OUR HOME TO MURDER ME.
IN MY RAGE I CHOSE TO DAMN THE WRETCH TO AN ETERNITY OF ANGUISH.
LEAVING HIM ALIVE HAS PROVEN TO BE MOST UNWISE.
THE FORCE OF HIS TRAINING BROUGHT HIM TO US AGAIN, WITH HORRIBLE CONSEQUENCE TO MY BROTHER, OMURA.
AND NOW FURTHER CONSEQUENCE TO MY ONLY LOVE, MY ADORA.
SOME OF YOU HAVE QUESTIONED MY JUDGMENT IN FORGIVING THIS WRETCH.
CAPTAIN...
YOU WERE RIGHT TO DO SO.
LET THIS REFUSE SERVE AS A REMINDER TO US ALL OF EXACTLY WHAT IT IS WE ARE UP AGAINST.
KILLERS SO BOLD AND DETERMINED THAT FIVE CENTURIES AT THE BOTTOM OF THE SEA DOES NOT DILUTE THEIR THIRST TO ANNIHILATE US.

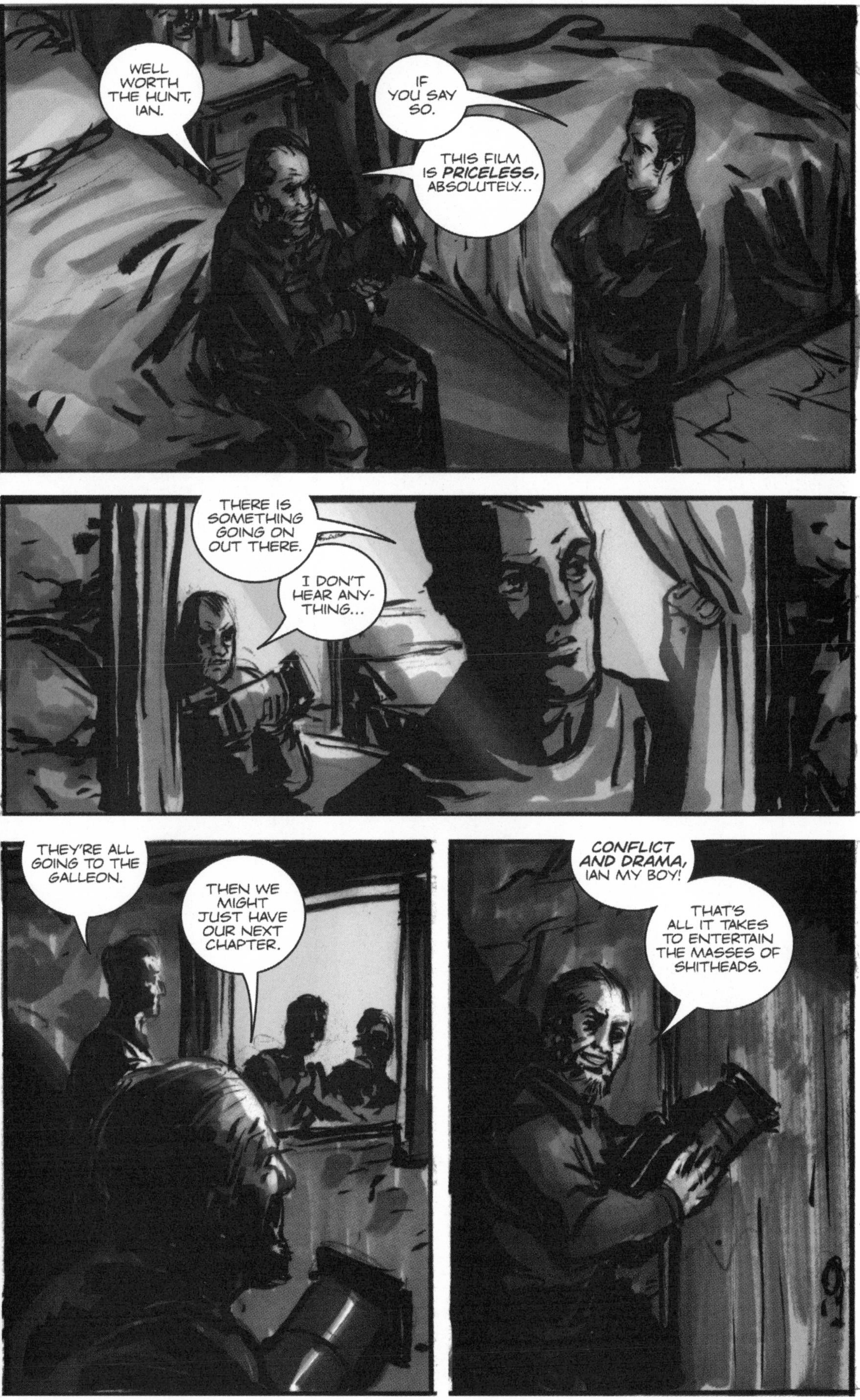
WELL WORTH THE HUNT, IAN.
IF YOU SAY SO.
THIS FILM IS **PRICELESS,** ABSOLUTELY...
THERE IS SOMETHING GOING ON OUT THERE.
I DON'T HEAR ANY-THING...
THEY'RE ALL GOING TO THE GALLEON.
THEN WE MIGHT JUST HAVE OUR NEXT CHAPTER.
CONFLICT AND DRAMA, IAN MY BOY!
THAT'S ALL IT TAKES TO ENTERTAIN THE MASSES OF SHITHEADS.

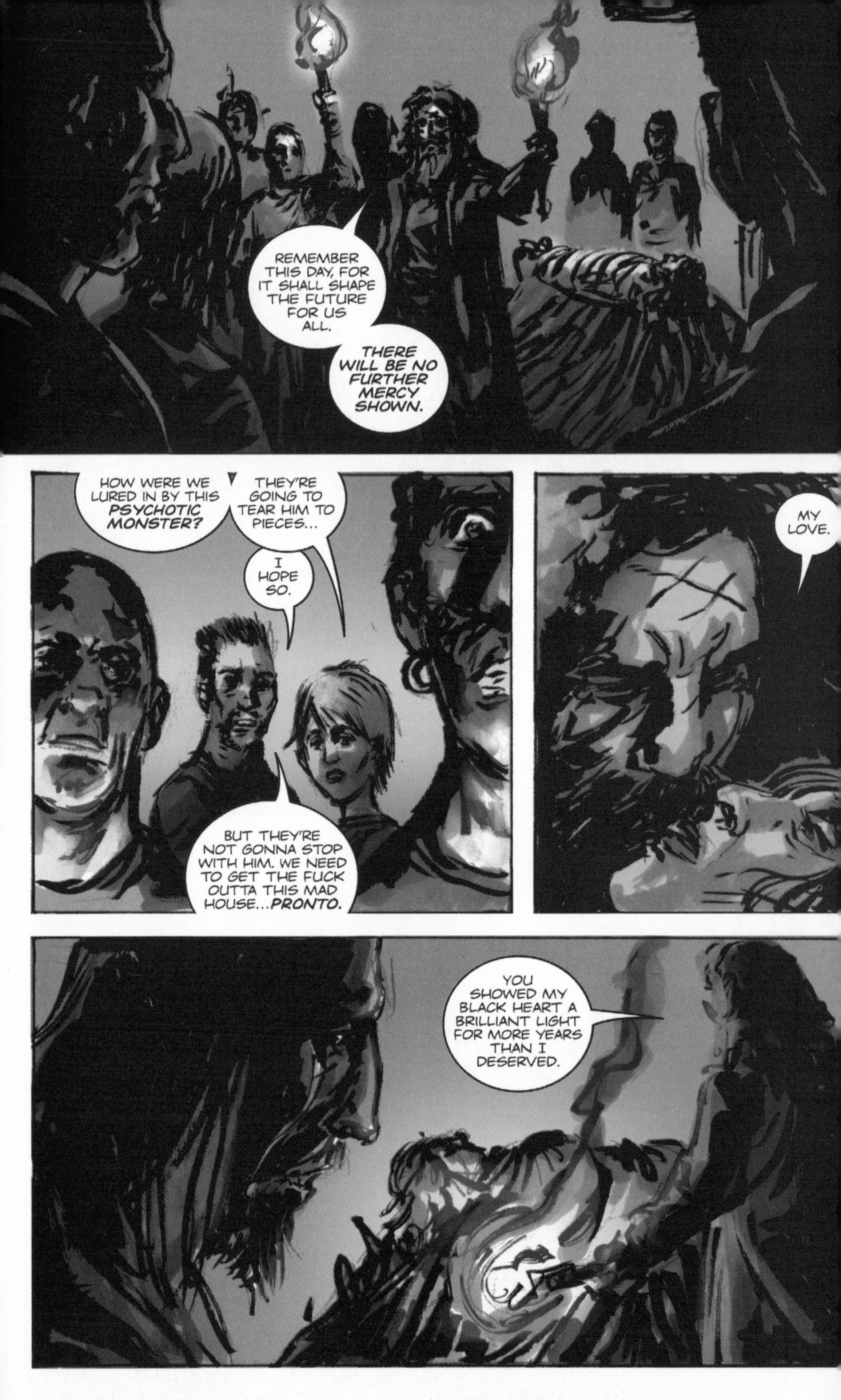
REMEMBER THIS DAY, FOR IT SHALL SHAPE THE FUTURE FOR US ALL.
THERE WILL BE NO FURTHER MERCY SHOWN.
HOW WERE WE LURED IN BY THIS PSYCHOTIC MONSTER?
THEY'RE GOING TO TEAR HIM TO PIECES...
I HOPE SO.
BUT THEY'RE NOT GONNA STOP WITH HIM. WE NEED TO GET THE FUCK OUTTA THIS MAD HOUSE...PRONTO.
MY LOVE.
YOU SHOWED MY BLACK HEART A BRILLIANT LIGHT FOR MORE YEARS THAN I DESERVED.

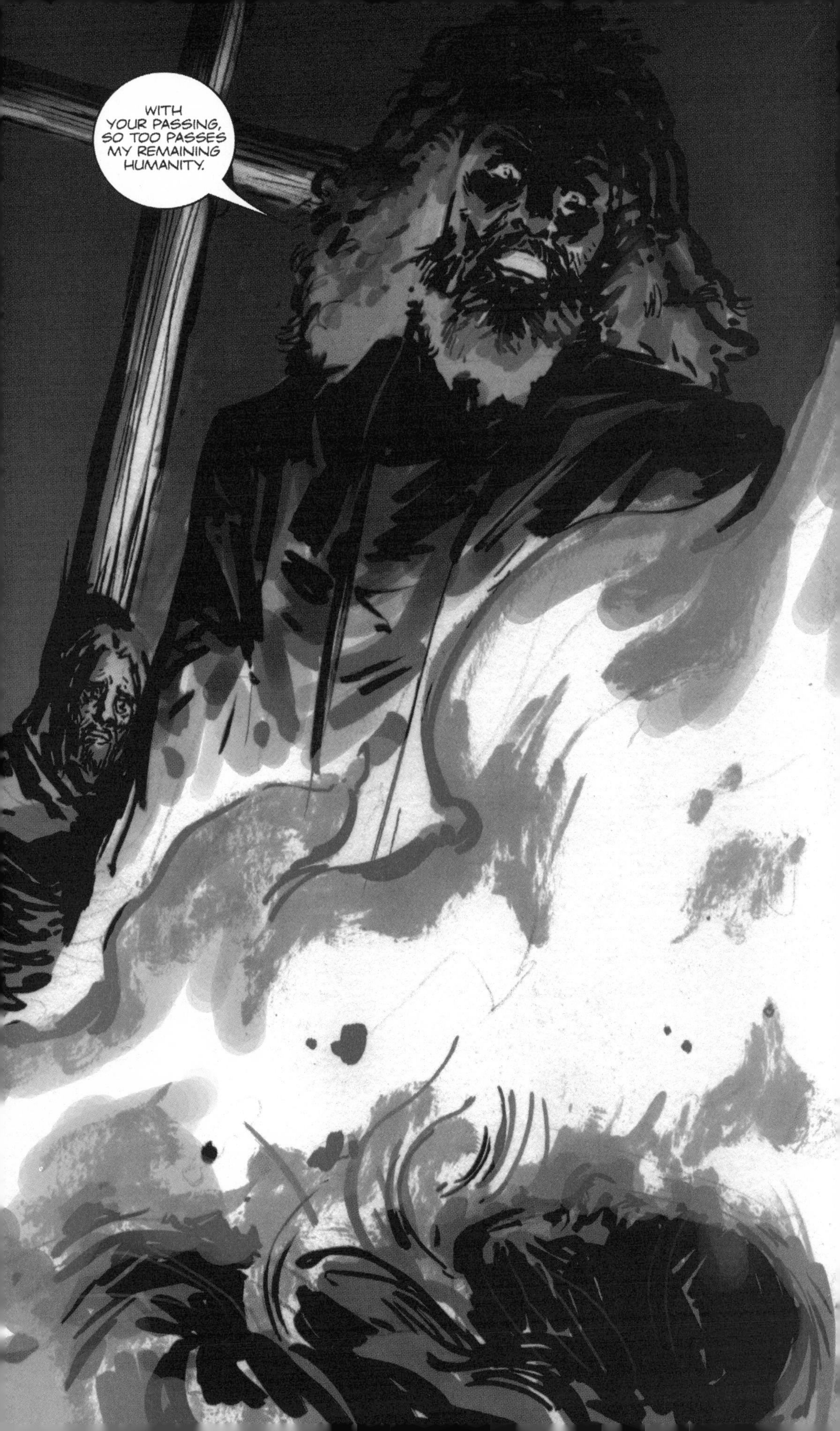
WITH YOUR PASSING, SO TOO PASSES MY REMAINING HUMANITY.

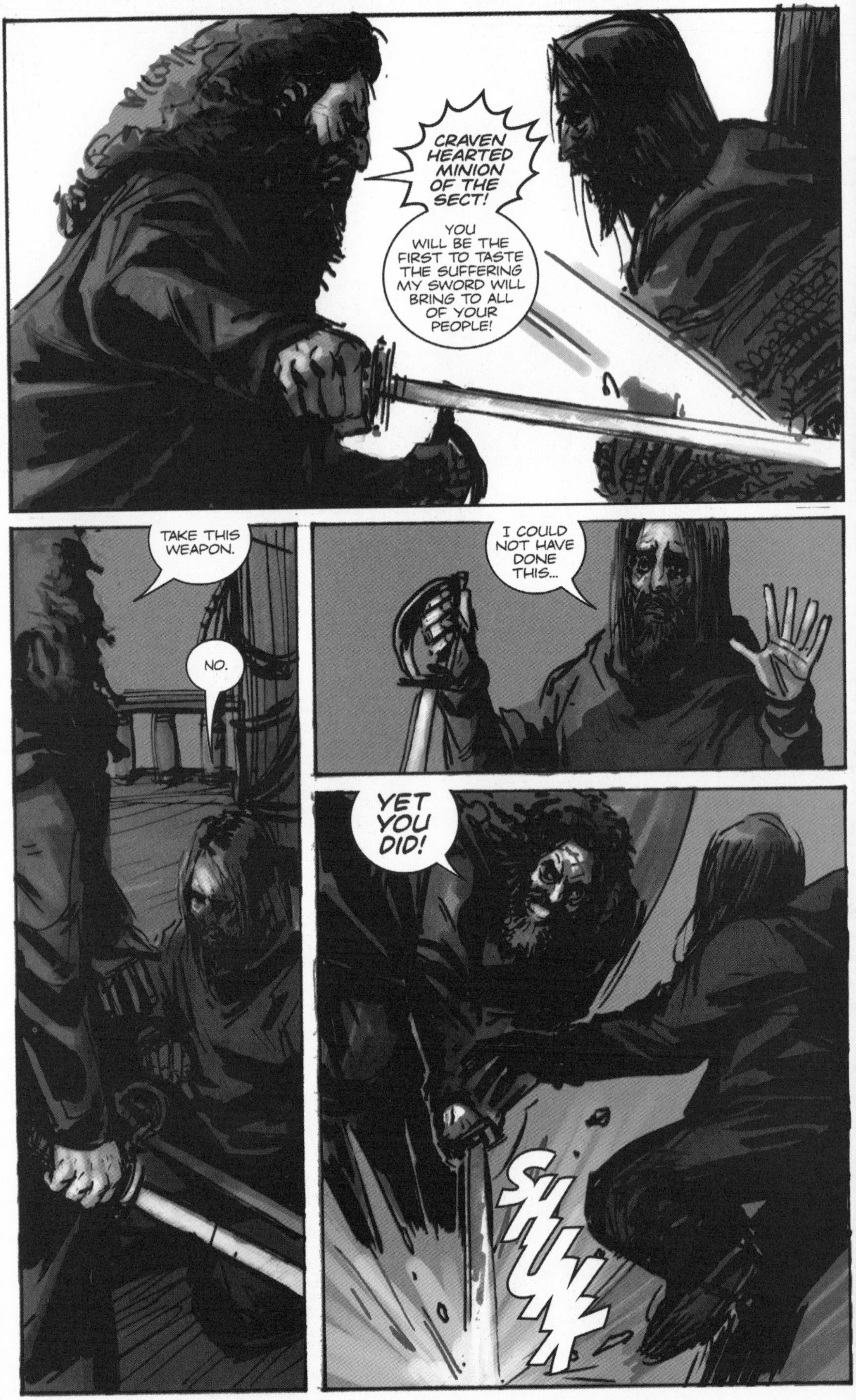
CRAVEN HEARTED MINION OF THE SECT!
YOU WILL BE THE FIRST TO TASTE THE SUFFERING MY SWORD WILL BRING TO ALL OF YOUR PEOPLE!
TAKE THIS WEAPON.
NO.
I COULD NOT HAVE DONE THIS...
YET YOU DID!
SHUNK

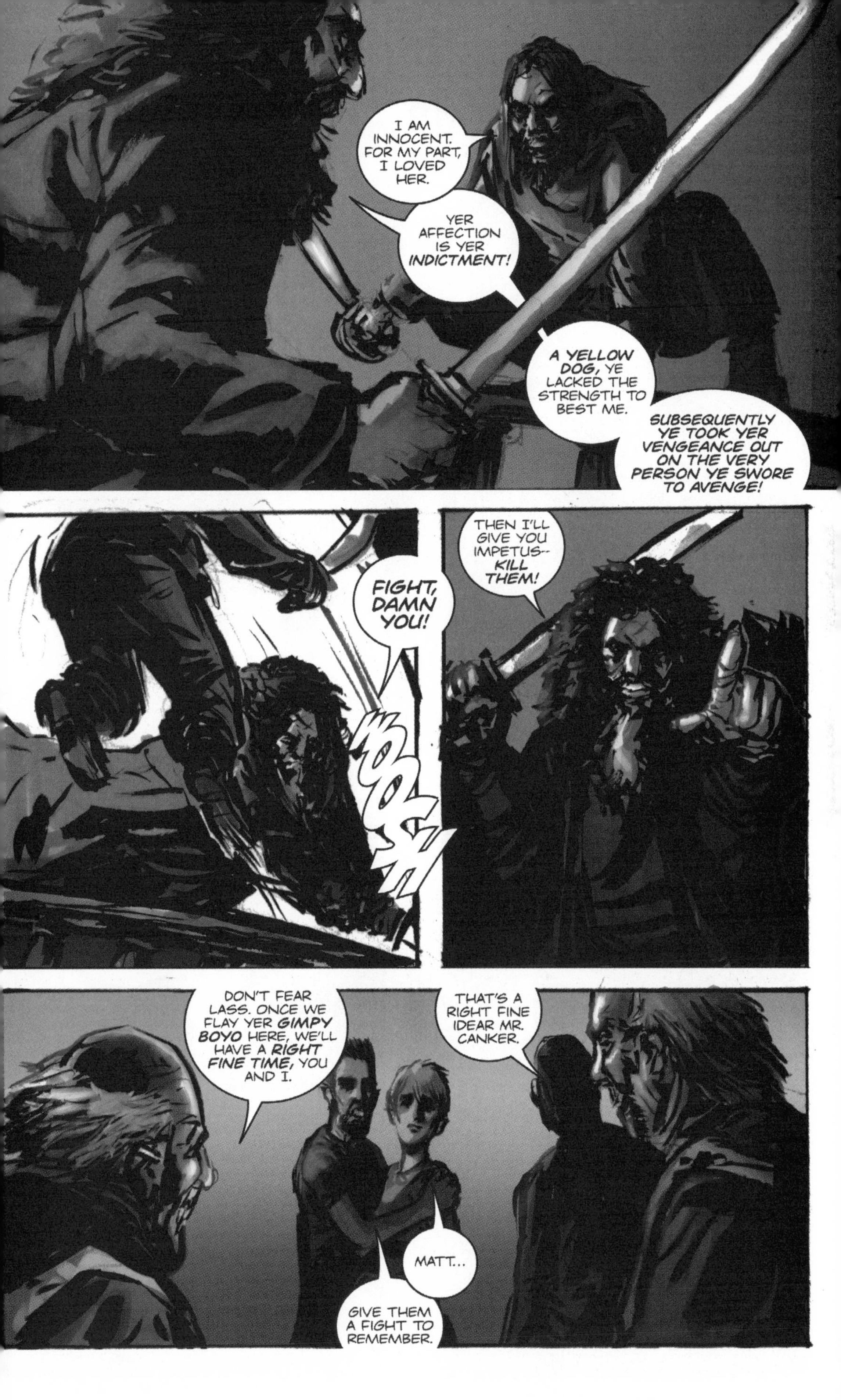
I AM INNOCENT. FOR MY PART, I LOVED HER.
YER AFFECTION IS YER INDICTMENT!
A YELLOW DOG, YE LACKED THE STRENGTH TO BEST ME.
SUBSEQUENTLY YE TOOK YER VENGEANCE OUT ON THE VERY PERSON YE SWORE TO AVENGE!
FIGHT, DAMN YOU!
WOOSH
THEN I'LL GIVE YOU IMPETUS-- KILL THEM!
DON'T FEAR LASS. ONCE WE FLAY YER GIMPY BOYO HERE, WE'LL HAVE A RIGHT FINE TIME, YOU AND I.
THAT'S A RIGHT FINE IDEAR MR. CANKER.
MATT...
GIVE THEM A FIGHT TO REMEMBER.

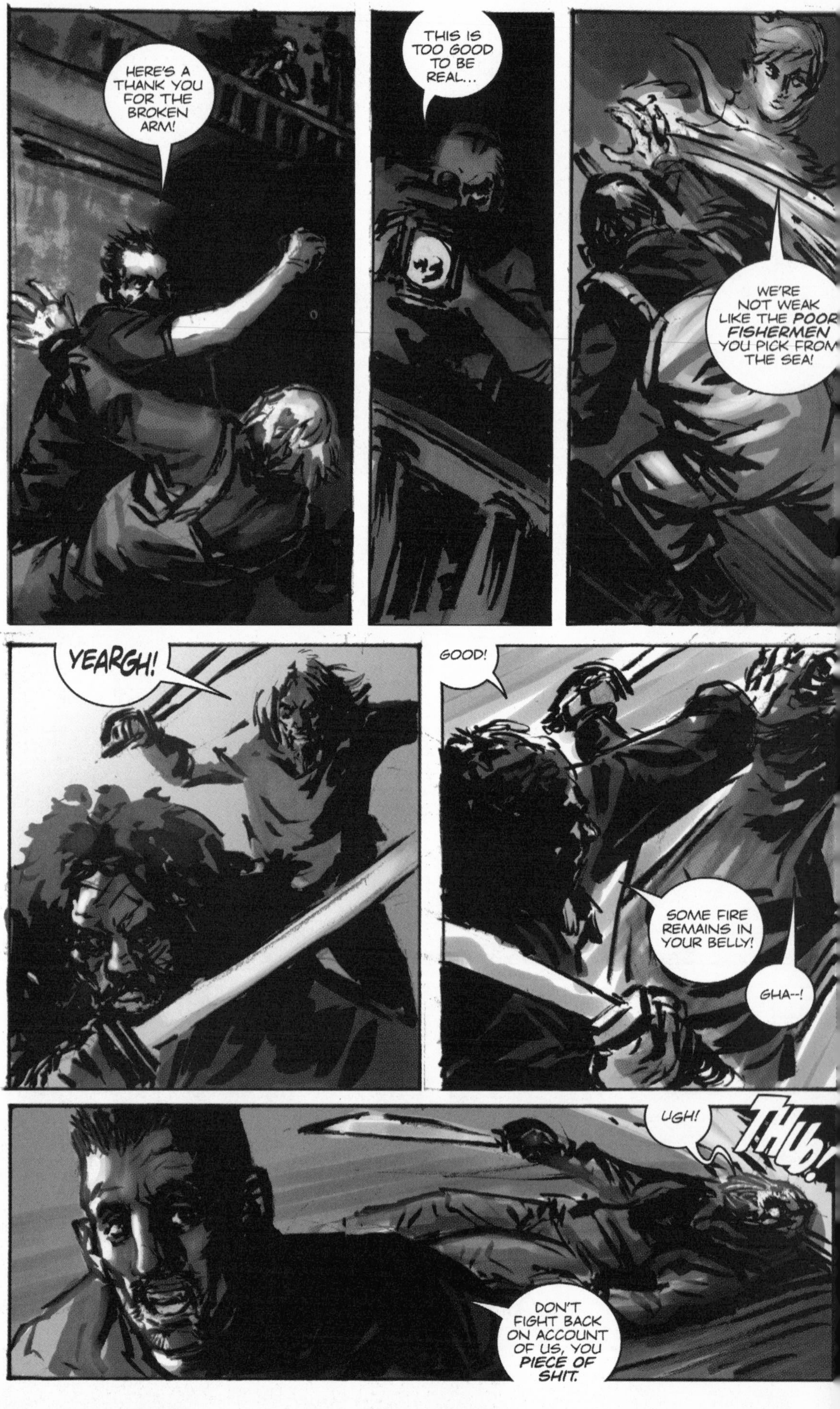
HERE'S A THANK YOU FOR THE BROKEN ARM!
THIS IS TOO GOOD TO BE REAL...
WE'RE NOT WEAK LIKE THE POOR FISHERMEN YOU PICK FROM THE SEA!
YEARGH!
GOOD!
SOME FIRE REMAINS IN YOUR BELLY!
GHA--!
UGH!
THUD!
DON'T FIGHT BACK ON ACCOUNT OF US, YOU PIECE OF SHIT.

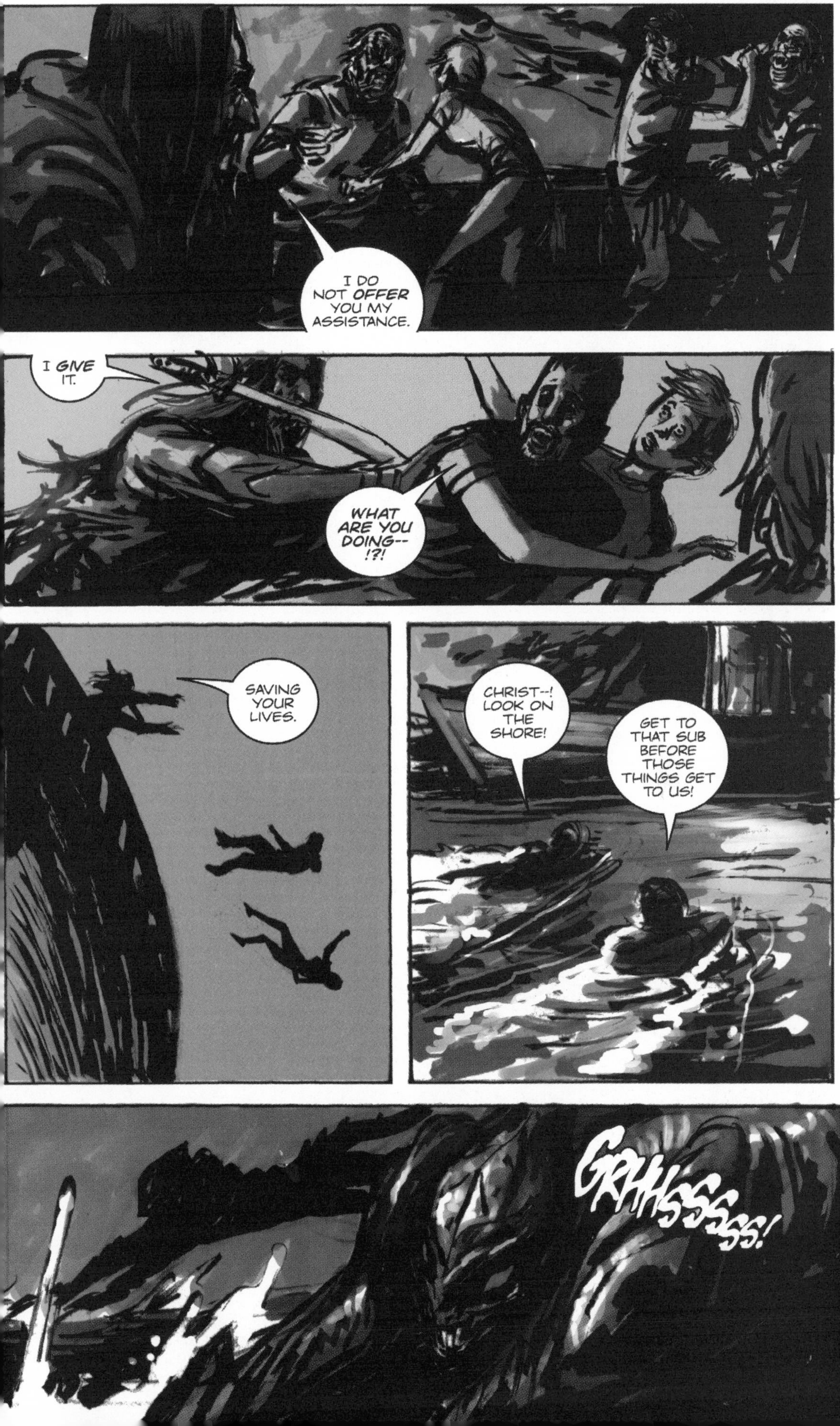
I DO NOT OFFER YOU MY ASSISTANCE.
I GIVE IT.
WHAT ARE YOU DOING--!?!
SAVING YOUR LIVES.
CHRIST--! LOOK ON THE SHORE!
GET TO THAT SUB BEFORE THOSE THINGS GET TO US!
GRHHSSSSSS!

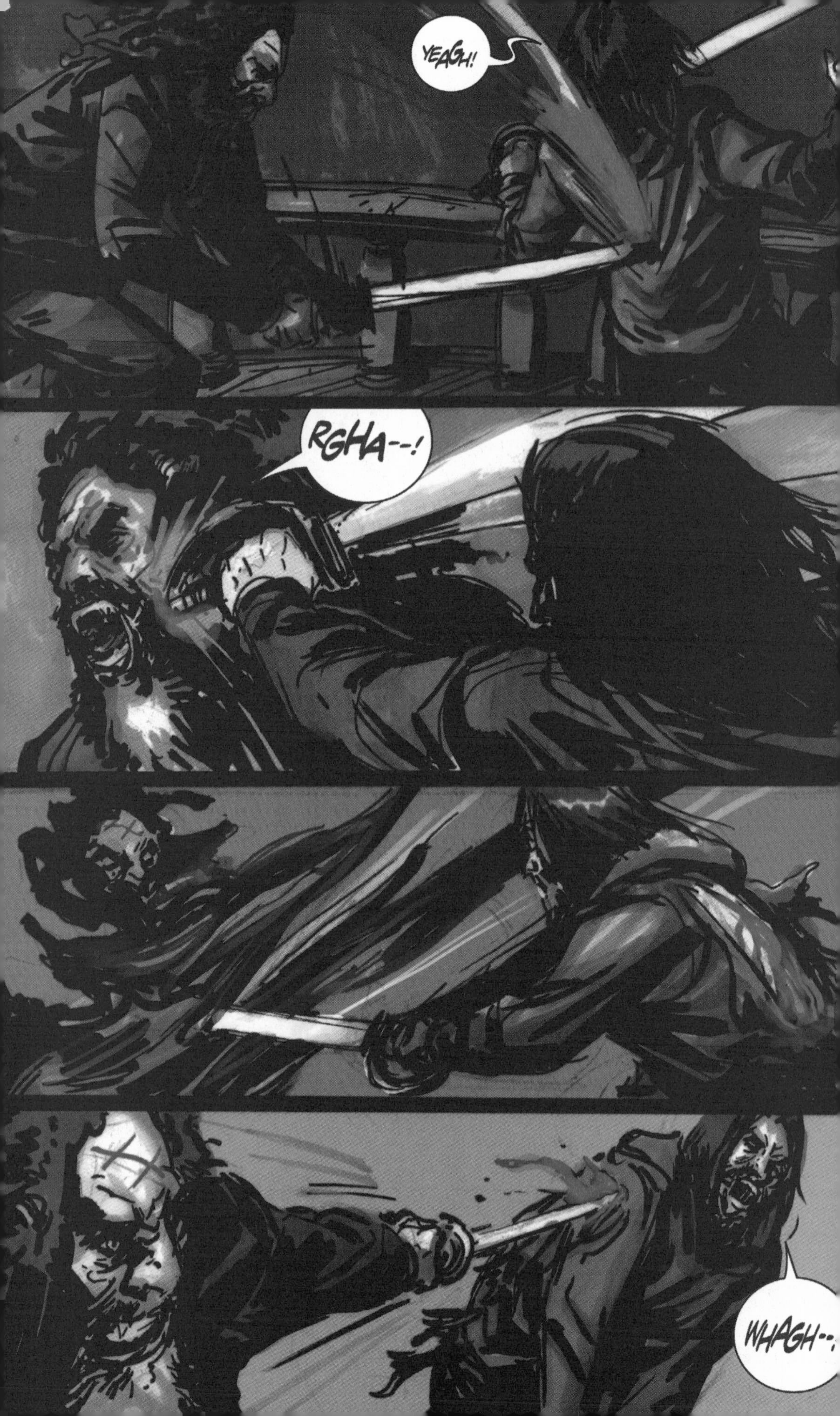
YEAGH!
RGHA--!
WHAGH--

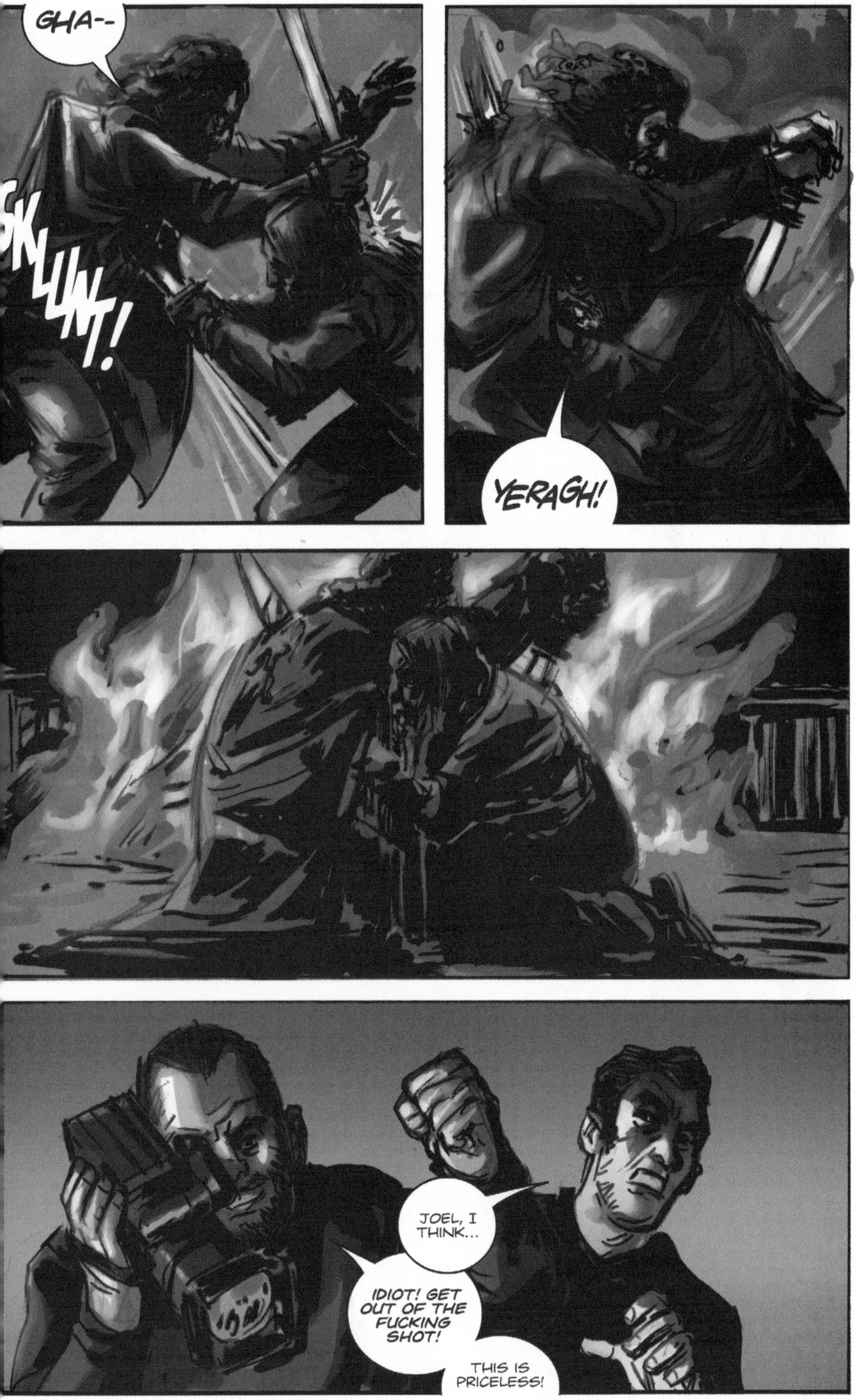
GHA--
SKLUNT!
YERAGH!
JOEL, I THINK...
IDIOT! GET OUT OF THE FUCKING SHOT!
THIS IS PRICELESS!

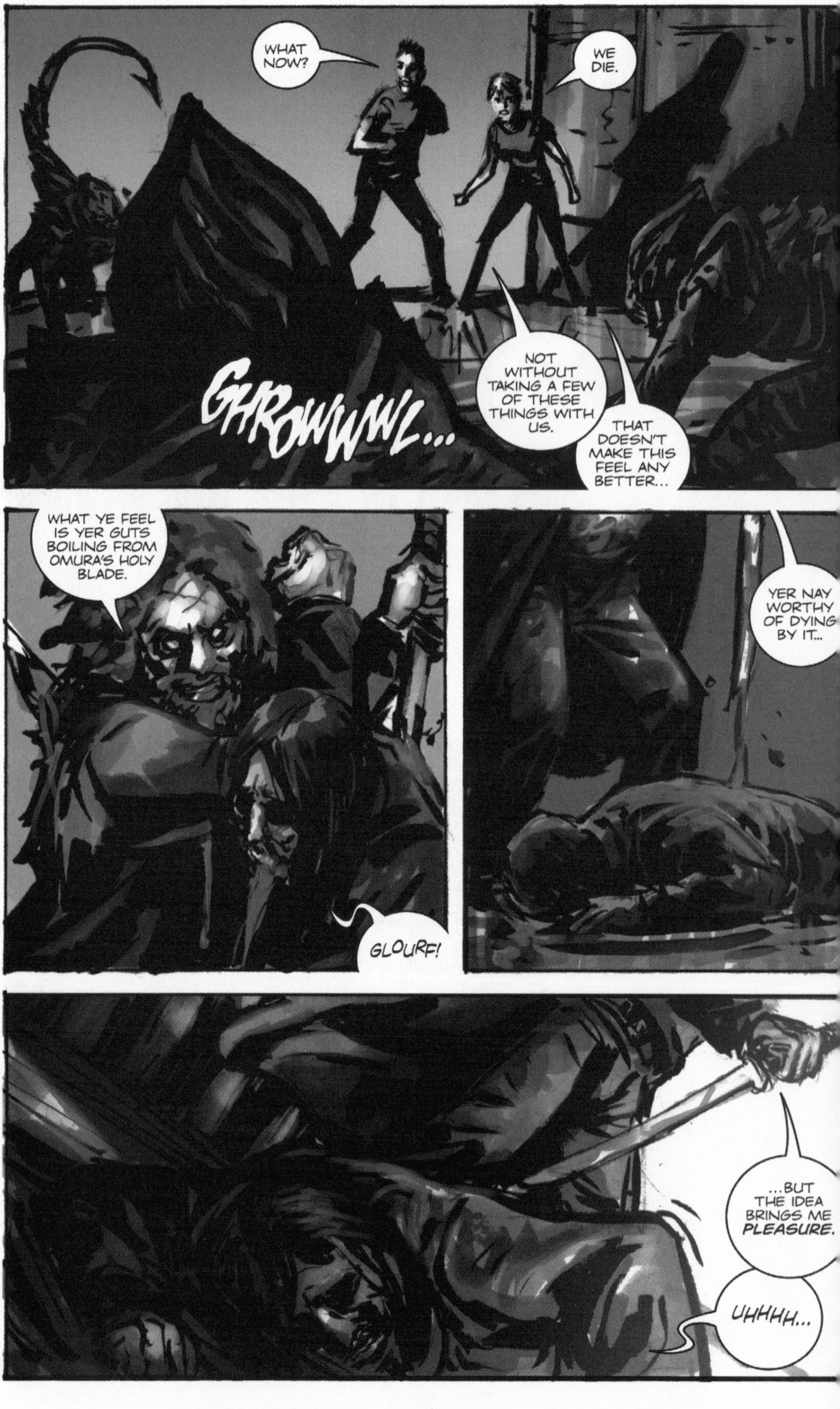

WHAT NOW?
WE DIE.
GHROWWWL...
NOT WITHOUT TAKING A FEW OF THESE THINGS WITH US.
THAT DOESN'T MAKE THIS FEEL ANY BETTER...
WHAT YE FEEL IS YER GUTS BOILING FROM OMURA'S HOLY BLADE.
GLOURF!
YER NAY WORTHY OF DYING BY IT...
...BUT THE IDEA BRINGS ME *PLEASURE.*
UHHHH...

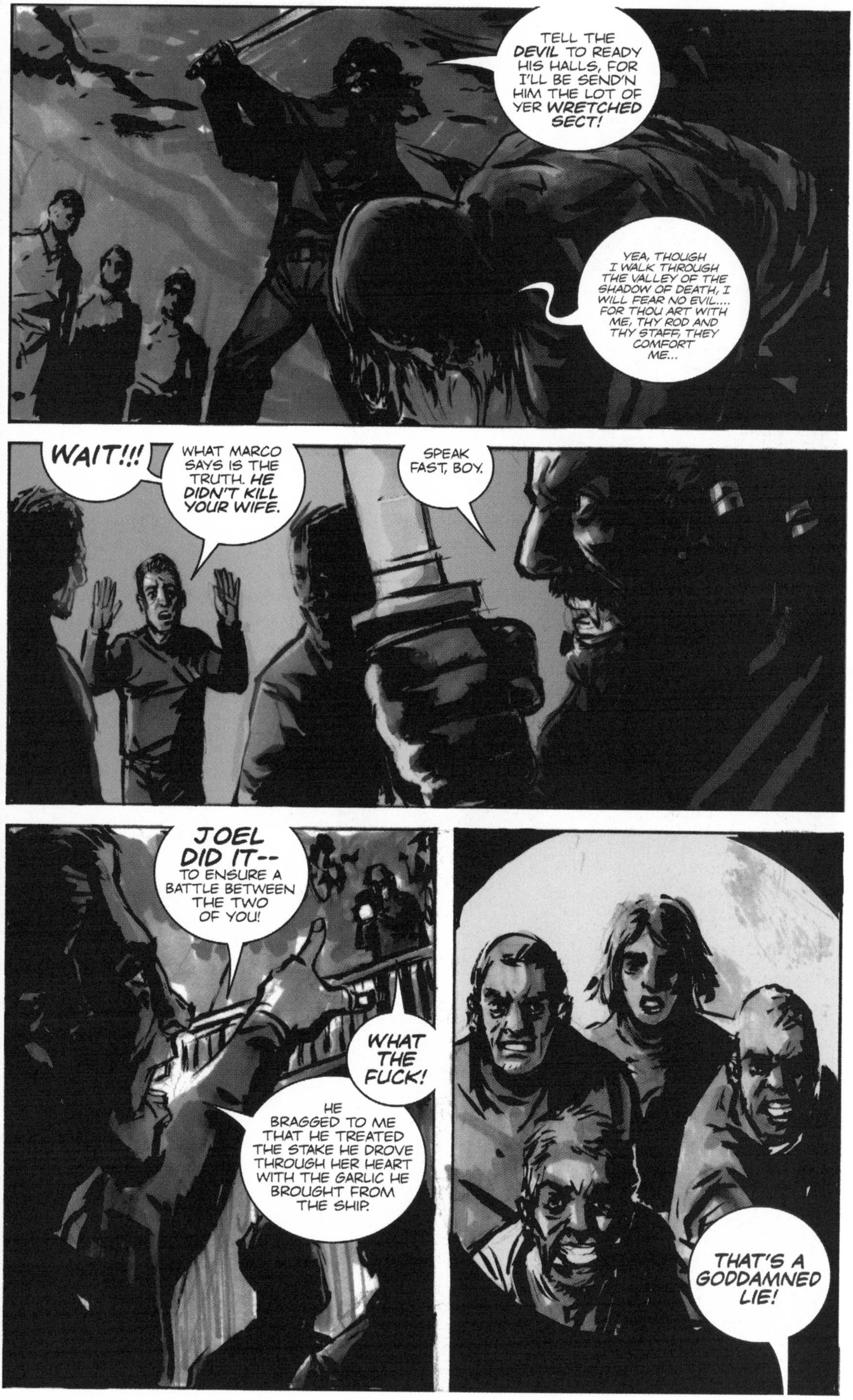
TELL THE DEVIL TO READY HIS HALLS, FOR I'LL BE SEND'N HIM THE LOT OF YER WRETCHED SECT!
YEA, THOUGH I WALK THROUGH THE VALLEY OF THE SHADOW OF DEATH, I WILL FEAR NO EVIL.... FOR THOU ART WITH ME, THY ROD AND THY STAFF, THEY COMFORT ME...
WAIT!!!
WHAT MARCO SAYS IS THE TRUTH. HE DIDN'T KILL YOUR WIFE.
SPEAK FAST, BOY.
JOEL DID IT-- TO ENSURE A BATTLE BETWEEN THE TWO OF YOU!
WHAT THE FUCK!
HE BRAGGED TO ME THAT HE TREATED THE STAKE HE DROVE THROUGH HER HEART WITH THE GARLIC HE BROUGHT FROM THE SHIP.
THAT'S A GODDAMNED LIE!

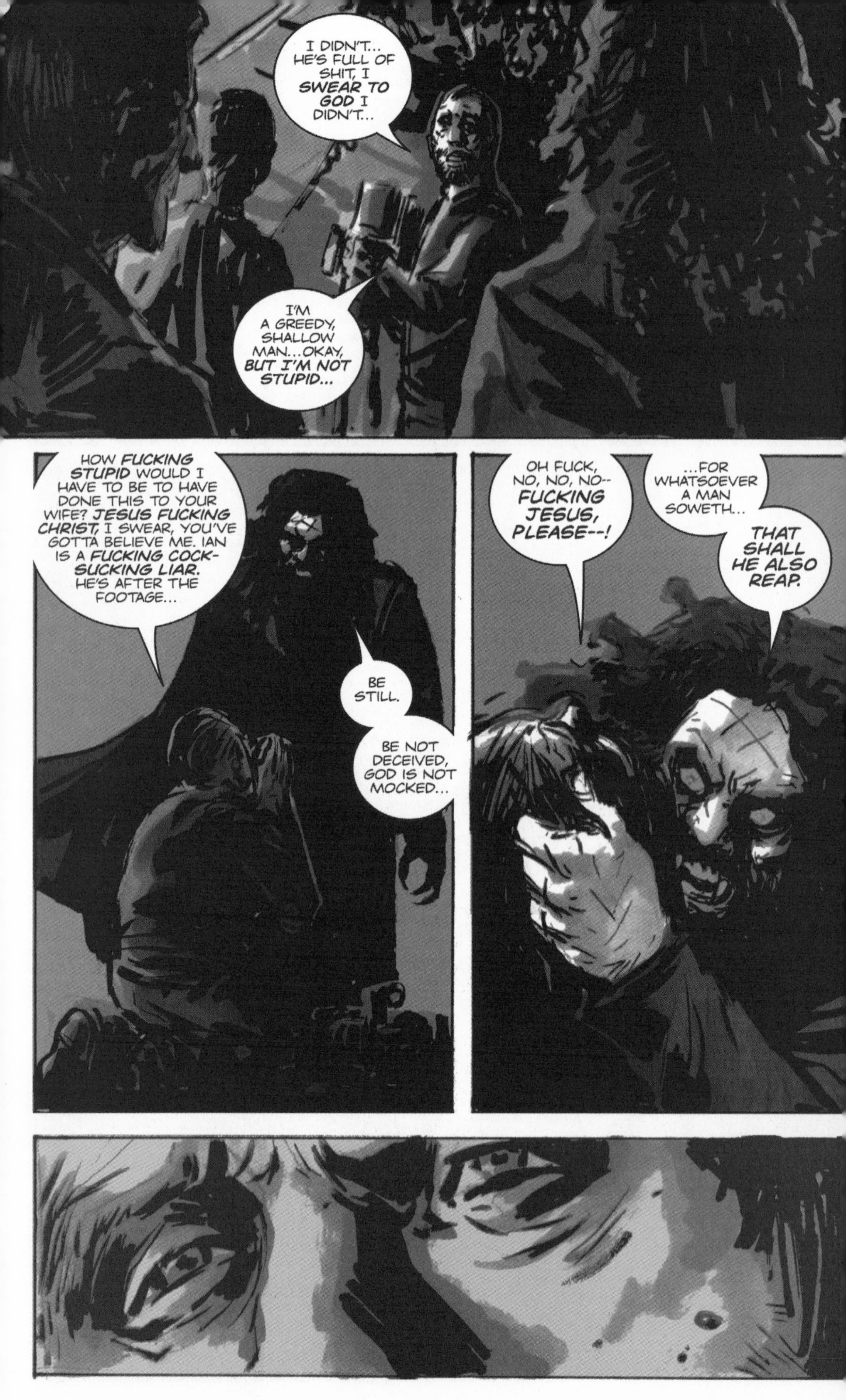

I DIDN'T... HE'S FULL OF SHIT, I **SWEAR TO GOD** I DIDN'T...
I'M A GREEDY, SHALLOW MAN...OKAY, **BUT I'M NOT STUPID...**
HOW **FUCKING STUPID** WOULD I HAVE TO BE TO HAVE DONE THIS TO YOUR WIFE? **JESUS FUCKING CHRIST,** I SWEAR, YOU'VE GOTTA BELIEVE ME. IAN IS A **FUCKING COCK-SUCKING LIAR.** HE'S AFTER THE FOOTAGE...
BE STILL.
BE NOT DECEIVED, GOD IS NOT MOCKED...
OH FUCK, NO, NO, NO-- **FUCKING JESUS, PLEASE--!**
...FOR WHATSOEVER A MAN SOWETH...
THAT SHALL HE ALSO REAP.

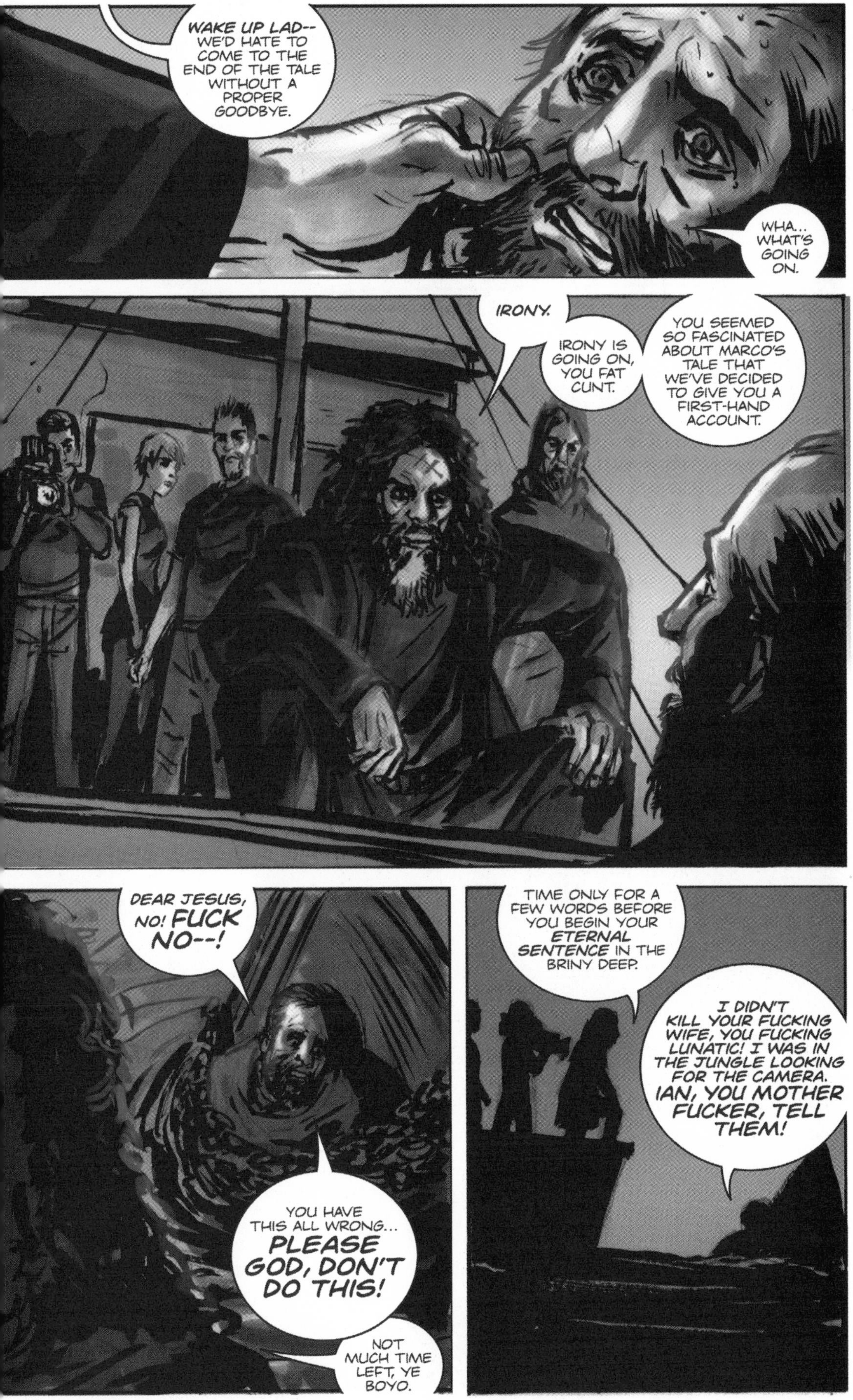
WAKE UP LAD-- WE'D HATE TO COME TO THE END OF THE TALE WITHOUT A PROPER GOODBYE.
WHA... WHAT'S GOING ON.
IRONY.
IRONY IS GOING ON, YOU FAT CUNT.
YOU SEEMED SO FASCINATED ABOUT MARCO'S TALE THAT WE'VE DECIDED TO GIVE YOU A FIRST-HAND ACCOUNT.
DEAR JESUS, NO! FUCK NO--!
YOU HAVE THIS ALL WRONG... PLEASE GOD, DON'T DO THIS!
NOT MUCH TIME LEFT, YE BOYO.
TIME ONLY FOR A FEW WORDS BEFORE YOU BEGIN YOUR ETERNAL SENTENCE IN THE BRINY DEEP.
I DIDN'T KILL YOUR FUCKING WIFE, YOU FUCKING LUNATIC! I WAS IN THE JUNGLE LOOKING FOR THE CAMERA. IAN, YOU MOTHER FUCKER, TELL THEM!

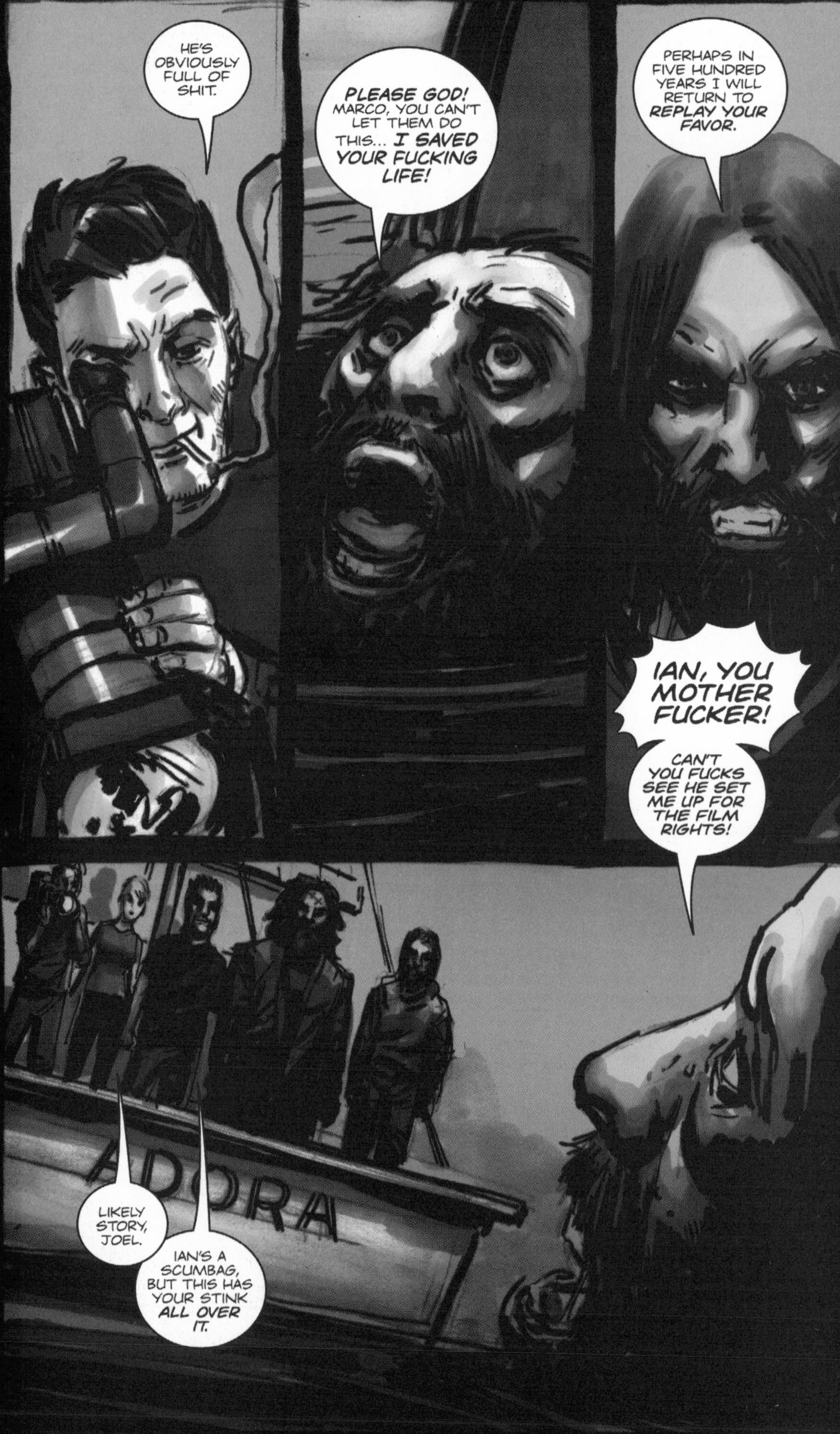
HE'S OBVIOUSLY FULL OF SHIT.
PLEASE GOD! MARCO, YOU CAN'T LET THEM DO THIS... I SAVED YOUR FUCKING LIFE!
PERHAPS IN FIVE HUNDRED YEARS I WILL RETURN TO REPLAY YOUR FAVOR.
IAN, YOU MOTHER FUCKER!
CAN'T YOU FUCKS SEE HE SET ME UP FOR THE FILM RIGHTS!
ADORA
LIKELY STORY, JOEL.
IAN'S A SCUMBAG, BUT THIS HAS YOUR STINK ALL OVER IT.

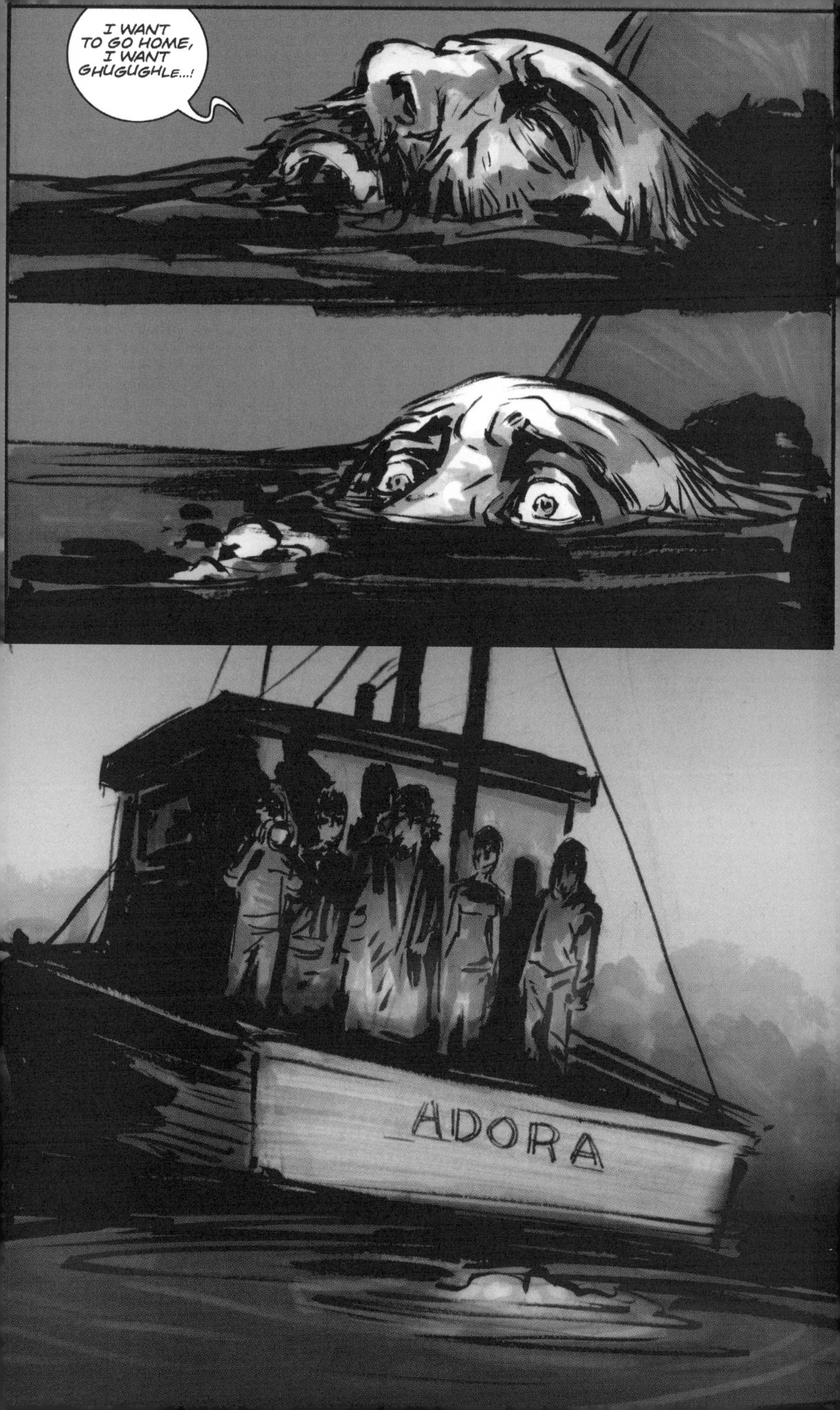
I WANT TO GO HOME, I WANT GHUGUGHLE...!
ADORA

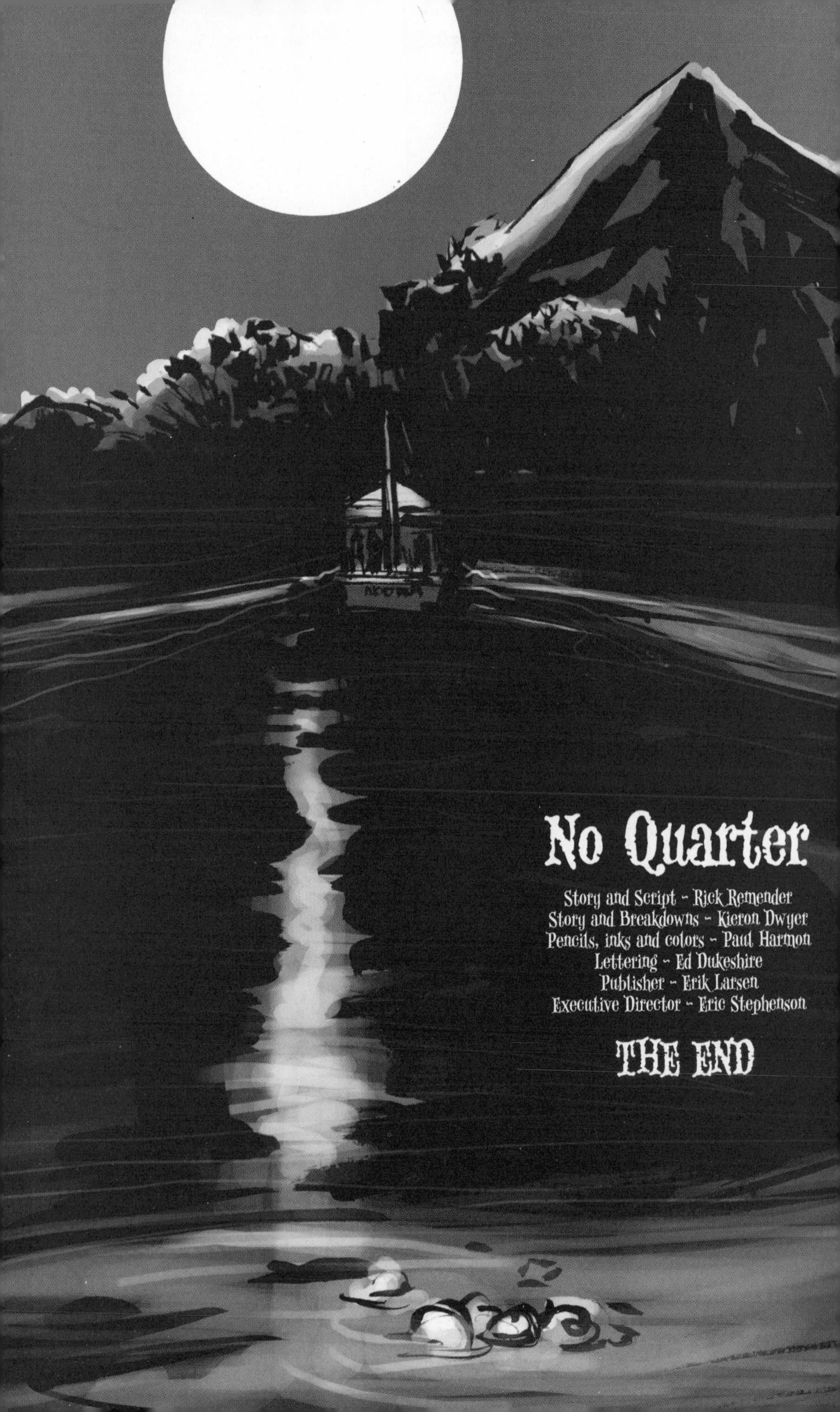
No Quarter
Story and Script - Rick Remender
Story and Breakdowns - Kieron Dwyer
Pencils, inks and colors - Paul Harmon
Lettering - Ed Dukeshire
Publisher - Erik Larsen
Executive Director - Eric Stephenson
THE END